STRAW MEN

STRAW
MEN

A FORMER AGENT RECOUNTS
HOW THE FBI CRUSHED THE
MOB IN LAS VEGAS

GARY MAGNESEN

Mill City Press

Mill City Press, Inc.
212 3rd Avenue North, Suite 290
Minneapolis, MN 55401
612.455.2294
www.millcitypublishing.com

ISBN - 978-1-936400-36-2
ISBN - 1-936400-36-7
LCCN - 2010934981

Cover Design by Wes Moore
Typeset by Madge Duffy

Printed in the United States of America

TABLE OF CONTENTS

– To my wife and children –

ACKNOWLEDGEMENTS

I want to thank my son, Greg, for his valuable assistance, and Adrienne, my daughter in law, for her excellent nuts and bolts editing. I would also like to acknowledge the newspaper reporters, columnists, and book authors who have given the public a peek into the dark world of organized crime. I especially want to thank former agents Dennis Arnoldy, Jerry Doherty, Mike Howie, Mike De Marco, Lynn Ferrin, and Fred Thorne for their friendship and priceless help in reconstructing the events related in this book. Also, a big thanks to Frank Cullotta for his candor and insights into the mob mindset and the selfless recounting of his remarkable life. I would be remiss if I didn't thank the men and women of non-FBI law enforcement who fight the good fight against the mob. I also acknowledge that band of FBI heroes who spent their blood, sweat, and tears in the worthy cause of fighting the dark powers that live among us. A big thanks also goes to editorial consultant Walter Bode for his great job of refining the manuscript. Finally, I would like to thank my wife, Diane, for her long suffering and encouragement.

PROLOGUE

There is a war being waged in the United States every day, every hour, every minute. This war is sometimes fought in the streets but more often it's carried out in the quiet of back rooms, social clubs, and FBI offices. This mortal combat occurs between the legions of darkness and the forces of law enforcement. On occasion, the war spills out on the pavements of America's cities, leaving a bullet-riddled victim sprawled in a pool of his own blood. On such occasions, media coverage gives a brief glimpse of the viciousness of the killers, but the real war is waged below the public radar screens.

Two powerful forces are gripped like heavyweight brawlers in a match to the finish, each side winning a battle or two but never relenting in its quest for dominance. The forces of drug cartels, street gangs, terrorist cabals and organized crime are the enemies of civilized society, constantly foraging for their life's blood – money and power. As a result, an imperfect wall has been erected between society and these predators - this barrier is law enforcement.

Many books have been written by experts who have established their credentials through study and research and an occasional interview with a cooperating criminal. My bona fides come from real life experience as a 26-year veteran of the Federal Bureau of Investigation. Twenty of those years were spent investigating what is known as Italian organized crime, otherwise labeled "OC." This book will detail a remarkable, true story of a nationwide conspiracy beginning in the cities of the Upper

Midwest and ending in the desert of Las Vegas. It's a story of conspiring men, vicious killers, and unsung heroes locked in a deadly battle of real life chess.

Law enforcement heroes know what this strife entails, as did Theodore Roosevelt, Police Commissioner for New York, when, in 1895, he said, "It is not the critic that counts, not the man who points out how the strong man stumbled, or where the doer of deeds could have done better. The credit belongs to the man who is actually in the arena; whose face is marred by the dust and sweat and blood; who strives valiantly, who errs and comes short again and again. . . .who knows the great enthusiasm, the great devotions and spends himself in a worthy cause, who at the best, knows in the end the triumph of high achievement, and who, at the worst if he fails, at least fails daring greatly so that his place shall never be with those cold and timid souls who know neither victory nor defeat."

The Mafia, or "black hand," has its roots planted deeply in the soil of Sicily, but the origin of this secret society is lost in antiquity. The "mob," or more correctly, "La Cosa Nostra" (LCN), which is translated as "our thing" or "this thing of ours," was and is a criminal organization that carries no official name among its ranks, thereby reinforcing the fiction that it doesn't exist. The Chicago mob is unique in the world of organized crime. It is the main powerhouse outside New York City, and its members refer to themselves as members of the "Outfit." There is no need to further detail the men who were instrumental in the growth of the LCN for the purposes of this book, but it is necessary to set the stage so that the reader will understand the full context of this true story.

Some of the foreign born Sicilian immigrants were carriers of the criminal virus that was allowed to breed in the slums of New York City. If immigration authorities had deported the criminal elements of these groups early on, we wouldn't be left to mop up the residue of their organizations today. Of course, the Italian mobsters weren't alone. There were Jewish, Germany, Polish, and Irish gangs that sprang up alongside the Italian gangsters and, inevitably, turf wars broke out between the competing groups. The spilled blood ran deep within all the factions, but the Italians won supremacy because of their organized approach. Several factions of the victorious Italian gangs remained, and it was cunningly decided that instead of continuing the war, they would maintain each group as an autonomous unit, overseen by a commission of high-ranking members from each group when conflicts arose between the gangs. These five New York City factions, otherwise known as "families," were named after their founders and continue to carry their names to this day. They are the Gambino, Genovese, Colombo, Lucchese, and Bonanno families.

Each man who is proposed for membership in the LCN is required to take an oath known as "omerta." This oath requires the participant to deny the very existence of the organization and much more. The member is never to cooperate with law enforcement authorities on penalty of death. The member must put the LCN ahead of himself and his natural family. He must follow orders and must never sleep with another member's wife. Anyone that comes to this point in his criminal career already knows the score, so all the rules don't need to be explained to him in the initiation ritual. Angelo Lonardo, the former boss of the Cleveland LCN family, once described this initiation ceremony to me. He said the secret ceremony is based on a perversion of Catholic emblems. The initiate is brought into a room where high-ranking members are seated. A gun and a knife are placed on a table in front of the initiate and he is given a picture of a saint, which is then burned in his cupped hands. Lonardo told me, "In the old days when the old 'mustaches' ran things, you know the old Mafia guys, you had to cut your finger and swear on your blood, but they don't always do that no more. The boss runs the show and says something like, 'You're now made. Don't turn against us or break the rules or you will die and burn in hell like that saint.'"

The LCN is not an equal opportunity employer. It is unfailingly discriminatory based on ethnic origin. A proposed member must be of Italian heritage through his father. If his heritage is only through his mother, he has no chance of membership. Those of other ethnic backgrounds need not bother to attempt to enter the inner sanctum, although they are certainly welcome as close associates under the uniting umbrella of the organization if they bring money into the coffers. Some of these associates are established as straw men, set up as fronts for a questionable enterprise while hiding the true owner. Strangely, even though these associates can be fabulously talented and bring untold wealth to the organization, they are frequently disparaged and slurred by members who consider themselves superior by heritage.

Additionally, the prospective member must have a criminal reputation and must have participated in at least one murder before he can be proposed for membership. This is known as "making your bones." This one insurmountable obstacle automatically excludes undercover agents from entering the unhallowed temples of mob membership. The ultimate sanction within the organization is death. If a member is ordered to kill someone, he has no alternative but to carry out the execution without question or face the ultimate penalty of losing his own life. Once a prospect has been admitted, he is said to have been "made." Many other organizations require loyalty oaths, but the oath is taken in the open and certainly doesn't require the commission of murder. For example, the military and the FBI require an oath, but it isn't secret and it certainly doesn't carry the ultimate penalty. This oath states, "I will support and defend the Constitution of the United States against all enemies, foreign and domestic; that I will bear true faith and allegiance to the same; that I take this obligation freely, without any mental reservation or purpose of evasion, and that I will well and faithfully discharge the duties of the office on which I am about to enter. So help me God."

The one element that makes the LCN a criminal conspiracy is its very organization, patterned after the Roman system. There is a boss, an under boss, and a consiglieri (counselor) at the head of each organized crime family. Below the triumvirate of leadership are the "capos, "captains" or "skippers" who are assigned over a number of "soldiers." These members belong to a "regime" or "crew" and each soldier has many associates who are not members. These associates can be ordinary criminals, businessmen, law enforcement officers, union officials, judges or politicians, anyone who can benefit the organization. As long as an individual has these important connections or is an "earner," he has value to the organization.

The family is a sole proprietorship run by a ruthless despot who has ultimate power. There are approximately 15 LCN families throughout the nation, with New York City having the most powerful families by far. The Chicago family, known as the "Outfit," is also very powerful, while the others are much smaller and less influential. The LCN is organized to obtain money through continuing illegal acts and, of course, part of each score, known as "tribute," passes from these earners upward in the organizational structure. This payment is absolutely mandatory upon penalty of death. Furthermore, envelopes containing cash are expected to be delivered to the boss on special occasions such as birthdays and Christmas.

Sometimes discipline or punishment is necessary to maintain order within the organization, and demands to carry out the discipline, a "hit" or "whack," is passed down the organizational structure where the orders are eventually carried out. These participatory sanctions ensure loyalty and discipline and assure the continuation of the organization. The question is often asked, "Why would someone want to join such an organization?" The simple answer is for respect and power – respect from criminal peers, respect by those in the ethnic neighborhoods, and, finally, a contorted sense of self-respect. You can't mess with a made guy without having the full force of the mob's power come down on you.

The main protagonist of the LCN is the FBI, as the mob is a national scourge and must be attacked on a nationwide scale. To my knowledge, there are only four means available to law enforcement to allow the penetration of the substantial secret bulwarks of organized crime. These penetrations can only occur through the use of informants, cooperating witnesses, undercover agents, or by the utilization of electronic listening devices, in other words, wiretaps and hidden microphones. This war is fought by law enforcement on all levels, and throughout this book, several notable heroes will be recognized as such.

My career as an agent with the Bureau began in November of 1970. After receiving 13 weeks of extensive and vigorous training in Washington, D.C., and at the Marine Base in Quantico, Virginia, I was assigned to the Minneapolis Field Division as a probationary agent where I investigated general criminal matters. These included bank robberies, thefts from interstate shipments, interstate transportation of stolen property, and fugitive matters. My first experience with an organized crime case occurred when I was assigned, along with many others in the office, to make numerous arrests in an illegal bookmaking case. I was surprised to learn that one of the arrestees in the massive sweep was an old friend I had met while going through basic training in the Air Force in 1964. At the time of the arrests, I wondered why the Bureau spent its time and manpower on such seemingly minor violations of federal law. These men seemed to be otherwise law abiding citizens who merely catered to the wants of those who desired to add to the excitement of sporting events by placing wagers on games.

After attending an organized crime training conference, my naiveté was washed away as it became evident that illegal gambling is a constant in all economies, and depending upon the prowess of the odds maker, it is a virtual lock as a moneymaker and, therefore, the lifeblood for organized crime. Large sums of money flow to those who control gambling operations, whether it is illegal casinos, card games, numbers operations, horse races, or sports gambling. When the LCN learns of such enterprises, it moves in like a hungry parasite and demands a "street tax," a piece of the earnings. The ancillary business of loan-sharking almost always pops up when illegal gambling thrives as losing bettors, more often than not, over- extend themselves in their exuberance for betting on their favorite teams. Bets with bookies are almost always taken over the phone because betting lines can change in a moment, and speed of action is essential. This means that the bets are based on credit, and it's human nature to spend more money when cash up front isn't required. Loan sharks are in the business of making money and they frown on deadbeats. They charge exorbitant interest, "vigorish" or "vig" as it is called, which can run from 5 to 10 % a week on the unpaid balance. Once the victim is placed in the grips of the loan shark's vice, he has the constant threat of injury or even death hanging over him.

After a year as a new agent, I was transferred to the Milwaukee Field Division where I continued general criminal investigations. I was then assigned as an undercover agent tasked with penetrating associates of the radical domestic terrorist organization known as the Weathermen. This group committed numerous bombings in the late 1960s and early 1970s, and many of its members were on the run as fugitives. Funding for the program eventually dried up, requiring me to cut my long hair and leave the life of a counter-culture pretender and return to the life of a regular agent. I was given my choice of investigative programs as a reward, and even though a seasoned agent counseled against it, I requested the organized crime squad. My mentor wrongly assured me that, "Organized crime investigations are too difficult and never lead to anything."

A typical FBI field office is organized very simply. There is a Special Agent in Charge (SAC), an Assistant Special Agent in Charge (ASAC,) and several supervisors. Each supervisor runs a squad and, depending upon the size of the office, the squads are broken down by investigative categories such as: bank robberies, white collar crimes, political corruption, counter terrorism, national security matters, fugitive apprehensions, organized crime (OC), and others. After nine years in Milwaukee, I was transferred to Las Vegas in October of 1980. Because of my experience, I was certified in federal court as an expert witness on organized crime. Before long, I was assigned as the primary relief supervisor of the OC squad and became the organized crime program coordinator for the Las Vegas Division. A coordinator can merely push paper, which was unacceptable to me, or he can actually coordinate and investigate at the same time. There's something in my DNA that requires me to be out in the trenches doing the dirty work, digging up evidence, and targeting every made guy in town. After my retirement, I authored a nationally distributed book, entitled *The Investigation,* and have been a guest on a number of radio talk shows. I am currently a consultant, along with former agent Dennis Arnoldy, for the Las Vegas Museum of Organized Crime and Law Enforcement scheduled to open in mid 2011, and I continue to hold a top-secret security clearance as I do contract security background investigations for the Bureau.

PART ONE

It Begins in Milwaukee

CHAPTER 1

There is no Hunting like the Hunting of Men

"Little cases, little problems – big cases, big problems."
– Charlie Parsons, former Las Vegas Organized Crime Supervisor

I carefully slid the key into the door lock. My heartbeat elevated, and I noticed my hand wasn't as steady as it had been when I received the key from the landlord the night before. The lock clicked ever so slightly and I could feel the tumblers slip into place. I whispered to my comrades, "Keep your eyes open, and don't take any chances." I slowly pushed the old door open, but it creaked, a sound much like stepping on a weathered, wooden porch. It seemed so loud in the early morning darkness – had Willie heard it? The fugitive's bedroom lay before us, down a narrow hallway. The landlord had drawn a diagram of the apartment's layout, so I knew the bedroom was at the end of the hall. As we crept down the narrow passageway, I was focused on the open bedroom door while three other agents concentrated on the periphery to ensure we weren't ambushed by someone from one of the other rooms. I was in the lead, the responsibility of the case agent, and I was carrying a Remington 870, 12-gauge shotgun with a pistol grip, a devastating close quarter's weapon. This movement down a narrow gauntlet is known in law enforcement as the funnel of death and is the most dangerous phase of an arrest of this nature. Any shot down the hall would surely have hit one of us. The adrenaline surged through my blood stream and gave me a rush that is difficult to describe. Perhaps Ernest Hemingway characterized this apprehension most closely in his short story, *On Blue Water,* when he wrote, "Certainly, there is no hunting like the hunting of men… and those who have hunted armed men long enough and liked it, never care for anything else thereafter."

I had been working bank robberies and had identified a serial bank robber. He was a huge man with a prison body builder's physique named Willie Davis who had recently been released from prison for armed robbery. Bank surveillance pictures tied the robber to three banks, and witnesses had positively identified Willie as the robber from a photo spread I had displayed to them. One of the female bank tellers who seemed to be a reluctant witness the first time I interviewed her turned out to be my strongest witness. When I showed her the photo spread, I instructed her, "Take your time. Look at the pictures and tell me if you see the guy that robbed you." She looked at the pictures ever so briefly and then slammed Willie's photo down on the table and stated emphatically, "That's him! That's the robber!" She absolutely had no doubt, and then she added, "Go get him." Another piece of the evidence against Willie was that his brother owned a two toned brown car that was know in 1972 as a "deuce and a quarter," a Buick Electra 225 which was described as the get away car by witnesses. I was able to track Willie to his apartment and after obtaining a warrant; a team of us went out to his shabby apartment at five o'clock in the morning so as to catch him in bed because I knew he was dangerous and had used two different handguns in the robberies.

The giant was sound asleep when I pointed the shotgun near his head and rudely awakened him. "FBI, you're under arrest. Don't move a muscle or you're dead!" He came to in an instant, his wide eyes alert and ready for anything, but he wisely lay still. I ordered him to roll over onto his belly very slowly and cross his legs as two pistols were retrieved from the nightstands on either side of his bed. He said nothing, but put his hands behind his back and was securely cuffed. He had obviously been through the drill before. I have no doubt that he would have gone for one of the guns had he been given the opportunity. Some years later I learned that Davis had been released from prison early and had taken a bank manager's family hostage and forced the terrified manager to go to the bank to retrieve ransom money. As a result, Willie was again sent to prison. This career criminal was a clear and present danger to society and should never have been released from prison after I got him. I'm convinced such a man can never be rehabilitated, as there is a hole in his character, a vacancy in his common decency. As a law enforcement officer, I wasn't concerned with why he had this deficiency. I leave that to the sociologists. I was only concerned with protecting society from a dangerous predator.

The late 1960s and early 70s was a time of national confusion and dissent over the Vietnam War. Some who had been drafted into the military didn't want to go, and the FBI was tasked with the unpleasant business of finding these deserters and returning them to the military, a job that wasn't particularly popular within the ranks of the Bureau. As a first office probationary agent in Minneapolis, I tracked down and arrested several deserters, including one from the Marine Corps. He was a thin, frail-appearing Marine. I had previously questioned his wife about the whereabouts of her husband, but she, understandably, lied to me and said she had no idea where he was. I knew she had lied, as a neighbor told me that the wanted man had been around earlier that day but had left shortly before my arrival. I, eventually, took him into custody and after booking him, I turned him over to the Marines and left him in a state of trembling fear. His wife called me after learning of his apprehension and screamed at me, accusing me of all kinds of evil against her and her husband, but I patiently let the words flow past me, not telling her that I had found her husband in the apartment of his former girlfriend. I didn't feel the wife needed any more pain at the time. The arrest bothered me for several years, not because I had made it, but because I may have sent the very passive, gentle man to his death in the jungles of Southeast Asia.

Some years later I was in Washington, D.C., on assignment and took the opportunity to visit the Vietnam War Memorial. I recall walking to the monument on a brisk, windy day, the autumn leaves blowing around my feet as I slowly strolled from FBI Headquarters on Pennsylvania Avenue, burdened by the possibility of finding the Minneapolis deserter's name engraved on the sacred wall. I walked slowly along the 246- foot black granite wall absorbing the magnitude of the 58,000-plus names engraved in the reflective stone. The stark contrast of small American flags, colorful flowers, a pair of pink baby shoes, as well as other remembrances left at the memorial as sacred offerings to the noble dead made my burden even heavier.

Major Michael O'Donnell, who was killed in action in Vietnam in 1978 made a profound request when he wrote before he was killed, "If you are able, save for them a place inside of you and save one backward glance when you are leaving for the place they can no longer go." I knew that two thirds of the dead had volunteered to serve in Vietnam, while the others were drafted into the divisive war. Nevertheless, they all died as a result of the war, so I made my backward glance as I searched the wall's name index. To my great relief, the deserter's name was not there. My concern had been lifted and I hope he has lived a long and useful life.

I continued working criminal cases in Scandinavia-influenced Minneapolis, Minnesota, which suited me well, as I was born in Norway and had immigrated to the United States with my parents at the age of three. Actually, my acceptance into the Bureau was a result of my Norwegian language proficiency and my ability to read and speak the Nordic languages. I was born during the Nazi occupation of Norway, and troubling stories told by my mother and father have embedded themselves in my psyche. For example, my great uncle, Bjarne Solberg, served in the City of Bergen Fire Department and was also a member of the Norwegian underground, but there were informers among them, and one day the Gestapo came for him. He was sent to the Dachau Concentration Camp in the heart of Germany and was assigned the vile task of placing many of the 25,000 emaciated, defiled bodies of deceased Jews into the ovens. The unspeakable conditions of the camp were a breeding ground for typhus, and he nearly died from the disease, compounded by malnutrition. He and hundreds of others were finally liberated after three excruciating years, by British and American Forces as they surged through Germany, crushing what was left of the Nazi Army. I visited Uncle Bjarne in Norway in the spring of 1966, but he wouldn't talk of his unspeakable experience as a war slave. His pleasant wife repeated the Norwegian phrase, "Du maa spise, jeg har mer i Kjokkene" (You must eat; I have more in the kitchen). She served us all manner of food and hand made pastries during the visit, perhaps an unconscious overreaction to Uncle Bjarne's years of deprivation.

The people of Norway resisted the Nazis the best way an occupied people could. For example, one of my uncles, as a teenage at the timer, pushed a German soldier off a steep mountain trail to his death. There was no German retribution, as it was thought his death was the result of an accidental fall. Other patriots fled to the mountains and fought a guerrilla war against the German army. My father often spoke of two childhood friends, who happened to be Jewish who were scooped up by the brown-shirted Gestapo and taken in for questioning. They were forced to identify other Jews so they could also be eliminated as if they were mere cockroaches. One of the young men was placed on a red hotplate and burned horribly. After the brutal questioning he had difficulty walking, and as he was being dragged to his cell by his arms, he broke free and dived through a fourth story window to his death. The other brother was never heard from again. Both of my parents stood firmly against the Nazi tyrants in their own way. For example, my father broke into a Nazi warehouse and took back many blankets and winter coats that had been confiscated by the Gestapo and returned them to those who needed them to survive the brutal Norwegian winters, a violation that would have been a virtual death sentence had he been caught. My mother secretly kept a Norwegian flag under the mattress of my baby buggy, knowing her defiance could have resulted in imprisonment or worse. After several years of Nazi occupation, and not long after the end of the war, my parents fled Europe for a better life in the United

States. Perhaps the injustices of World War II and the atrocities committed against innocents by the Nazis planted a seed within me, a seed that grew and blossomed into my trying to make things right and bring about justice when I became an agent.

As a first office probationary agent, the first year of employment is considered on-the-job training. Cases are assigned, but a training agent keeps an eye on you and helps out when needed. One of the first cases assigned to me in Minneapolis was a fugitive case where a man was wanted for violating a federal crime. A photo and general description of the fugitive were contained in the lead communication, including the fact that the subject had a small scar on his chest. The address of his mother, who lived in a suburb of Minneapolis, was also provided. On its face the case seemed simple enough, but things don't always go as planned. My partner, another first office agent named Brent Thueson, and I went out and quickly arrested the fugitive at his mother's home. I'm 6'1" but Thueson towered over me by three inches, so we presented a formidable duo to the fugitive. We hooked him up without incident and proceeded to the office for processing. On the way, the FBI office contacted us on the Bureau radio and said the mother had called and said that we had the wrong guy. I responded, "What do you mean we have the wrong guy? He's the right guy. We compared him against his picture and I'm sure it's him." They came back, "He has an identical twin brother and the mother said you have the wrong brother." I pulled over and Brent and I both looked at the fugitive and asked, "Is that right? Are you the wrong brother?" He nodded. "Yeah. I didn't say anything cause I didn't want you to put my brother in jail." Now that was true loyalty to a brother. Certainly I have often seen the exact opposite, where one brother turns against the other because of greed or for a legal advantage. With the new information, we turned around and found the identical twin, who was purported to be the real fugitive, standing outside waiting for us on the curb. I pulled up his shirt to check for the telltale scar and, amazingly, he had one almost identical to his brother's. Now we had a real problem. Were they playing a game with us, or were they telling the truth? We solved the conundrum by taking them both, and when we got to the office, a fingerprint comparison quickly determined that they were telling the truth and the innocent twin was released.

The Minneapolis Field Division was one of the notorious destinations used by J. Edgar Hoover, who will forever be known in the Bureau as "The Director," as a disciplinary office. That is to say, if an agent screwed up and Hoover determined that the offense was sufficient enough to warrant a sanction of transfer, then Hoover, who hated cold weather, sent the malefactors to Minnesota, Montana, or the Dakotas, where he hoped they would suffer in the cold. The Minnesota winter is relentless. It begins in early October and doesn't let up until May. I recall a one-week period where the January high temperature never rose above zero and the low dropped to 10 below zero.

As a result of Hoover's eccentric policy, there were several agents with drinking problems assigned to Minneapolis. This was before such problem drinkers were actually helped by counseling and other programs. Hoover, who refused to understand the foibles of his agents, had numerous ways to reprimand and he used these methods liberally. When it came time for the annual inspection of the office, the SAC would send the men on "road trips" in a humanitarian effort to protect them so they wouldn't be present when the inspectors arrived, because they often had a price on their heads set by Hoover. One of these men had a promising stolen check case that needed attention, so it was assigned to me, as he was away on one of the legendary road trips.

The Director, understandably, wanted "his Bureau" to be without reproach and, therefore was extremely sensitive to any potential public perception problem. Unfortunately, his unbending and often naive expectations resulted in ridiculous rulings. One such example was having factory installed air conditioning and AM radios removed from Bureau cars even though they were, by that point in time, included in the standard accessory package. He feared the public's perception of agents driving around like big shots would hurt the Bureau's image. In spite of his many idiosyncrasies, Hoover had molded an investigative agency that was second to none in the world, and he demanded excellence.

I had barely had the opportunity to review the skimpy stolen check case file when I received a phone call from a police detective. As it turned out, the local police had arrested a man attempting to cash a stolen check, and after running the check number in the stolen property computer file of the FBI's National Crime Information Center (NCIC), they determined the check was part of a large number of instruments stolen from an Allstate Insurance claims office in a Minneapolis suburb. The checks were drawn on an out of state bank, thereby qualifying for the federal violation of Interstate Transportation of Stolen Property Statute. Thueson and I went to the suburban police department and, after advising the blond, bespectacled check passer of his rights, he decided to cooperate. He realized he had gotten himself into a mess and wanted out of it. First he told us of a plan to hit the

Allstate office again. Then he went on to give us the names of all the conspirators in the check-passing ring. That night, along with police, I waited for the burglars to appear at the claims office. There were five of us crouched behind some trees waiting to ambush the burglars. I sat leaning against a tall oak tree, and after about three hours of anguished waiting, two men showed up at about 1:00 a.m. and made forced entry by kicking in a side door to the small, single-story office building. They were inside the office for about 15 minutes, but when they came out, they were met with the distinctive metallic racking sounds of shotguns and orders yelled out, "Police! Hands up! Don't move!" The two immediately froze and raised their hands. As they did, two thick packets of blank checks slid out from under one of the men's coats and fell to the ground.

Many of the previously stolen checks had been cashed at grocery stores where surveillance photos had been taken at the customer service counters, and with the names of the participants provided by the witness, we were able to match the photos, finger-prints and handwriting found on the checks with the various co-conspirators. Within weeks, we had swept up the whole gang, consisting of the burglars and six others. They all pled guilty and were sentenced to five years in prison, except for one of them who was a hard-nosed ex con who had threatened me when Brent Thueson and I went to interview him in jail. The judge didn't care for his threat to "climb across the table and kick your ass," so he sent him to prison for a maximum of seven years. Those words had cost him an additional two years of his sorry life. I was fortunate, as a first office agent, to have such a successful, multi conspirator prosecution. Not long after I was assigned to the Milwaukee Field Office, where I first came in contact with organized crime.

Organized crime is a continuing criminal conspiracy, an illegal enterprise, a virus that found its breeding ground in the Italian neighborhoods of large American cities. To paraphrase a famous book title, this is a tale of five cities. Three of these viral petri dishes were the predominantly industrial centers clustered around the deep, gray waters of the Great Lakes. A fourth is located at the center of the U.S., almost equidistant north to south and east to west. The fifth city is nestled in a valley of sparse desert meadows.

The first city in our tale is Milwaukee, set on the shores of Lake Michigan. It has a history similar to that of other Great Lake cities. Its name comes from the Native American word "Millioke," meaning "good and beautiful land," which it certainly is. Just to the east of the city is Lake Michigan, the second largest of the Great Lakes. It is 118 miles wide and 300 miles long. Its size and average depth of 280 feet presents, an extraordinary ecological system with weather variants that frequently change the inland sea's disposition. I have shared its tranquility on board a friend's cabin cruiser anchored off shore as our families watched the 4th of July fireworks explode over the city in the annual celebration, and I have often stood along the bluffs overlooking Lake Michigan and felt the gentle sea breezes as they moved off the inland sea in the summer. I have also huddled with my back to the darts of ferocious gales as they rip off the lake and spew their venom on the city in the dead of winter. The state of Wisconsin is pocked with hundreds of lakes gouged out of the fertile soil by huge pre-human glaciers, and it is also blessed with thickly forested

GARY MAGNESEN

tracts of land where pioneer farmers made their stand against the wilderness and the forces of nature.

Milwaukee, Wisconsin, was once a city of ethnic neighborhoods. Immigrants of German decent settled on the northwest side, African Americans moved to the north-central area, while Poles and Slavs settled on the south side. There are more bars in the city than anywhere else I've been. It seems that there is a neighborhood watering hole in nearly every locality where community members congregate for pizza, homemade sausage, or fish freshly caught from the waters of Lake Michigan. Most of the time, these congregations are friendly gatherings, but the down side is that Milwaukee has the nation's highest rate of beer alcoholism.

Over time Milwaukee became an industrial hotbed and, as everyone knows, became famous for the brewing of beer. German immigrants poured into the city in the mid-1800s and Milwaukee was known as the "German Athens." The infamous Al Capone, living only two hours south in Cicero, Illinois, owned a home in one of the suburbs of the Dairy State. When he wanted a breath of fresh air from the stress of Chicago, he would visit Milwaukee and, at Capone's urging, bootlegging took hold there. At the same general time, newly arriving, hardworking Italian immigrants settled in Milwaukee's 3rd Ward, near the Milwaukee River, and developed a thriving produce market that exists to this day. They expanded their sphere of influence and grew in numbers as the population burgeoned. Most lived honest, productive lives, but the Italian-American malcontents, criminals, and tough guys were the pool from which the LCN would draw new members.

Of course, time passes and children raised in the ethnic

22

neighborhoods grow up, marry, and often move away from the old neighborhoods, thereby homogenizing the population, but many of these neighborhoods still exist to this day. When I was assigned to the Milwaukee Division in early 1972, a small pocket of ethnic Italians held residency north of Wisconsin Avenue, not far from Lake Michigan. Frank Balistrieri, the boss of the Milwaukee LCN family had moved out of the old neighborhood in 1960 and settled into a large two story, brown, brick mansion on Shepard Street in the exclusive suburb of Shorewood. There was a perpetual investigative case opened on Balistrieri, but nothing of any real significance was done on it. A few surveillances, notations of license tags, recording of the names of known associates, and information from various sources kept the case barely alive, as if it were on life support. Intelligence can be invaluable, but if it doesn't lead to any action, it has no value as far as I'm concerned. At the time, the closest I got to an organized crime investigation was when another agent pointed out Frank Balistrieri's house located in a bedroom suburb north of the metropolis of Milwaukee.

My desire is to make this book an accurate account of my career. Certainly, not all the cases assigned to me or cases I was involved in will be recounted here, but let it suffice to say there were hundreds of them. An accurate account also means exposing flaws in the bureaucratic system. Unfortunately, the Bureau is plagued by many of the same ills and foibles that inhabit all mankind, as the organization and its members are not perfect. There are some self serving agents whose purpose is to satisfy their own egos or personal wants at the detriment of the Bureau's mission. There is public perception that all FBI agents are hard driving, fearless pursuers of justice, but, unhappily, there are a few who have ego problems, or those who are lazy and don't want to stretch out and leave their comfort zone and merely mark time till their retirement. I recall an agent we referred to as the "mortician," as he looked like a walking corpse and was, for all intents, worthless as an agent. I have often compared FBI agents to Air Force pilots. Pilots are central to the military mission of the Air Force, so when fighter pilots go on a raid, every pilot must carry his load as well as protect the wings of other pilots. If one pilot merely circles the combat area while his comrades are engaged in the fight, he is useless. Sadly, such agents are frequently moved to squads where they can hide and merely push paper. If a pilot can't fly, he shouldn't be a pilot. If an agent can't pull his load as an investigator, he should be demoted to a clerical employee. This is not to disparage FBI clerical employees - they are invaluable and do a great job but their job is not that of an agent.

There are also, on occasion, problems with leadership within the Bureau. For example, there was an SAC who we nicknamed "Fast Eddy" because at 8:15 sharp, every morning, he would sweep through the various squad rooms in the office, walking at a frenetic pace, obsessively snapping his fingers and ordering all agents out of the office. This, he explained, was because all the crooks were out on the street and not in the office. He gave no consideration to the time needed to prepare the volumes of paperwork required to document investigations or the time consuming research needed to properly tie suspects to crimes. As a result of this insane policy, we were forced to come in early and stay late in order to accomplish anything. Another inexplicable practice was for "The Fast One" to temporarily assign a newly transferred agent to assist resident agents in small towns in northern Wisconsin or the Dakotas while their wives and families languished in motel rooms, desperate to shop for a new home and get settled. These idiotic road trips caused untold difficulties within families, and certainly caused disdain for the boss. For a time I thought I had landed in a lunatic asylum, but after Fast Eddy retired we learned he had an inoperable brain tumor, which eventually took his life. The tumor surely affected his erratic behavior but that fact didn't mitigate the misery he caused.

Our relief at the retirement of Fast Eddy was short lived when the new SAC arrived. He was an uncompromising man of questionable experience who quickly became embroiled in a dispute with the United States Attorney. Because of the conflict between the heads of the two agencies, we were ordered not to speak with anyone in the U.S. Attorney's office, but to only communicate by written reports. This is an impossible situation, as face-to-face contact with prosecutors is absolutely essential for any kind of success. I happened to be in the middle of an extensive investigation of the Outlaws Motorcycle Gang, and a member of the gang had been arrested in another county and wanted to cooperate to lighten his sentence. He was represented by an attorney who wouldn't allow his client to cooperate until he had full assurance of a deal from the U.S. Attorney's Office. An Assistant U. S. Attorney (AUSA) and I traveled to meet the gangster and his lawyer, and after a proffer of evidence, he was given assurance in writing that we would recommend a reduced charge based upon his full and truthful testimony regarding arsons and bombings committed by the gang. I wrote my report and, of course, included the fact that the AUSA had been present and had rendered a legal opinion.

The stubborn SAC saw the report and went ballistic, as I had broken his ridiculous and unworkable rule. Instead of personally confronting me and allowing me to explain that my interview of the biker had occurred before his silly edict, he ordered the Assistant Special Agent in Charge to verbally reprimand me and reassign the case to another agent. I wasn't high on the ASAC's list of favorites anyway, because I didn't carouse the bars with him after work. He didn't have the guts to back me, and I was on the punishment list for some time and was unfairly given all sorts of menial assignments. On one occasion I was ordered to fly from Milwaukee, after working a full shift, to a small town in Michigan to deliver some evidence needed in a trial. When I was met by the Michigan agent, he wondered why it was necessary for me to personally deliver the evidence as the trial was set for several weeks in the future and the evidence could easily have been shipped by Bureau mail. I was perceived by the SAC to be a troublemaker, or as he said "a smart money guy," a thorn in the side of the powers to be. Unfortunately, it's the nature of all bureaucracies to eliminate the free thinkers, the thorns, and the doers that may stumble from time to time and cause minor problems. Agents are often seen as interchangeable or mere "bodies" that can be moved around like pawns. This is simplistic and short sighted at the very least. The Bureau would do well to fit its needs with specific agent's abilities instead of throwing all agents into a homogeneous pot. To say the least, this was a very difficult time for me and caused me to search for other employment. This ridiculous episode nearly drove me from the Bureau, but, luckily, I outlasted the fool and before long, the dawn brought a new SAC, John Glover, who may have been the finest administrator of my career. He was excellently assisted by ASAC Bob Butler who took a hands-on approach by helping the street agents do their job.

Not all frustrations came from within the Bureau. At that time the largest pornographer in the nation was a man named Reuben Sturman, a mob connected multimillionaire out of Cleveland, Ohio, and part of his porno profits went to the LCN in that city. He had a large warehouse distributorship in Milwaukee that supplied pornographic material to retail stores west of Ohio, so I focused on the distributorship. Pornography prosecutions are very difficult, as you are required to prove that the scenes depicted are counter to local community standards, so we focused on child pornography and bestiality, which are despicable and against all known community standards. With the cooperation of an agent in Waukegan, Illinois, I set up a simple undercover operation with the agent posing as a truck-stop operator and working out of a friendly truck stop. He recorded a phone conversation with the manager of the Milwaukee pornography distributorship and told her that he could sell countless movies and magazines of child porn and bestiality to truckers. The manager agreed but said she needed to obtain approval from Sturman before she could send those "special" products. Phone records showed a long distance telephone call to Sturman's private office number from the warehouse manager shortly after the first conversation with the undercover agent, and a shipping document for the requested videos was initialed by Sturman himself. We had the manager cold on tape when she contacted the agent, admitting Sturman's approval. Numerous videos and magazines were delivered from Milwaukee to Illinois, fulfilling the interstate shipment requirement, with a promise of many more deliveries to come.

As a new agent, I was once told by a veteran agent, "You won't have problems making cases on the bad guys - the guys with black hats. It's the guys with the white hats that will cause you the most problems." I've found his warning to be true. One of these white hats was the newly appointed United States Attorney (USA) in Milwaukee, who was very liberal and refused to prosecute the Sturman case because he believed there was no such thing as pornography. There was no convincing him otherwise even though subordinates pushed for prosecution. The attorney's personal opinion should not have had any sway, as the violation of the pornography law should have been left up to the community standards, in other words, determined by a jury. My frustration with the decision was palpable but there was nothing more I could do about it. There was no logical excuse for not going forward with the case.

At this point in time, organized crime investigations were far from my specialty as I continued to work general criminal matters. For example, there had been a spat of extortions against banks in Milwaukee. A man would call the financial institution and ask for the manager of a small branch. When the manager came on the line, he would be told that his wife had been kidnapped and would be held until he withdrew a certain amount of money from the bank vault and paid the ransom. The manager, understandably, would panic and try to call his wife at home, but the caller already knew she was out because he had watched her leave the house. Because this was in a day before cellular phones, the manager had no way of making contact with his wife, so he was willing to do anything in order to get his wife back. Usually the manager had enough sense to call the FBI, and we would swing into action. There is always a moment of truth in such extortions and, similarly, in kidnappings for ransom. It occurs at the ransom drop site. No matter how much he jerks the victim around, the perpetrator must eventually show up for the money. That is why the crime is so stupid and uncommon today.

I remember one case in particular where the pickup was made by a skinny, 19-year-old kid. We spotted him as soon as he came near the trashcan drop site. He wandered around scanning the area for unusual cars or people and then he stood for a time moving his gaze back and forth from the trashcan to his surroundings. I happened to be in a car with a veteran agent named Don Reilly, a hard-nosed New Yorker. He was an old timer who had no patience with such cases and was in no physical condition to chase a very fast teenager. While sitting with Reilly as we waited for the pickup, I was subjected to a series of complaints about the case. He griped, "The rotten bastards that pull these jobs should be shot. I haven't got time to be sitting out here with this crap. If someone comes for the pickup, I might run him down." The kid couldn't stand it any longer so he tentatively walked to the can, leaned in, and grabbed the money package and took off down an alley behind some business like an Olympic sprinter, holding the moneybag as if it were a baton. Two agents were chasing him on foot when Reilly gunned the engine and pursued the kid down the alley at full throttle. I thought Reilly was going to plow into the runner. "Don, are you nuts? Whatever you do, don't kill the kid!" He gritted his teeth and mumbled, "Don't worry about it. I won't kill him."

We passed the pursuing agents, and to my surprise and relief,

Don slowed down and ran the kid up against a fence with the car, pinning him. The robber, uninjured, was so frightened he wet his pants - the dark stain testifying against him. After that experience, he was more than willing to cooperate and gave up the mastermind of the several similar extortions. I learned over time that Reilly just liked complaining about things. Not long after, Don was pursuing a bank robber in his car and, as he entered an intersection with lights and siren on, he was T-boned by another car. I was in a vehicle behind Reilly with the ASAC, and saw the cars collide. The impact caused an explosion of smoke and flying glass. Don's car was pushed 50 feet or more before it came to a stop, and we jumped out to give assistance. Don was stretched out on the front seat covered with window glass and bleeding from his head. He moaned as we removed his sidearm from its holster and tried to help him. Moments later, an ambulance arrived and Don was taken to the hospital for treatment. He was released the next day with superficial wounds.

Not long after the auto pursuit, a dentist's son was kidnapped while on his way to school in Onalaska, Wisconsin. The small town is located in the Eastern part of the state along the Mississippi River, and the FBI was called to provide assistance to the small, rural sheriff's department. We responded with about 10 agents. An investigation ensued and, again, the pickup point was the perpetrator's undoing. The kidnapper moved us around from drop-site to drop-site in the hilly farmland. A call would come in to a pay phone, usually located in front of a small country store or service station, giving instructions for the drop, and a then a note would be found at the new drop-site directing the ransom bearer to another spot. This cat and mouse game continued as we moved east from the Mississippi River into the rolling farm fields of the surrounding area. It was getting dark, and this caused us great chagrin, as we were aware that the headlights of the covering cars would give us away in the open, little traveled country. He moved us onto dirt roads, and it became evident that it was an impossible situation for us and we had to back off. Unfortunately, the kidnapper had seen the headlights of the pursuing cars, and it appeared that our efforts had been futile. Luckily, one of the deputies had noticed a car he recognized near two of the drop sites and he knew the driver. At this point we backed off and disappeared, but it was too late for the suspect who had been identified. A full court background investigation determined that the man's grandmother owned an old, abandoned farm in the next county, and inspection by agents and deputies found the 16 year old victim tied up in a dilapidated chicken coop on the neglected property. He was cold and bug bitten, but otherwise he was well. It was obvious that the kidnapper intended to kill the boy by just leaving him there to die after receiving the ransom, because the boy could surely identify the perpetrator if he let the victim live.

We received permission to use a house across the street from the perpetrator's residence and set up surveillance on him and his car. We were instructed to arrest him if he made any attempt to leave his house, but otherwise we should wait for search warrants, which were being prepared. Within a few hours the warrants were obtained, and agents and deputies found the jerk hiding under his bed. He was pulled out by his ankles, and special agent Dennis Condon and I transported him to the nearest U.S. Magistrate, located 140 miles away in Madison. The kidnapper was placed in the rear seat, behind the passenger side of the car, and I sat next to him. The trip was made in complete silence, the man leaning his head against the back of the front seat for the entire trip as if he didn't want to look at us. Try as I might, I can't remember his name, nor can I recall what he looked like even though I sat next to him in the back seat for nearly three hours. I guess I didn't want to look at him either.

Sometime later, on May 15, 1977, the SAC received a phone call from FBI headquarters. He was informed that Presidential candidate George Wallace had been shot four times in the abdomen while at a campaign rally in Laurel, Maryland. Three others had also received wounds, including an Alabama State Trooper, a campaign volunteer, and a Secret Service agent. The shooter had been arrested at the scene, and his driver's license identified him as Arthur Bremer of Milwaukee. Our supervisor assigned Special Agent Fred Thorne as case agent, and he and agent Jack Hunt were immediately dispatched to secure Bremer's apartment until a search warrant could be obtained. The supervisor exclaimed, "Go check it out, then we'll report our results and close out the case in the morning." He couldn't have been more wrong. When Fred and Jack arrived, they found two over zealous Secret Service agents and a journalist picking through the hovel. Thorne, a native of New Orleans and a veteran Air Force officer, was a very competent investigator who, as a first office agent in Iowa, had engaged a bank robber in a close quarters gun battle after the robber had killed a police detective. The bank robber ended up face down and dead as a result of the gunfight.

A conflict of badges and jurisdiction ensued with the two Secret Service agents and it was resolved that the Bureau had investigative preference in presidential candidate assassination matters. This jurisdictional problem had been resolved after the assassination of President John F. Kennedy, when it was determined that the FBI had primary investigative authority in such cases. A case of this magnitude is a pull no punches investigation where the whole office is thrown into the fray. The questions needing timely answering were: Why did Bremer commit the crime? Did he act alone? If not, who else was part of the conspiracy? And, is anyone else in danger? Investigative organization is absolutely essential in a case such as this and assignments were made and followed up on. SAC, Fast Eddy, was set aside, as the Bureau was aware of his ineptitude and a senior inspector from Washington, D.C., was put in charge of the overall investigation. I received the assignment of identifying and tracing the sources of Bremer's finances. I determined that Bremer had been employed as a busboy at the Milwaukee Athletic Club but had lost his job because he "talked to himself," and this,understandably, bothered the members. He then worked as a janitor at South Division High School, his alma mater, during which time he lived at home, so he was able to save $1,500 from his menial jobs. For reasons never determined, he moved his money through various banks, perhaps in an effort to hide it. When he was arrested after following the presidential campaign in his blue 1967 American Motors Rambler, he only had $1.73 left in his checking account. Mug shots of Bremer taken immediately after his arrest showed a distinct indentation of a boot print on the side of his face where a Maryland State Trooper had held his head down on the floor of the police cruiser to protect him from any retaliation as the attempted assassin was being spirited away to jail.

Our concerted and exhaustive efforts produced a 1,000 page investigative report in three days. In it, we proved Bremer had acted alone and was self-financed in his twisted fantasy. It was also determined that Bremer, abused at home as a child by both parents, was a loner with no one to turn to. This is a proven blueprint for disaster, a cauldron that so many have the misfortune to endure and resulted in the fledgling sociopath turning inward to create his own reality. Bremer could easily have evolved into a serial killer or rapist, but he determined to be something else. He wrote in his diary, "It is my personal plan to assassinate by pistol either Richard Nixon or George Wallace.... to do something bold and dramatic, forceful and dynamic, a statement of my manhood for the world to see." George Wallace was personally convinced that a conspiracy was afoot to kill him and that someone had financed the efforts of Bremer, but after being shown the investigative record, he realized that his very serious wounds were the result of a single nut's actions.

The pitiful Bremer was released from prison on November 9, 2007, after serving nearly 30 years in prison. He had shot four people who were only spared from death because of sheer luck. It's my belief that luck shouldn't be a factor in determining the difference between murder and attempted murder. He intended to kill Governor Wallace and should have been charged with "unsuccessful murder." In my opinion, that non- existent law should carry the same punishment as a successful murder. His premeditated intent was the same. The factor of chance shouldn't play a role.

Some years later, I found myself speeding north on Highway 94 out of Racine County, where I had been assisting the agents in the area in catching up on some of their cases. After hearing the report of "an agent down" over the Bureau radio, I dropped everything and headed for Milwaukee. There is nothing more alarming or gut wrenching than hearing those words. Thoughts raced through my mind. Who was it? What happened? Can I get there in time to help in some way? I later learned that on the previous day, two police officers had attempted to take a man named Jacob Cohen into custody in a Chicago neighborhood bar on a cold, winter afternoon. The burglar resisted and was somehow able to disarm one of the cops as they struggled during the attempted arrest. Cohen killed both officers with one of the service revolvers and escaped. The Chicago Police Department called the Milwaukee FBI after determining that Cohen had a girlfriend who lived in an apartment on Stowell Avenue on Milwaukee's east side. They said they were on their way and requested assistance in determining if Cohen was at the apartment. The SAC and ASAC and agents from the fugitive-bank robbery squad responded to the police request. Some of the agents remained outside near the rear of the four-story building as others entered the apartment complex and received permission to go inside an apartment on the floor just below the target dwelling. They listened for footsteps from above but heard none. They asked the elderly resident if she had heard any movement in the apartment above her and she said she hadn't.

At this point everyone felt the fugitive was not there so Agent Dick Carr walked to the rear of the apartment, through the kitchen and out the back door leading to a wooden landing. There were stairs connecting all the rear landings, and Cohen, who must have heard or seen the activity, came creeping down the stairs from above. Carr was caught completely by surprise as Cohen; carrying the Chicago police service revolver in one hand and a .45 caliber semi automatic in the other, shot Dick in the chest. He staggered and fell backward onto his back before he had a chance to draw his weapon. Then everything happened in an instant as the outside agents moved toward the building. Fred Thorne fired off a shot with his shotgun, as did Bud Hall. Cohen fell, but his adrenaline flooded through his veins and he got up running. He was able to evade the pursuing agents by cutting around the corner of the building, but the agents tracked his blood trail in the snow to a house on Bradford Street, some few blocks away. One of the agents had obviously hit Cohen, but they had no way of knowing how serious his injury was. It was later determined that he had been hit in the hand by buckshot, blowing part of it off. Reinforcements from the police department and the FBI responded to the scene in an effort to bring justice to the man who was thought to have murdered two cops and an FBI agent.

When I arrived in Milwaukee, I was directed to the crime scene apartment where I saw Dick's blood pooled on the floor. It was beginning to congeal and had the consistency of tomato ketchup. It looked like a gallon of the stuff was spread out like a crimson cloth, and I was convinced no one could have survived such extensive blood loss. Thankfully, I was wrong. Dick had miraculously survived the near fatal shot because of quick first aid measures taken by ASAC Edward Best, a former Marine. After we completed our assignment at the crime scene, I drove home. I had to get my shoes off. The soles were soaked in Dick's blood and I would never wear them again.

I learned, prior to my departure from the crime scene, that

the killer came out of the house of refuge holding a fourteen-year-old boy as a hostage and was moving toward a car provided to him for a negotiated getaway. The swat team had set up a block away, and a sniper planned to shoot Cohen through the windshield as he drove down the street with his hostage. When Cohen came out of the house, he held the .45 caliber pistol to the boy's temple, but unknown to him, Joseph Del Campo, an agent who had positioned himself on the roof of a neighboring house, waited for an opportunity to end the standoff with his .357 magnum revolver. Del Campo was wearing a white sweater given to him by his wife for Christmas and as he climbed onto the roof, he had cut his hand. He told me later, "Blood was dripping down from my hand and I was just trying to keep it from staining my sweater. It didn't hurt, but there were drops of blood all over the roof." Del Campo waited for a safe, open shot. His chance came when the teenager slipped slightly on some ice and slid down somewhat, giving Del Campo a clear shot at the killer's neck, and he took it. The killer fell dead, his spine severed. Case closed.

Bob Walsh and I were assigned as undercover agents not long after the Bradford Street incident. We were assigned an old white, beat up 1960 Dodge van to drive. We grew our hair long and sprouted beards and spent time around neighborhood co-ops and other counter culture gatherings in Madison, Wisconsin, where we tried to get close to Weathermen wannabes and associates. Walsh, the son of an FBI agent and the brother of another, eventually went on to become SAC in San Diego and San Francisco. We weren't spying on these groups, but were looking for fugitives or trying to pick up street talk as to the whereabouts of any of the "Weathermen" fugitives who we knew had strong ties to the

Madison anti war sub culture. We were careful not to set foot on the University of Wisconsin campus, as we didn't want anyone accusing the FBI of spying on students.

The Weathermen group was the radical arm of the Students for a Democratic Society (SDS) that had sprung up in the 1960s as a violent leftist protest group opposed to the Vietnam War. They had committed several bombings across the country, including the Pentagon, U.S. Capitol and the Madison campus, where they had bombed the mathematics building. A graduate student was studying late into the night when the building was bombed. He was killed by the effects of the blast, and several others were injured. After a time, not being successful in making any inroads as to the whereabouts of the fugitives, Bob complained, "This seems to be a dead end. I don't think we're accomplishing anything." I agreed with him. "I don't like this either, but we can't just go in and quit, it wouldn't look good." We subsequently learned that the Weathermen fugitives had gone deeply underground and had broken off all contact with past associates, so our undercover project was shut down after six months. Interestingly, Bill Ayers and his wife, Bernardin Dorn, were two of the fugitives we were looking for, but years later when they were finally brought to justice, the charges were dismissed because of a legal technicality and they were never prosecuted. Ayers has admitted his participation in some of the bombings, but today, he and his wife, Bernardin, are considered respected members of the Chicago educational community.

As a reward for our undercover work, Walsh and I were assigned to the organized crime squad run by ASAC Ed Best, an expert on the mob. Bob and I opened a case on bookmakers

Sam and Dennis Librizzi, brothers who operated Libby's Sports Lounge. I assisted Bob on the case, and we prepared a wiretap on Sam's phones. This was a great learning experience for me because I became familiar with all the intricacies of wiretaps, and the preparation of affidavits, and the proper handling of tapes, logs, and transcripts. The authorizing judge granted 30 days of monitoring, but the moment we went up on the two lines we had constant betting action. After about fifteen days, Bob concluded, "I can't see why we need the full 30 days. We're picking up constant action and it's the same thing over and over again. Let's bring this thing down."

Bob and I conducted a few surveillances inside Libby's Sports Lounge together during the investigation. The bar was usually packed, noisy and filled with sports fans. I don't drink, so Bob and I had a system we developed to deal with that situation. We ordered two beers and Bob would drink half of his, and then we would quickly switch bottles and he would work on mine. We often chuckled at our clever drinking scheme as Bob said, "This is a great deal for me," but I complained, "Yeah, it's a great deal for you, but I don't have anything to drink. It would look goofy if I had a beer and a Coke in front of me." After a while, the surveillance became tedious, as the script was the same, over and over. We wrote our observations on cocktail napkins used as rough surveillance logs that would be properly recorded later. They would read something like: "Un male approaches DL (Dennis Librizzi). They talk. Un PM (pays money) to DL," or "DL PM to Un." One of us would get up and follow the unknown (Un) male out to the parking lot and jot down the license tag to identify the bettor. This would go on until we were finished with the surveillance. In any event, Bob always left the surveillance with a smile, and I always drove. About 20 days after the initiation of the tap, we conducted searches, and not long after, grand jury indictments were obtained and the Librizzi boys went to prison for a while.

On one occasion Bob and I were out working when we heard loud yelling and a gunshot. We looked across the street and saw a uniformed store security guard holding a .44 magnum revolver and standing over another man lying on the ground, writhing in pain. I jumped out of the car and ran across the street while Bob retrieved the first aid kid from the trunk of the Bureau car. I identified myself to the jittery guard and told him to put his gun away, as a gathering crowd was becoming unruly. Bob radioed the office to report the incident and asked for ambulance and police response, while I was trying to attend to the victim, a robber who had stolen a very expensive coat that he was still clutching. The bleeding man cried out, "He shot me! Can you believe that? He shot me!" Using gauze from the first aid kit, I applied direct pressure to his heavily bleeding thigh, but it was obvious the femoral artery had been severed and I knew from my medic training as a member of an aero-medical evacuation team in the Air Force Reserve that he would soon bleed to death without proper intervention. Blood was pumping out in a stream at a remarkable rate and was splashing on the sidewalk, so I removed the thief's belt and tightened it around his thigh as a tourniquet, chocking off the spurting arterial flow. The robber moaned in pain and I told him, "I have to stop the bleeding or you'll die right here on the street." He kept saying, "He shot me over a damn coat!" When the police and medical personnel arrived, I got up and walked into the nearest store's restroom and washed the blood from my hands. Then Bob and I quietly slipped away. There was a small piece in the paper the next day reporting that "a doctor" on the scene had saved the thief's life. Bob recommended me for a letter of commendation, but our supervisor said, "I would agree if he had saved the life of an innocent victim, but he saved a criminal. I don't think the Bureau would buy that."

As I was getting my feet wet on the new squad, a confidential informant provided information about a plan to beat up a chef who worked for Sally Papia, girlfriend of Chicago Outfit member "Big Frank" Buccieri. Sally was known as the "Milwaukee Queen Bee of Organized Crime" she owned and operated Sally's Steak House, a highly rated restaurant located in the Knickerbocker Hotel in Milwaukee and frequent meeting place for politicians and businessmen. Sally was a raven-haired firecracker of a woman. I once described her as "Elizabeth Taylor on a bad day." She had assembled a loyal crew of employees who were mobster wannabes. Russell Enea was an arrogant little man who threw his weight around as Sally's general manager. Jimmy Jennaro was her well-dressed maitre d' who was more of a ladies man than a tough guy, and Max Adonnis was the restaurant host who had his hands in a number of illegal pies, including illegal drugs. Frank Balistrieri resented Papia's restaurant's success and thought she was a threat to his power, as she brought Chicago Outfit guys to his town, where they often dined at Sally's place and never bothered to pay their respects to him. Balistrieri was once heard describing her as "an Outfit wannabe in a friggin' skirt." It was rumored that he once considered having her killed, but thought better of it.

Sally saw herself as a big shot but was, in reality, a hard-hearted she-wolf who had become very upset with one of her cooks. She had paid for the chef's schooling, but he had left her employ to open his own restaurant. In retaliation, his restaurant, the Northridge Inn, was torched and burned to the ground. One of the arsonists, Joseph Vincent Basile, a curly-headed, chubby friend of Sally, was recorded by a cooperating witness and was overheard to say, "The old man's [Frank Balistrieri] hysterical, absolutely hysterical . . . Frankie Bal scooped me up with a pistol. He says, 'Why did you burn the joint down without telling me?'" Basile went on to say, "She [referring to Papia] ain't got the clout to be doin' this. It probably came through the back door with some friends of hers in Chicago, and it turns out her friends are callin' Frank and givin' the friggin' details, and he don't like it . . . He's more concerned with people goin' around him." But Sally, ever vindictive, wasn't satisfied with torching the restaurant. She also ordered the crushing of the cook's hands.

The Milwaukee Police Department's Detective Bureau was notified about the potential threat to the chef, and, fortunately, two detectives were on their way to interview the victim that evening when they spotted a car cruising slowly in the area of the chef's residence. The cops pulled the suspicious vehicle over and began questioning the two occupants, when they spotted two baseball bats partially hidden under the front seat of the car. The men were immediately arrested for having concealed weapons and for suspicion of attempted assault. The next morning, I got a call from one of the detectives who told me that one of the hitters wanted to talk, but he didn't trust the police and would only speak to the FBI. We hurriedly set up an interview where the detectives, an Assistant United States Attorney, and I would be present.

Jack Schlecter was a monster. He was the meanest looking guy I have ever met. He stood 6' 6" and weighed over 250 pounds. One of his eyes was partially closed and constantly oozed a foul liquid, a result of a childhood injury. If you'd have met him in the shadows," flesh-eating Cyclops" would have come to mind – an apparition out of the adventures of Sinbad. Remarkably, he and I hit it off for some reason. It turned out that he wasn't nearly as mean as he looked. He stated emphatically, "I don't trust the cops. I only want to talk to an FBI agent." I said, "That's fine, but the police have jurisdiction at this point I want them to be here." He reluctantly led us through the whole scenario and explained how he had set fire to the cook's restaurant on orders from Basile and how he, along with his partner, were to have grabbed the cook and brought him to a garage where Sally's employees, Max Adonnis and Russell Enea, would be waiting. Apparently Adonnis and Enea got cold feet and hired Schlecter to do the dirty work, so he and Herbie Holland, owner of a massage parlor, were given the job by Jimmy Jennaro. Jimmy had told the hitters to "break the wrists of the cook so he can never work again." He informed the hitters that the cook had given notice to Sally that he was leaving to start up on his own. Sally was furious. She wouldn't let him go because she had spent a lot of money on him by sending him to chef's school and he had no right to leave her, "ever." Schlecter said he and Holland intended to "hold the kid down and smash his hands with the bats, but the cops got us first."

Based on Schlecter's proffer, a deal was struck and it was agreed that if he cooperated completely, the charges against him would be dropped. He made bond, as did his partner, and they both went back to their lives. Unknown to anyone but the government, Schlecter was wired for several meetings with the various co conspirators, all Sally's minions. The taped evidence, from the mouths of the conspirators, was devastating.

The day before indictments were returned on September 24, 1975, my ASAC suggested, "Let's have lunch at Sally's before everything comes tumbling down tomorrow." This idea appealed to me, so we had a great steak lunch as I pointed out the various players in the drama that was about to unfold. The impressed ASAC willingly paid for the expensive meal, which was fine with me. The next day agents fanned out and arrested the mobster wannabes - Sally, Jimmy Jennaro, Joseph Basile, Herbie Holland and Max Adonnis. Adonnis was not what his name suggested. He was a large, powerfully built man with a surly personality and only one arm. The two agents who took him into custody were a bit flustered at handcuffing a one armed man but they finally cuffed his arm to the back of his belt. The roundup was completed when the ASAC and I arrested general manager Russell Enea as he sat in his business office at the rear of Sally's restaurant.

The trial of the Queen Bee and her co-conspirators was covered by all Milwaukee media outlets, and Sally's name and face were flashed on television screens and in newspapers day after day. The excellent Assistant United States Attorney prosecuting the high profile case was Thomas E. Brown, who began his opening statement by looking directly at Papia and saying, "Sally and her pathetic goons burned down a restaurant and tried to crush a man's hands for daring to leave her and venture out on his own. The government is going to prove that what goes around comes around." This proved to be prophetic as well as dramatic, even though the defendants pulled out all the stops by acquiring the best defense attorneys money could buy. An interesting aside is that Joseph Balistrieri, attorney son of LCN boss Frank Balistrieri, and Sally's avowed enemy, ended up defending her. I always wondered about those strange bedfellows, but it could be that old man Balistrieri wanted to learn what Sally was actually up to in his city or, perhaps, "Big Frank" Buccieri leaned on Balistrieri to provide a defense for his paramour. Interestingly, I have often observed that defendants are somewhat jovial and upbeat for the first couple of days of a trial. They have usually been convinced by their attorneys that they can beat the charges against them, and so the true gravity of the occasion doesn't begin to sink in until the evidence mounts to suffocate them. When it does, they realize that they are looking at serious prison time and their demeanor changes dramatically. The defense attorneys did a good job, but they were up against a wall of overwhelming evidence with the tapes and a very good government attorney.

This was the trial where I learned how truly miserable it is to be a case agent in a multiple defendant case. It's Bureau policy that the case agent always sits with the prosecutor at the prosecutor's table during the entire trial, and as there were six defendants, that means a minimum of six defense attorneys. Most cases consist of assembling the evidence and witnesses and arranging for the witnesses to testify, but when extraordinary means are used, such as taped evidence, then the case agent becomes a key witness, and necessarily the main target of the defense, because the tapes are central to the case. After testifying on direct examination about the tapes and everything surrounding them, the six attorneys took their crack at me, and by the time I was finished, I felt like a punching bag. Joe Balistrieri started off, as he represented the main defendant. After he finished, the next attorney stepped up. Luckily, by the time the sixth lawyer came at me, he had no substantive questions left to ask and merely re-asked questions already answered. The last attorney was frustrated at his lowly position and asked me about the handling of the tapes. I responded, "It's Bureau policy that we..." He rudely interrupted, "I don't care what FBI policy is, answer the question!" I just stared at him in disgust as the judge reprimanded him. After my time in the witness chair, I concluded that I never wanted to go through that again, but, of course, I did. This pounding by the defense sometimes keeps agents from pursuing the difficult cases because they don't want to deal with the abuse or the problems that naturally come with such cases. This is by no means an excuse for these timid agents but it is a reality. In any event, Sally and her crew of steakhouse mobsters were all found guilty and sent to prison for extortion and conspiracy. Before going to prison Sally was given the opportunity to cooperate with the government on other cases, but she rebuffed me by saying, "I'll never be a stool pigeon."

CHAPTER 2

Two Murders

*"There is no prosecutable evidence of
organized crime activity in Milwaukee."*

– Harold Breier, former Milwaukee Chief of Police

Milwaukee is a place where you can go to the best German restaurants, purchase the finest bratwurst or homemade Polish Kielbasa and, fresh fish and chips. While living in Milwaukee, my favorite restaurant was Karl Rausch's. The restaurant is set in a Bavarian theme and the food is marvelous. My preferred dish was the fleischplatte, which means meat-plate. It consisted of a heaping mound of a pork chop, sausage, ham hock and wiener schnitzel with peas, red potatoes, and sauerkraut – delicious! The city is the home of Harley Davidson, Briggs and Stratton, Milwaukee Tool, and Schlitz Brewing, but there is another side to the city, a dark underbelly where men grapple for power and riches.

Old man Vito Guardalabene ran the Milwaukee mob until his death in 1921. A succession of bosses filled the position over time, until John Alioto seized power in 1952. The Milwaukee LCN has always been small and tightly connected to Chicago, and it certainly is not a major power on the national scene, but its control in parts of the city was profound. Like many of history's ascendants to power, Frank Peter "Frankie Bal" Balistrieri married into a position of power by joining in matrimony with Alioto's daughter. Frank took power in 1961 with the death of his father-in-law, but he was never liked nor respected by the lesser members. He was, by all accounts, an egotistical, self-absorbed, and selfish man. To a degree, he was not made of the sterner stuff of other LCN members because he considered himself educated, as he had attended college for a time. Furthermore, his two sons were college educated and licensed attorneys, and he relied on their knowledge and expertise to run his more sophisticated earning schemes. Balistrieri was convicted of income tax evasion in 1967 and served a short stretch in prison, but the pretender to the throne was not what I would term a tough guy who had made his bones on the mean streets, although it is said by some that he was an adept remote controlled bomber in his youth and had a proficiency for blowing up his enemies. This, to my knowledge, has never been corroborated.

The Milwaukee LCN in the 1970s was unique in many respects. It was a small, somewhat sophisticated group that existed for the sole benefit of Frankie Bal. The lesser members did their own things, but were never a real factor in the family. Balistrieri used his two sons as his consiglieris, and his brother Peter Frank Balistrieri, acted as his underboss when it was necessary. Frankie Bal had long since enlisted street enforcer Steve Di Salvo, whom he used as a hammer to collect the street tax and maintain discipline. Di Salvo, certainly not a formidable physical presence, was balding, bespectacled and only 5'9" and weighed 170 pounds. It isn't the physical size of the mobster that intimidates, however - it's the size of his power and his ability to get you maimed or killed that causes fear.

There was a chill in the air at 7:10 in the morning of September of 1975. Many of the leaves were off the trees and had been swept up by wind or rakes in preparation for the onslaught of the Wisconsin winter, when August "Augie" Maniaci walked out the rear door of his house in the Little Italy section of town wrapped in a sweater. It was his usual practice to warm up the car before his wife joined him for a short ride to her work at the Prize Steak Joint, where she was employed as a cook. Augie wasn't employed, as is the case with many mobsters. He preferred to let his wife do the hard work of earning a regular living while he schemed and committed various illegal jobs as opportunities came up. Augie casually backed his car out of the garage and into the alley that ran behind the block of houses, as he had done hundreds of times before. He immediately noticed there was something wrong with one of the back wheels, so he got out of the car to investigate. As he bent down to inspect the slashed right rear tire, a blur of a man moved across the alley, his breath lingering behind him in a tiny cloud as he pointed his pistol and shot the kneeling man in the torso. Augie, a man in his 60s, slumped against the wheel well of his car, his lung punctured. Before he could react, let alone defend himself, the coup d' grace was administered at point blank range with several shots fired into his skull, right behind the ear. The pencil eraser-sized projectiles slammed into the soft tissue of the brain and chopped the organ into cerebral coleslaw. Unseen by the shooter, a 14-year-old newspaper boy had entered the south end of the alley as the assassin carried out the murder. The boy, who had finished his paper route, was on his way to school as he approached the area of the shooting. He saw the shooter point his pistol at the fallen man, but although it jerked slightly a few times, he heard no sound. The boy froze momentarily as the shooter jumped a low fence like a world-class hurdler and was gone. The description of the athletic shooter jumping the fence was evidence that the man was relatively young and in good physical condition. The boy rallied to Maniaci's aid, but there was nothing he could do. The traumatized youth was then joined by a hysterical Mrs. Maniaci. In desperation, the boy ran to a neighbor's house and called the police.

Augie Maniaci had hated Frankie Bal for as long as he could remember. He never considered him a legitimate LCN boss and had accused Balistrieri of marrying into the mob. Maniaci, an old school LCN member, showed utter contempt for the boss and made his feelings known to others in the family. Balistrieri, in return, detested Maniaci and his brother, Vincent, and considered them to be a cancer to his authority. Sources informed us that Balistrieri had had a sit-down with Augie three weeks prior to his murder because Balistrieri wanted a piece of a score Maniaci had made. We don't know what the result was, but in all probability, Balistrieri was unsuccessful. Just one week before the hit, street enforcer Steve Di Salvo was seen in a violent argument with Maniaci in the parking lot of the Prize Steak Joint. After the Di Salvo confrontation, Balistrieri, according to an informant, had said, referring to Maniaci, "I've got to get that little sonofabitch before he gets me." We can certainly infer that Maniaci must have threatened Frank during their meeting, thereby irrevocably sealing his fate.

Frank Balistrieri was the son of Sicilian immigrants. His father was a lowly cinder ash hauler, but little Frank would have none of that. He would be something more; he would be a man of respect, sophistication, and power. "Fancy Pants," as he was known by his detractors, was a derisive nickname resulting from

Balistrieri's fastidiousness of dress, perhaps as a subconscious overreaction to his humble roots. He was also sometimes called "The Trumpet Player," as he had played the instrument in his high school band. He was a small, finely featured man who wore custom made suits, tailored shirts, and two-inch elevated heels to raise him from his 5' 6" height. His face was pale, almost sickly in appearance, but his eyes were the true reflection of his soul. They were dark, like those of a shark. I once described them as " . . . dead eyes in the body of a living man." Somehow, Fancy Pants had convinced Chicago mobsters to authorize the hit on Maniaci because there was no one in Milwaukee that could have pulled off such a professional murder. In all likelihood, he had used the accusation that Augie was a snitch in order to get the okay and a helping hand from the Outfit. The diminutive megalomaniac loved his power. He once stated to an informant, "Every once in a while, you have to teach somebody a lesson," and that is exactly what the murder accomplished in Milwaukee. The professional killing of Maniaci was precisely the kind of hit that Chicago mobsters could pull off, and this reinforced the hard fact that if you crossed Frankie Bal, he could surely have you killed.

The Milwaukee Police homicide unit and a few special agents responded to the scene of the murder and a survey of Maniaci's neighbors revealed that a paperboy might have been in the area when the shooting occurred. He was soon identified and interviewed at his home. The boy was terrified and traumatized beyond anything a young boy should endure, but he did his best in cooperating with authorities. When he was questioned by detectives, he wet his lips and began speaking haltingly. "I was on my way to school. I turned into the alley and saw Mr. Maniaci fall down. Then I saw a guy running toward Mr. Maniaci. He was carrying a pistol, it was big…long. He shot Mr. Maniaci." The boy began to shake. "He saw me. He looked right at me."

The boy was asked the key question by detectives: "What do you remember? Let's start with the man you saw. What did the man look like?"

The boy shook his head. "I couldn't see his face. He was tall. He had a hood over his head. He looked at me."

The detective stated, somewhat sarcastically, "If he looked at you, you would have seen his face."

The boy shook his head. "I can't remember."

Another detective inquired, "Did he point his gun at you?"

The boy shook his head again as if trying to emphasize his helplessness. "No, but he saw me!"

The questioning continued. "Did you see where he went after he shot Mr. Maniaci?"

The boy responded, "No. He came out from behind a garage across from Mr. Maniaci's house. He must have been waiting for him. After he shot Mr. Maniaci, he ran fast back across the alley and jumped the fence. He flew over it. Then he took off."

The lead detective asked, "What was he wearing?"

Again the boy shook his head. "All I remember is his shirt."

The detective followed up, "What color was it?"

The boy looked straight ahead and answered mechanically, "It was dark colored."

Exasperated the detective asked, "Can you remember anything else?"

The boy shook his head emphatically. "No."

A routine neighborhood canvas by agents and detectives

uncovered a witness who saw a strange car in the neighborhood on the morning of the shooting. A number of photos of known Chicago hitters were displayed for the witness and she identified the probable getaway driver as Charles "Chuck" Nicoletti. It was later determined that Nicoletti had been a close friend of Augie Maniaci and would have been aware of Maniaci's daily pattern of behavior. Nicoletti was a deceptively handsome man with silver hair who had come out of a totally dysfunctional Chicago family. At the age of 13 he killed his own father, but it was considered justifiable homicide by the court, as his father was proven to be a violent, abusive man. Little "Chuckie" had pleaded self-defense, and the jury took that into consideration. Tragically, heavily abused boys often turn to crime or act out in other violent ways. Chuck evolved into an Outfit hitman and had an estimated tally of 20 mob-related kills to his credit.

A couple of weeks after Maniaci's murder, a street department crew was cleaning out drain grates emptying into the Milwaukee River not far from Maniaci's house when they discovered a partially rusted Browning semi-automatic pistol fitted with a silencer. A serial number trace determined it had come from the Tamiami Gun Store in Miami, Florida. Unfortunately, the trace of the gun ended at the gun store as no records could be found for the sale of the pistol. The weapon had obviously been ditched in the drain by the shooter after his escape from the murder scene. The recovered gun was cleaned up and test fired, positively tying the bullet recovered from Maniaci's torso to the murder weapon.

We had drained all investigative possibilities out of the murder case and as we discussed the matter, case agent Bob Walsh concluded, "We're at a dead end. We can't identify the shooter and can't prove Nicoletti was part of the hit. The gun is a dead end and the grand jury investigation has led us nowhere." Fred Thorne, who had just attended a forensic hypnotism training session, was convinced that the boy knew more than he consciously remembered. He said, "I'm sure the kid has details in his brain, locked securely away in a mental vault as a result of the trauma he has experienced." It was decided that Thorne would pursue this investigative avenue, and some months later, Fred was able to arrange for an expert in forensic hypnosis to travel to Milwaukee for the purpose of unlocking the secrets held tightly in the boy's brain. Dr. William S. Kroger, psychiatrist and professor of Clinical Anesthesiology at UCLA School of Medicine flew to Milwaukee along with a Los Angeles Police forensic artist. The boy was brought to a neutral site a comfortable, non-threatening room in the classic Pfister Hotel across the street from the federal building, to meet with Dr. Kroger. After introductions and some small talk, the psychiatrist spoke gently to the boy. "This won't be painful in any way. I want you to relax. Do you like the beach?"

The boy nodded. "Yes."

The professor smiled. "Good. Lie down on the bed and close your eyes. Picture yourself on the beach. The waves are coming in. You can hear the water. The sun is warm, and you are stretched out on a towel. Can you see yourself on the beach?"

The boy began to relax. "Yeah."

The process continued. "Now, relax - breathe slowly. Can you feel the warm sun?'

"Yeah."

"Just lie there for a while. Enjoy the moment. Now you're beginning to feel sleepy. Your eyes are closed. You're drifting away.

It's so peaceful, so safe, so warm. Now I'm going to ask you to do some things. Lift your right arm."

The boy complied. This was done to test the boy's depth of trance, and he held it there for a time without any strain or movement.

"Now, son, lift your right leg off the bed."

The boy complied. He held his leg off the bed for some time without any difficulty.

"Drop your arm and leg. Mr. Thorne is going to ask you some questions."

Thorne began the questioning, which would result in the development of details never imagined. He asked, "Do you remember the morning when you saw Mr. Maniaci fall behind his car?"

"Yeah."

"Do you remember a man running toward Mr. Maniaci?"

"Yeah." The boy seemed to be viewing a movie.

"Now, take your time. Can you see the man clearly?"

"Yeah."

"What is the running man wearing?"

"He has a dark, long sleeved sweatshirt or tee shirt. It's probably gray."

Thorne continued. "Can you see the gun? What does it look like?"

"It's a pistol. It's long, real long, but there's no sound."

"What hand is he holding the gun in?"

"His right hand."

"What kind of pants is the man wearing?"

"They are blue Levis."

"You mean blue denims?"

"No. Levis."

"How do you know they are Levis brand?"

"Because I can see the little red tag on the right back pocket."

"What kind of shoes is he wearing?"

"They're dark blue sneakers, Nikes."

"How can you be sure they are Nike brand?"

"I can see the white swoosh mark on the side."

Thorne was astounded at the boy's locked memory for detail. "Now we are going to focus on his face. You can see it, can't you?"

The boy paused briefly, "Yes, I see it."

"I want you to describe the face. Start with the hair."

The boy said, "He was wearing a hood over his head, but I can see the front part of his hair. His hair is dark and parted on the left side and he had marks on his face."

"You mean cuts or a birthmark?"

"No, like grooves or holes."

"You mean pockmarks?" "Yeah, pockmarks."

"How old do you think he is?" "I can't say, maybe 22. His hair made him look young."

"How tall was he?"

"I would say 6 feet."

"How much did he weigh?"

"About 140, 150 pounds."

The remarkable opening of the young man's hidden consciousness proves the human brain's capacity to store even the most minute details of events. The debriefing process continued as the boy described the face of the man he had seen but had defensively locked out of his remembrance. After Thorne's questioning, the forensic artist began sketching a face on her drawing pad, starting with general details such as the shape of his face and the pattern of his hair. Then she asked the boy more detailed questions as she refined the features: "Were his eyes like this? How about his nose?" Each time a change was made on the sketchpad and the artist's rendering was shown to the boy. After several tedious refinements the picture was complete. The drawing showed a thin, young, "v" jawed man with a pockmarked face and a full head of hair. The boy was satisfied with the finished product and said the drawing looked just like the shooter.

At the conclusion of the process, Fred proudly returned to the office carrying the artist's rendering as if it were a trophy. He walked into the OC squad and showed it to Walsh and myself. "I just got back from the hypnosis of the paperboy. Look at this drawing. The kid said it looks just like the shooter. Do you know who it could be?" I was familiar with many of the known Chicago Outfit hitmen and had accumulated numerous photographs of them sent to me by our Chicago office. I looked at it for mere seconds and I told him emphatically, "That's Paul Schiro. It looks just like him. Even the pockmarks on the drawing indicate it's Schiro. His face is covered with them." I dug out a photo of Schiro from my collection of mobster mug shots and we compared the drawing with the picture. Remarkably, they were very nearly identical. We were convinced we had our man. We were also aware that Schiro, known as a cold-blooded killer, was one of Outfit member Tony Spilotro's hit crew.

Not long after, Thorne returned to the newspaper boy and showed him a photo spread, including a picture of Schiro. The boy stated, pointing to the photo of Schiro, "That's the guy who shot Mr. Maniaci." We were elated at our success. As a result, homicide detectives presented the murder case to then Deputy District Attorney Thomas Schneider, a diminutive pit bull terrier who, once he got his teeth into the flesh of a criminal, never let go. Schneider, who was later appointed as United States Attorney for the Eastern District of Wisconsin, opined that the hypnotism, although extremely helpful in gleaning necessary details and potentially identifying the killer, would not be recognized in a court of law as it was considered too suggestive. He instructed, "If the young man is given the chance to personally observe Paul Schiro in a lineup, and if he identifies him as the shooter, I will prosecute the case." He prepared an arrest warrant giving the police authority to make the apprehension, but stressed, "If the identification isn't 100% positive, I will have to drop the charge of first degree murder against Schiro."

An old time agent, jaded by years of fighting various crimes, once asked me, "Why worry about mobsters killing other mobsters? Why waste time investigating them? They just kill each other." This is one of the conundrums of aggressively investigating mob hits. Who cares if they kill each other – after all, they're all killers. I answered the best I could. "They don't just kill each other. The fact is, they kill whoever can cause them harm, and sometimes that can be innocent people. I look at it somewhat philosophically. If a hooker is raped by a John, it's still rape. If a killer gets murdered, it's still murder. Besides, it gives law enforcement the opportunity to delve into the mob's operations and, perhaps, score a few points and maybe lock some of them away."

On October 18, 1977, the two Milwaukee detectives, the

newspaper boy, prosecutor Tom Schneider, and I flew to Mesa, Arizona, where we were met by two Mesa detectives. Although it was winter, the climate of the Valley of the Sun was a relief from the refrigerator of Milwaukee. We went to Schiro's residence early the next morning and knocked on the door of his modest, ranch-style stucco home. He came to the door and was immediately placed under arrest without incident. He had no reaction, no questions, and no sign of concern. He was transported to the Maricopa County Jail, where he was processed and taken to the lineup room and placed in a lineup with five other men who had his general physical characteristics. A homogeneous lineup is very important. You can't have a midget, a fat man, a bald guy, a one-legged man, and Santa Claus standing next to the subject who is 5'9" and has thick black hair because the lineup participants need to look similar to the subject in order to authenticate the identification.

There was palpable tension in the small viewing room with one-way glass as the young man struggled to remember the man he had seen so very briefly in the alley. Schneider told the boy, "When we open the curtain, look at the men in front of you. Take your time. They will be standing with numbers one through six below them on the floor. You pick out the man you saw shoot Mr. Maniaci and tell us which one it is. If you can't pick him out, then tell us." The small curtain was opened slowly on the one-way glass window like it was opening night on Broadway. No one said a word, as we didn't want to taint any identification. The boy stared at each man in the lineup for some time. Our anticipation was acute. Finally, the boy whispered, "I don't know. It might be number two, but I can't say for sure. I was scared. I don't remember very much." All of us just looked at each other but nothing was said. We knew the young man had only been willing to come part way and then fear took over. It happened that suspect number two was Paul Schiro, but the ID was much too weak to take the case to trial. The boy had obviously panicked at the sight of the killer, since he had already identified Schiro from a photo spread and he looked exactly the same as the photo. The dark ghosts had smiled on one of their own and we were, of course, extremely disappointed. Remarkably, Schiro never asked what murder he was arrested for. As a matter of fact, he didn't say one word. He was as cold as a frozen fish. He was a man who killed people he had never met only because someone told him to do so – his soul was obviously dead and his lack of a normal reaction was that of a morally deficient human being. We went home empty handed and frustrated beyond words because we knew a guilty, cold-blooded murderer had gone free.

Some time later, another member of the Milwaukee mob, Vincent Maniaci (Augie's younger brother), was the subject of FBI surveillance, and Steve Di Salvo and another unknown man were observed in the vicinity of Vince's home. Vince was a likable person, known as a funny man, always telling jokes and stories, but he was also a mobster who was despised by Balistrieri. The next day, Chuck Nicoletti was observed in Vince's neighborhood driving a car rented by John Balistrieri. We knew something was up and expected Vince to be the subject of the next vindictive murder ordered by Frank Balistrieri, but we couldn't be sure. We assumed, wrongly, that if a hit were to come, it would be similar to Augie's killing - by way of a shooter in the morning when he left for work. The next morning we were watching as Vince got in his car and drove off on his way to work as a cook at Alioto's Restaurant. Vince realized something was wrong when he pushed down on the accelerator because the car wouldn't go faster than 20 miles an hour. We watched him pull over and open the hood of his white Oldsmobile to check for the problem, but what he saw shocked him. He jumped back from his car, quickly walked some distance away, went directly to a pay phone, and, realizing he had no options, called the police. When he had peered under the hood, he had seen the ultimate death package. A bundle of twenty sticks of dynamite, wrapped together in electrical tape, had been placed at the rear of the engine block and wired to the ignition by alligator clips. He had pumped the accelerator two times, as was his custom, before starting the car and, luckily, the accelerator rod had pushed against the bomb, thereby impeding the speed of the car. It had also loosened one of the clips wired to the ignition, thereby inactivating the bomb.

The Milwaukee Police Department bomb squad responded quickly and without so much as a "What's going on" or "What are the details," the two detectives ran to the car and began tinkering with the bomb. I couldn't believe their foolish bravery or total insanity and determined that I never wanted to be around guys who were that crazy. In any event, after visually examining the device, it was reported that if the bomb had ignited, it would have blown Vince and his car into small scraps and certainly would have caused catastrophic collateral damage. The bomb was dismantled, and it was determined that the red arrow brand dynamite been stolen from a mine site in West Virginia in 1975.

On August 11, 1977, Special Agent Al Ness and I were on our way to debrief an informant and we were discussing what we needed to get from the informant. Al was a veteran of the Air Force who had been assigned to the National Security Agency monitoring Soviet military air traffic. He was a direct descendant of Elliot Ness, the man who took down Al Capone. Al stated, "My guy knows Sam Librizzi well. He lays off bets to him regularly so decide what you want from him." I responded, "Yeah, I have a list of questions I want to ask him." Al continued, "I've got some money to pay my guy for the last information he gave. Hopefully he'll buy us lunch. He usually does." As we drove along through the Italian section of town, we spotted a short, mopey-looking guy getting out of a shiny, black Ford with Illinois tags. Instinct is often developed when working the streets and when you know your adversary and neighborhoods as well as we did, any deviance from the norm can be a signal to an astute investigator. I told Al, "Let's stick around. This smells like something to me." He agreed, "Yeah, that mopey-looking guy is up to something. The way he's looking around makes me think he doesn't belong here." The Ford sped off, leaving its passenger behind, but we were able to get the tag number. We determined the black Ford was registered to Merry Montelleone, wife of John "Johnny Apes" Montelleone, a Chicago Outfit member. The mope was dressed in an unkempt gray, long sleeved work shirt with matching pants and ball cap. He stood on the street corner like some vagrant as we made a U-turn a few blocks away to come back for a better look. As we did so, a white over red Cadillac that I recognized as Peter Balistrieri's car pulled up and the mope got in. They sped off, but we now were coming the other way, so we had to wait for traffic before making another U-turn, and by the time we made the turn, they were gone. The mope was eventually identified as Nicholas George

Montos, known in the underworld as a "mechanic," a bomb making expert. It was later determined that he was the same man seen with Steve Di Salvo near Vince Maniaci's house before the dynamite bomb was discovered. We were sure we had identified the bomber, but we couldn't prove it at that point.

Hollywood productions always make everything so easy, crimes are cleaned up in an hour or so, and there are almost always car chases and gunfights in every episode. That, of course, is understandable – it's entertainment. The real world of crime fighting, particularly organized crime fighting, takes a long time to unravel. Most organized crimes are hidden and seldom surface on their own, and the order of investigation is often reversed. For example, the FBI knows who the crooks are, but we don't have a crime to tie them to. The murders committed by mobsters are usually professionally done and are very difficult to solve, as little evidence is available. The result of these hurdles is tedious surveillances, developing of informants, and dealing with their sometimes outrageous behavior, to say nothing of hours of monitoring electronic surveillances. Even when listening to wiretaps or microphones, the conversations are often coded or difficult to sort out. An example of this difficulty in determining what is going on is a conversation we monitored between Frankie Bal and his son, John:

Frank asks, "Did you take care of that thing?"

John: "What thing?"

Frank: "You know, that guy over there at that place."

John: "Oh, yeah, it's okay, don't worry about it."

On June 30, 1978, Milwaukee illegal bookmaker August "Augie" Palmisano, was getting into his car parked in the parking garage of the Juneau Village apartment complex. The bartender inserted the key into the ignition and the car lifted off the concrete floor and erupted in flames. The explosion was so violent that 21 other cars were also damaged by the blast. We later learned that Augie had refused to pay street tax to Balistrieri and, thus, had received the same reward as Augie Maniaci - eternal something. We arrived on the scene after Palmisano's body cooled down and he had assumed room temperature. The enclosed garage held a distinct sour odor of smoke and burned flesh as we examined the remains of what was left of the car. We could see the remains of Augie's nude body within the twisted metal that was once his late model automobile. His clothes had been scorched off by the blast and his carcass was singed much like a large roasted turkey. His face had been ripped and burned, rendering him unrecognizable, and the once tall man's legs and feet were mangled by the force of the horrific explosion. After the bombing, the cold-hearted Balistrieri was overheard by an informant to say, referring to Palmisano, "He called me a name to my face, now he doesn't have a face." The informant told us that Palmisano had had utter contempt for The Trumpet Player and had no fear of the diminutive Steve Di Salvo. Augie was somehow in denial, as he believed he was safe and beyond the grasp of the hated boss, but he was dead wrong. We later learned that Joseph Aiuppa, mob boss of Chicago, had approved the killing of Palmisano but was skeptical of Frankie Bal's motivation for the hit. He had told an associate, "The guy probably combed his hair wrong and Balistrieri didn't like it."

Nicholas "The Mope" Montos was subpoenaed before the federal grand jury in September of 1980, but he refused to testify and was sent to jail for contempt for the term of the grand jury, as was John Montelleone. Montos, like so many others, had grown up on the mean streets of Chicago and was known as a consummate safe cracker and hit man. He only stood 5'5," but was a man without any mercy. He was twice installed on the FBI's Ten Most Wanted list, the only man ever to be so "honored." He was a professional thug who never stopped his criminal activities, and even at the advanced age of 78, he tried to rob an antique store in Brookline, Massachusetts, with a .22 caliber semi-automatic pistol, fitted with a silencer. Unfortunately for him, he ran into the feisty 73-year-old proprietor of the store who beat him with a baseball bat. Sonia Paine bragged when the police came to take Montos, only a shell of the man he had once been, "I beat the hell out of him." The mope was sent to prison for attempted robbery and died alone in his cell at the age of 92, a fitting reward for a lifelong crime spree.

Grand jury subpoenas were issued for Frank Balistrieri and Peter Balistrieri in an effort to determine their whereabouts on the day of the murder of Palmisano and to have Peter tell us who he had picked up in his car and why. Fred Thorne and I went to Peter's house, but when he came to the door he refused to open it. We identified ourselves. "We're with the FBI. We have a grand jury subpoena for you." He responded, "I ain't gonna open the door. Go away." I slid the subpoena through the mail slot in his door, where it was immediately attacked by his dog and ripped to shreds. Fred and I started to laugh and Fred informed Peter, "You've been served, and so has your dog." A day later, I went to serve Frankie Bal with a subpoena, and Fred Thorne took one to Steve Di Salvo. When we returned to the office and shared our experiences, I told Fred, "Balistrieri refused to come to the door.

He spoke to me through his second story window that he had partially opened. He told me, "I don't open my door for anybody. Talk to my son, Joe, about the subpoena." Fred recounted, "I've got you beat. When I went to serve Di Salvo, he opened the door and was surprised to see me. He told me, 'I thought you were the paperboy.' I smiled and said, 'Well, in a way I am,' and served the subpoena – 'here's the paper.'" The attempt at obtaining information from the brothers and Di Salvo was unsuccessful, as all three, through Joseph Balistrieri, advised the Assistant United States Attorney that they would take the fifth if they appeared before the grand jury. We couldn't grant them immunity as they were our targets, but in spite of the rebuff, we had no intention of giving up.

By this time, Bob Walsh had been transferred to FBI Headquarters and the case was assigned to another agent. Al Ness and I were very upset about the assignment of the case, as we knew the new case agent well and were convinced that he couldn't handle it. As a result of our complaints, the ASAC publicly said, "We have a couple of prima donnas on the squad who think they are better than anyone else. Let me tell you, no one on this squad is better than anyone else. Everyone is the same. You big shots keep your mouths shut or find another squad."

Al and I were furious. Al turned to me and said, "Let's get out of here and go to lunch at the Aegean." We both left the squad room and drove the short distance to the restaurant in silence, seething with anger. We were seated at the Greek eatery in a quiet corner booth. Al ordered a salad and I asked for string beans and beef medallions and lots of fresh bread. While we were waiting for our food, Al asked, "Why did that little jerk call us out in front of the whole frigging squad? That should have been done privately. Did you ever say you were better than others on the squad?" I responded, "Of course not. There are several guys that could handle the case. I just said the wrong guy got the case. As far as I'm concerned, Balistrieri is safe again. Nothing will be done. Everyone knows you and I have the most institutional knowledge about the Milwaukee mob and that little creep, Fancy Pants." He agreed. "I don't understand why the ASAC called us prima donnas just because we expressed our opinions. This is bullshit as far as I'm concerned." I added, "The boss doesn't like me anyway. He called me a smart money guy. He thinks I manipulate everything, so it's possible the blame may have spilled out on you because . . ." Al interrupted, "No, the boss doesn't like me, either. I guess we'll both be on the shit-list for a while." I was resigned to our fate. "Yeah, well, I'm already on that list." We ate our lunch in relative silence as we both contemplated what to do. Later, Al requested a transfer to Madison, Wisconsin, and before long, he left in disgust. I decided to hang on, as I loved organized crime work – it fit me so well.

Our dire predictions were fulfilled when the annual inspection of the office determined that the agent who had the case on Frank Balistrieri deserved an unprecedented letter of censure for investigative inaction. I have never seen that done before or since. In any event, the case was then reassigned to me. The case file was thick and filled with surveillance reports, spot checks, and other surface intelligence. I wanted actionable intelligence, information that I could sink my investigative teeth into, so I began turning over rocks to develop more substantial information. I began interviewing various people who had had minor dealings with

Frankie Bal or his sons in an effort to glean bits and pieces that might add up to something.

Some time later, Agent Mike Potkonjak initiated an undercover operation targeting Balistrieri's hidden control of a vending machine business known as Alioto Distributing. I traveled with Potkonjak to Chicago to set up the purchase of vending machines from a Windy City manufacturer. Later, gifted undercover agent Gail T. Cobb, using the undercover name Tony Conte opened a company with the Chicago machines and began to compete with Balistrieri's Alioto Vending Company. Cobb's company was named Conte's Best Vending Company. Cobb contacted some of Alioto's clients and offered them a better deal, but they refused to change vending companies. Cobb made no real progress until FBI undercover agent extraordinaire Joe Pistone, using the undercover name Donnie Brasco, stepped into the picture to help Cobb gain credibility with Balistrieri. Over a period of time, Pistone had infiltrated the New York, Bonanno family and had developed strong mob credentials. Pistone set up a meeting with Balistrieri through a Bonanno soldier named Benjamin "Lefty Guns" Ruggerio who was anxious to make some money on the deal. During a preliminary meeting, Ruggerio, who believed Cobb was a criminal associate of Pistone, asked Cobb if he was "connected to anybody?" By this, he meant, was he associated with any mob guys? Cobb responded, "I'm trying to do my own thing." Ruggerio was shocked and said, "I'm surprised Balistrieri let you get this far without muscling in on you." He continued by describing Balistrieri as "crazy." Ruggerio then added, "Balistrieri can't be controlled by New York or anybody else. He's controlled by Chicago."

After a number of telephone calls, Ruggerio was able to

contact Rockford, Illinois mobster, 80-year-old Joe Zito, and he
agreed to be an intermediary between Ruggerio and Balistrieri.
A meeting was held between and Zito, Ruggerio, and Pistone
and Frank Balistrieri, Steve Di Salvo, and Peter Balistrieri at
one of Balistrieri's joints, the Centre Stage Dinner Playhouse.
They resolved some issues and then moved the meeting to
another of Balistrieri's places, Snugs Restaurant, where Balistrieri
was introduced to Cobb using the name Tony Conte. When
Balistrieri heard the name he stiffened and said, "Tony Conte?
We were gonna hit you. We thought you were the 'G." Balistrieri's
admission sent chills through Cobb as he realized he was nearly
a dead man as Balistrieri thought he was with the government.
Balistrieri went on to tell Cobb, "We've been looking for you all
week. We were looking to kill you. You've got the white Cadillac,
an apartment in Greenfield, and a store out on Farwell." Cobb
suddenly realized he had been followed and Balistrieri knew all
about him. Balistrieri said three men had been watching Cobb,
and they were just about to move against him. He told Cobb
that he was about to have him killed because he had moved in
as a competitor to his Alioto Vending Company without his
permission. Balistrieri explained that Cobb was lucky they had
now met and proper arrangements could be made. The fortuitous
meeting with Balistrieri had undoubtedly saved Cobb's life, but
now that he was sponsored by Ruggerio everything would be
fine. Not long after, Balistrieri's son, Joseph drew up a contract
with Cobb giving Balistrieri a piece of Cobb's vending company.
For reasons never fully understood at the time, Balistrieri later
cancelled the contract and turned his back on Cobb, Ruggerio
and the Bonanno family. Later, we learned that Balistrieri had

informed the Chicago Outfit about the contract and the secret agreement with the Bonanno family and he was ordered to have no contact with the New York mob as they didn't want them to have a toe-hold in their territory.

Not long after receiving the case assignment on Balistrieri and, therefore, the Milwaukee LCN, I followed him from his home to a small bar in the northeast part of town, where he sat alone at a table, nursing a drink for a time. I sat at the bar with a Coke. He didn't pay any attention to me, obviously not recognizing me. Then he got up after a while and went to a phone booth located in the lobby. There were two side-by-side booths with a wooden wall dividing them, so I slipped into the other compartment. I could hear Balistrieri yelling at someone on the other end of the line, but his words were muffled and I couldn't make out what he was saying. I wondered if I would ever be able to harness enough evidence to bring him down. There I was, so close, and yet he was so far out of my grasp.

Some time later, I took my wife to the Centre Stage Dinner Playhouse, one of his secretly owned properties, to scope it out for future reference. My wife and I found the food at the Centre Stage to be lousy, cold and stale. The show was the same even though the headliner was Emmy winning comedian Sid Caesar. He put on a less than entertaining one man comedy act and appeared pitifully old and worn out. I remembered Caesar as the star of "Your Show of Shows" television program that ran from 1950 to 1954. My parents and I used to watch it regularly. He was a comedic genius and one of the most popular comedians of the day. It was sad to see his decline, but that wasn't the end of the story. Balistrieri had hired Tony Pepito a big, tough kid who had just been released from prison, to be a bouncer at his club. Pepito approached a massage parlor operator at the request of Mr. Caesar and procured a prostitute for him. I subsequently interviewed the hooker, and she was willing to testify against Caesar if it was necessary, as he had paid her for her services. Assistant District Attorney Tom Schneider subpoenaed Sid Caesar from Hollywood to testify against Pepito for pimping. Caesar fought the effort, but was forced to testify and wept as he admitted he was " . . . down on my luck and very lonely in Milwaukee."

Balistrieri opened and closed a number of businesses over time. These businesses were fronted by his sons. They were: the Centre Stage, the Ad Lib, the Brass Rail, the Downtowner, Gallaghers, the Tradewinds, La Scalla, Leonardo's, Joey's Place, and the Shorecrest Hotel, and Snugs Restaurant. Some of the places were strip joints and others were legitimate bars that offered world-class entertainers such as Vic Damon and Bill Haley and the Comets until Frankie Bal drained the clubs of their profits and they drifted into oblivion. Fancy Pants also promoted prize fights, but this also ended for the same reason.

Soon after being assigned as case agent, I followed Frankie Bal to the apartment of John Alioto, nephew of the former boss, small time bookie and straw man for Alioto Distributing. As I sat outside the building, a light bulb went on in my head prompting me to call Mike De Marco, another member of the organized crime squad, on the car radio. I told him, "Mike, come over to Humboldt Street. I just had a great idea." That became the genesis of a full out electronics attack on Balistrieri and the Milwaukee LCN.

CHAPTER 3

Full-Court Press

"The first time I heard the word Mafia
was when I read it in the newspapers."
--Frank Balistrieri

In 1970, a game changing law was passed by Congress. It's called the Racketeer Influenced and Corrupt Organizations Act, otherwise known as RICO. The law gave the FBI a sledgehammer to be used against organized crime. It's designed to attack illegal enterprises run for the benefit of the mob and other crooked organizations. Under the law, if you are able to show a pattern of racketeering activity by a group of individuals, you can not only attack the individual but the whole enterprise by proving certain predicate crimes. Some of the many predicate state and local crimes are: murder, extortion, illegal gambling, and so on, exactly those crimes committed by the mob. If at least two of these crimes can be proven to be essential in the acquisition, maintenance or conduct of an enterprise, the RICO law has been violated. The law has criminal penalties as well as civil remedies. With the new weapon, the FBI could pull all the various mob crimes into one tightly wrapped package and attack the LCN at its very heart.

Special Agent Mike De Marco had recently been transferred from the New York City Division to Milwaukee. He is the son of Italian immigrants who chased the American dream by putting himself through night school while working as a clerk in the Newark Field Office of the FBI. His extensive clerical experience was just what was needed at that particular time in Milwaukee, as we were about to embark on an all-out electronic surveillance of Balistrieri, necessitating the orderly flow of paper and coordination of efforts. After his retirement from the Bureau, Mike became the director of security for Milwaukee's Summerfest, the largest music festival in the United States.

I had called Mike on the Bureau radio to share an idea with him. Within twenty minutes he pulled up and got in my car. He asked, "What's up Mugsy?" He always called me Mugsy. I said, "Mike, I've been thinking. Frankie Bal is in Frank Alioto's place. Who knows what's going on, he's probably picking up money. We're blind as far as Balistrieri is concerned. We need some eyes and ears on him, and I think we have enough probable cause to go up on Balistrieri. And maybe we can talk the new SAC into forming a surveillance squad to watch him." Mike thought for a minute. "We'll have to dig through what we have and see where the holes are and try to fill them. It will be a lot of work." I responded, "Yeah, I know, but look at us. We don't know what's going on. He does his thing and we do ours – what good is that?"

That informal conversation was the spark that lit the fuse on a full-court press to bring down the Milwaukee LCN family. We began kicking around ideas, reviewing the evidence we were aware of and what we needed. Mike immediately volunteered to write the affidavit in support of obtaining a judicial wire tape order on Balistrieri, and we agreed that we would both run the case together. I would attend to scheduling of agents, the review of tapes, and coordination of the surveillance squad. We returned to the office, anxious to get started, and we began pulling together all the evidence we had on Balistrieri.

Mike and I reviewed the case with SAC John Glover and the ASAC Bob Butler and they expressed excitement at the prospect and assured us that whatever we needed would be provided. This was vital because we knew the case would expand, but we had no idea as to what extent. An eight man surveillance team was established, and they were tasked with determining Balistrieri's movements, contacts, and finding other potential targets for monitoring purposes. Additionally, within days I was able to develop an informant who knew Milwaukee mobster Frank Alioto, so we set up a scenario where the informant and Alioto drove to Rockford, Illinois, some two hours away, to attend the horse races. We had pre-wired the car and taped their conversations during the drive. They engaged in conversation throughout the trip, and Alioto complained about Balistrieri and his management style and how everybody was left out of the loop. He mentioned "some big deal" Fancy Pants was involved in. He said, "Nobody knows what it is, but he has been going back and forth to Chicago a lot." During the drive, the informant asked about the Augie Palmisano bombing and Alioto responded with a sly smirk. "He was a big informant. He had a direct line to the FBI." The informant then asked, "Who killed him?" Alioto responded, "The syndicate, positively, I know that.

I know that for sure, you know what I mean? These were special guys, they brought them in special."

Obtaining authorization to intercept oral communications in criminal cases is a very intensive and daunting process, not at all a simple matter as shown on television. This authorization is obtained through what is known as Title III of the Omnibus Crime Control and Safe Streets Act of 1968. In the Bureau, this is known as a "T III." This is entirely different than consensual monitoring of conversations where one of the parties agrees to the monitoring. For a T III, an affidavit must be prepared detailing the probable cause, a legal term for "more likely than not," that we had for eavesdropping on Balistrieri. The document must specify who the target of the proposed intercept is and exactly why that person or persons are the target. For example, you must spell out what crimes are being suspected and what evidence is available as probable cause to show those crimes are being committed. The most difficult part is showing that a specific telephone or location is being used in furtherance of the crimes specified. You must be able to swear that there is probable cause that subject A is talking about a specific crime over phone A or at location A. De Marco's 110 page initial rough draft RICO affidavit was then reviewed by the Milwaukee office's legal counsel, then it went to an Assistant United States Attorney for review. After some massaging and filling in needed legal gaps it was forwarded to the FBI's Organized Crime Section in Washington D.C., and to the U.S. Department of Justice for their review.

There is a saying in the Bureau: "Nothing is impossible for the person who doesn't have to it." Headquarters always wants more probable cause to bolster the affidavit but sometimes additional details are impossible to obtain. That's why we apply for the T III authorization to begin with. At this point in the investigation, the FBI is on the outside looking in, and it's impossible to know exactly what is going on without eyes or ears on the inside. We were lucky to have Bob Walsh, my old partner in the Librizzi bookmaking case, in the Organized Crime Section of FBI headquarters to help shepherd the affidavit through the process. After some back and forth and sometimes contentious negotiations, the finished product was signed off by the Bureau and a specially designated Deputy Attorney General.

In the final step, the affidavit is presented to a federal judge and the affiant who prepared the document swears to its truthfulness. The judge then decides whether there is sufficient probable cause and, hopefully, signs the order to execute. When a surreptitiously placed microphone is requested, an order to break and enter is also required. The judge's order to execute is only authorized for up to 30 days, and then judicial authority must be renewed and the daunting process begins again. If there are several monitoring targets, the process becomes even more complicated. In addition, the judge must receive timely reports as to the progress of the monitoring. Mike and I knew that we had an uphill climb on our hands, but we were willing to commit to it.

Our first target was Frank Balistrieri's home phone. The installation was a relatively simple matter, but as the surveillances progressed, we learned that Frankie Bal often frequented Leonardo's and La Scalla restaurants. Both places were owned, on paper, by his sons. He was treated with the utmost deference at both establishments and was always seated at the same booths, where he often met with various known criminal associates. As a result, we added Leonardo's and La Scalla to our target list. This necessitated breaking and entering and placing microphones in his personal booths.

We scheduled the monitoring for 16 hours a day as Balistrieri was a late riser and stayed out until closing time at 2 a.m. The SAC gave us a separate wing of the office where we set up shop and I spent my time reviewing the monitored conversations from the previous day. This task was made easier because the monitoring agents kept contemporaneous logs of each conversation and highlighted those conversations considered important. This daily review was a tedious process and extremely time consuming. We used two separate tape recorders on each target. One tape was sealed and kept in a locked vault as the original while the second tape was used as a work copy. When I found a good conversation, I made a third tape of that specific conversation. Then that tape was sent to the typing pool for transcription. Upon completion, the rough transcript was reviewed by me for accuracy and returned to the pool for final typing. The pertinent transcripts, surveillance reports, and additional new evidence was then reviewed by De Marco, who correlated the information into the next affidavit. We gave our case the code name of "Bellwether," which is defined as someone who is followed by sheep-like others.

At this point we had approximately 12 agents a day working the case, but by the time we finished we had as many as 30 agents, plus several clerical employees working for us. As our targets increased, the review process became overwhelming, so Fred Thorne who was somewhat familiar with the case, was assigned as another co-case agent. I knew he would be a great addition to out team. We were like the three musketeers and worked extremely well together. I don't recall a single instance of serious disagreement or conflict of any kind between us during the often tense two year investigation. In the meantime, the always affable De Marco sat at his desk with papers stacked all over it and wrote and wrote and wrote, never complaining and never missing a deadline. When I first joined the Bureau, agents would dictate reports to stenographers who would come to our desks and type the material. Then we began using dictation machines and the reports would be typed by typists. Many agents, however, preferred to handwrite the material for submission to the typing pool. Mike preferred this method and said, "When I have the words in front of me, they make more sense and I can do it better this way."

To make things more difficult, we decided to target Dennis and Sam Librizzi's bookmaking operation on top of everything else. Mike proposed, "Mugsy, why not go after them, too? They're Frankie Bal's guys, and maybe he will come up on their wires." I agreed. "Good, but that makes more work, more affidavits, more monitoring – everything." He responded with a shrug of his shoulders "Yeah." The decision was made. Dennis, as he had done in the past, took bets out of his business, Libby's Lounge, Sam took telephone action in the late afternoon, before the games started, at his home on Brady Street. When we first began to monitor Sam's two telephones, we immediately picked up betting and bookmaking activity.

The calls ran like this: "Sammy, this is number 25, give me Duke, minus 6 for a dime." In this call, the bettor, using the code name "number 25," placed a $1,000 bet on the Duke University basketball team that was favored by six points over their opponent. Another call followed immediately. "This is Johnny the Genius, give me the dog on number 8 for a nickel and the favorite on number 12 for two dimes." This bettor placed two bets. The first wager was on a team identified as "number 8." The bettor and the bookie work off identical sheets listing games to be played by number, and the bet was on the underdog team for $500. The second bet was on the favored team according to the point spread set in game number 12 for $2,000. The next call came in quickly. "Sam, this is Benny the Bum. Give me the over on 18 for two bucks." This bettor placed a $200 bet on his belief that the total combined scores on game number 18 would exceed the number set by the bookie.

The biggest sports betting seasons are during college and pro basketball and college and pro football, with the largest betting day being on Super Bowl Sunday. Settle up day during football season is on Tuesdays, a day after the Monday night football game. Basketball is usually settled the same day to keep things simple. The Librizzi settle up was usually done at Libby's, where the losers came in to pay what they owed and the winners picked up their money. The only problem faced by bookies, besides law enforcement, is collecting from deadbeat losers. The Librizzis they tried to handle these situations themselves, but if they were unsuccessful, the job fell to Steve Di Salvo, The Trumpet Player's street collector. Di Salvo had a ferocious temper. He was loyal to Frankie Bal but, as far as we knew, hadn't committed a murder since the 1963 killing of a vending machine operator. His street reputation was enough to frighten most men.

At this point, the microphones in the restaurants weren't producing much of value because of the overwhelming background noise and were considered "dry holes," but we would soon hit the mother load. I said, "Mike, we're still just picking around the perimeter. We need to penetrate deeper into his world." Mike agreed, "I think we have developed enough probable cause for the installation of a mic in John's office." I agreed, "You're right, let's do it." John Balistrieri's office was located inside the Balistrieri-owned, high-end Shorecrest Residence Hotel. John, unlike his brother, was a dark, brooding man who specialized in financial matters. I always felt he was the "Michael Corleone"-type character portrayed in the movie *The Godfather*. We learned that the Shorecrest property was financed was financed through a $500,000 deposit of Teamster money by Teamster trustee Frank Ranney into the Milwaukee Continental Bank and Trust. As a result of the capital guarantee, a loan in that same amount was given to the Balistrieris to buy the Shorecrest. Unlike John, brother Joseph had a law office downtown and was a practicing attorney. Joe was the gregarious, glad-handing, outgoing type who enjoyed the good life and the spotlight. John, although a licensed attorney, ran the various family businesses out of his office, and the surveillance team had placed his father, Joseph, and Steve Di Salvo in the office along with John on a number of occasions. The hotel was well protected by security, and all exterior doors were locked at night. John drove a midnight blue Mercedes convertible and had an assigned parking spot outside the hotel, so we always knew when he was present at the Shorecrest office. The overriding problem confronting us was how were we going to install a microphone in John's office with such tight security.

Squad member Rick Prokop obtained blueprints for the Shorecrest from the city building department, and De Marco, Prokop, and I scoured the plans for the best way to make surreptitious entry. Prokop, a veteran of the Coast Guard and a man with ice water in his veins, stated, "As far as I can tell, the only way to insert the mic into the office would be through the ceiling or through the floor. We can't go through the ceiling because there's an occupied apartment directly above the office. The best bet would be to install the mic through the basement ceiling into the floor the office." Mike and I agreed. Mike stated, "The front desk is almost always manned and it's right across from the door to the office. That makes entry through the door impossible." I added, "The seemingly insurmountable question is, how do we gain access to the basement?" Prokop answered, "We need the Bureau's help. We need an expert lock guy." We enlisted the aid of a lock expert from FBI headquarters. He flew out to Milwaukee and we discussed our plans with him. The court order to break and enter and install and service a microphone in John's office had been obtained, so now it was a matter of getting into the locked building. After discussing our problem, the lock expert informed us that he could get through any lock as long as he had enough time, and since we may need to make entry more than once, he wanted to make a key for the front door. Mike and I just looked at him with surprise and Mike asked, "What do you mean the front door? Wouldn't it make more sense to go through another more secluded door?" He responded, "Yeah, it normally would, but we would attract more attention from the security guards by hanging around some dark, back door. All I need is a cooperative, cool-headed female agent to help me. I promise, we can pull it off."

The next night our plans were set in motion. We had surveillance on the primary targets and in the vicinity of the hotel, and the SAC was on the street in case we were discovered by local police. Thorne once bragged, "We knew exactly when the milkman delivered, when the bakery brought their goods, when people who regularly walked their dogs in front of the Shorecrest came, and when the police made their regular patrols." We didn't feel comfortable telling the police department of our plans because there had been persistent rumors that a few officers were close to the Balistrieris. A police cruiser actually pulled around the rear of the hotel during the operation and surely would have caught us had we tried to make entry through a back door. The lock expert and Special Agent Berdie Pasinelli, the wife of then Racine, Wisconsin, chief of police, acted as though they were lovers and had had a few too many drinks. They hung around the front door, embraced against the wall and front door, all the time a key was being fitted and made. The wait was excruciating, but finally, Pasinelli walked away. The lock expert entered the building (with court authorization to do to so) in order to ensure that the key would work in the basement door. A short time later, we heard the cheerful report over the radio, "Everything is good." We let out a cheer, and the next night (actually early the next morning) Prokop, De Marco, the ASAC, and I made entry into the belly of the hotel.

The four of us slipped in the front door unobserved and went directly down some stairs to the concrete walled basement. I felt like we were in some bunker awaiting an attack. Sheets, pillowcases, and other laundry were stacked on tables giving us some cover, and several commercial sized clothes washers lined one of the walls. We helped Prokop make careful measurements with a twenty-five foot tape measure based on the blueprints, but we found that once inside the confines of the laundry room, exact measurements were impossible because of the thick walls and laundry tables placed throughout the bunker. We couldn't get a straight measurement over the piles of laundry. We never discussed our feelings with one another at the time, but my heart was pounding and every sound was a signal for alarm. At the same time, the adrenaline rush was savored because I knew we were on the brink of something extraordinary. All of our efforts and hopes hung on the success of the installation. When Prokop began drilling a hole in the 18-inch reinforced concrete, the fine powder of pulverized cement fell like snowflakes on his head, causing us to chuckle nervously. He spit out some dust and just shook his head and kept drilling. The drill was exceptionally quiet, but our senses were on edge and we were on high alert, so the noise seemed amplified in our ears. The thought ran through my mind, what happens if we're discovered by security? Will we be able to convince the guard to cooperate with us and not tell his bosses of our plan? Would his sense of loyalty to the U.S. be enough, or would we need to threaten him with charges of obstruction of justice if he ratted us out? Thankfully, none of those questions would need answering. Finally, the microphone was slowly pushed up through the hole into the upper floor. The feeling of satisfaction was indescribable as we set about cleaning up the damning cement dust.

We later learned that the Milwaukee newspapers, as was their practice, had been monitoring our radio traffic during our operation. This was before the FBI benefited from encrypted radios, and it certainly would have resulted in the story being blasted out for all the world to see and would have ruined everything. Our concern for absolute security proved to be well founded and our careful use of coded language in our radio communications during the entire operation was successful. We had designated a name of a bird for each subject: Frankie Bal was the "pigeon," Joe was the "turkey," John was the "hawk," the Shorecrest was the "henhouse," and police cruisers were designated the "fox." The media had no idea what we were talking about. Later I was told by a reporter that he knew the FBI was up to something big, but he couldn't figure out where we were or what we were doing with all the references to various fowl.

We returned to the office and remained there anxiously awaiting the arrival of John at his office. While we waited we recounted stories of experiences during the installation. Mike said, "We were really sweating it down in that basement. We would have been trapped if a guard came to check." Fred piped in, "Jack Fraser and I were in the van parked across the street from the henhouse. We had the engine off and were just sitting there. Suddenly, a car came into the lot with its lights off. We immediately knew something was up, so we just watched. The car stopped and two guys got out and started pulling wheels off a car parked next to us. We couldn't believe it, so we jumped out of the van with our guns drawn and scared the hell out of them. We told them to get out of there or we'd kill them. They never know who we were."

When John arrived at his office, we were very curious to listen to the quality of the device. When we turned on the mic, however, our exuberance was dashed, as all we could hear were footsteps and muted speech. I asked Prokop, "What happened? Is the mic bad?" He responded, "No, the mic is good. I tested it - it works." His frustration was obvious. "I think we missed the office and came up in the hallway just outside the damn office where it does us no good at all." I responded, "This means we have to go in again, right?" Reluctantly, he nodded "Yeah." So we redid the installation, but this time we merely measured one foot from the first drill hole. On the second try, we hit pay dirt. The mic was pushed up to the bottom of the carpet in the office and the listening device proved to be worth all of our blood, sweat, and tears. Most of the time, we picked up the one sided conversations of John on the telephone as he maneuvered and manipulated the family's finances, but from time to time we caught priceless meetings in the office.

We were now inside the belly of the beast and were monitoring three microphones and three telephone lines. We were no longer deaf and blind. All of our electronic surveillances necessitated 12 tape recorders and an average of three monitoring agent per eight hour shift, to say nothing of the administrative functions that were nearly overwhelming, but after many months we were ready for the big dance. The Three Musketeers were exited. Fred said, "This is the big one. The finale to a great operation." Mike enthusiastically added, "It's like waiting for Christmas to come when you were a little kid. This is the closest we have ever come to success on the La Cosa Nostra in Milwaukee."

One of the problems with monitoring microphones, sometimes called "bugs" or mics, is that you are only authorized to listen when one of the targeted subjects is present. This means the target must be physically placed at the microphone location. Additionally, the bugs do not discriminate between sounds, so music and restaurant noise are also picked up along with the conversations, and sometimes pertinent statements are covered by secondary noise. This becomes extremely frustrating, but it is what it is. Also, we are only authorized to listen to "pertinent" conversations and "non-pertinent" conversations must be minimized. The problem with this is that conversations often change course and may begin innocently, then change to criminal discussions; plus, the participants often speak using code. For example, Balistrieri once received an incoming telephone call. The conversation began, "Happy birthday, Frank. How do you feel?" Frank responded, "Good, I feel good. I don't feel any older, I feel good."

The caller continued, "What about that guy we talked about? Did you get the money?"

Frank responded curtly, "Yeah."

Furthermore, some callers may be totally innocent and not have anything to do with criminal activity, so the monitoring agent has to be on his toes.

Before long, we hit the jackpot the floor microphone. On November 7,1979, we were monitoring Frankie Bal and his son, John, when we heard a conversation about subpoenas being issued in the murder cases of Augie Maniaci and Augie Palmisano. These subpoenas were served on various people, including Vincent Maniaci, who had fled to Hawaii after finding the dynamite bomb in his car. Frankie Bal was heard to say, "You know that, that guy from Hawaii, ah, that comedian, he called Joey at home today. Now he's calling up and he's afraid to come here. See that's the fear. And we got him and his brother and he knows that. See, that's the respect I have in this town." The conversation continued. "See, there might be, they may try to nail Pete (Balistrieri), Steve (DiSalvo), or me, or something like that so they can, they might have pictures. I don't think they have any witnesses. I can't conceive that we, that. We were very careful about nobody seeing us . . . The serious part about one of the guys that they subpoenaed is a guy [Montos] that's highly ah, get ah, real, real, real good information on the boom." Then Joseph, who had joined the conversation, asked, "Subpoenas, up here?

Holy smoke." We were very pleased. The mic had paid off. They were actually discussing the murder of Augie Maniaci and the attempted bombing of his brother, Vincent Maniaci. We fully expected to obtain much more over the mic.

CHAPTER 4

The Kansas City Connection

"This thing is spreading. I wonder where it will lead?"

--Former Special Agent Mike De Marco

We felt we had found a rich vein of gold in the microphone overhears from John Balistrieri's office and anticipated hitting the mother-load before we were through, hoping that it would give us enough to bring down the Balistrieri mob. We were given a boost toward our goal by an unexpected development. Unbeknownst to us in the Milwaukee FBI office, agents in the Kansas City Division were in the midst of a full-scale investigation of their city's Cosa Nostra family, including mob boss Nick Civella, his brother Carl "Corky" Civella, and chief enforcer Carl "Tuffy" De Luna. The case began with the 1978 murders of the Spero brothers, two rival gangsters, which led the Kansas City office to begin wiretaps in an effort to solve those crimes. Headed by Agent William Ouseley, the Kansas City (KC) case was at about the same stage as ours, but the two investigations didn't converge until late 1979.

Kansas City, Missouri, the second town in our tale of five cities, was an expansive area frequented by the indigenous Kkaze Indian tribe, who hunted the countless bison that roamed the plains of Kansas and western Missouri and gave the town its name. White settlers found the land ideal for farming and eventually Kansas City, Missouri, was incorporated in March of 1853. The city, famous for its barbecue, is located very near the geographical center point of the United States being nearly equally centered north to south and east to west.

Kansas City has a storied past in the annals of the FBI because on July 17, 1933, notorious murderer and career criminal Frank Nash was being transported from Union Railway Station to Leavenworth Penitentiary when three men, including "Pretty Boy Floyd," attacked the transport car with machineguns in an effort to free Nash. Tragically, Nash, three police officers, and FBI agent R.J. Caffrey were killed in the flurry of bullets. This slaughter became known as "The Kansas City Massacre." The LCN infected Kansas City in 1912 when the Di Giovanni brothers, two Sicilian Mafiosi, arrived in the city and began plying their dark trade. As time passed, the Kansas City mob grew and prospered, beginning during Prohibition, as the city's thirst for banned liquor was satisfied by illegal bootleggers. Political corruption allowed the mob to thrive, as is often the case, and various bosses have ruled the family since 1931, when the organization developed into a structured illegal enterprise. It is estimated that there are 20 to 30 made members of the LCN residing in the Kansas City area.

Giuseppe Nicoli "Nick" Civella was born in the northeast section of Kansas City around 1912. As a child, Civella had no desire to waste his time in school and ran the streets as an uncontrollable troublemaker. At the age of 10 he was arrested for vagrancy, and he subsequently dropped out of school. As he aged, his career as a criminal advanced from auto theft and robbery to illegal gambling and bootlegging. He was a tough guy, a real blue collar hood who rose in the organization through sheer violence to become boss of the Kansas City LCN, a satellite version of the much larger Chicago mob. Civella became the fifth boss of the family in 1953.

Civella, although not formally educated, had the street smarts of a feral cat. Like many old time mobsters, he had white hair and looked to be an ordinary grandfather, until he opened his foul mouth. Civella was the son of Italian immigrants and was the exact opposite of Frank Balistrieri. He never wore a suit, kept a low profile, and was truly a hard-core mobster. He was also one of the first men to be entered into Nevada's "Black Book" of those excluded from entering any Nevada casino. He once sarcastically said, "I even deny, to my knowledge, that organized crime exists in Kansas City. I am not a joiner. I am not even a member of the Knights of Columbus."

There was nothing Civella wouldn't do to achieve his illegal goals and maintain his power. Unlike the mobsters portrayed in the movies who live in palatial mansions, he worked out of his small neighborhood grocery store. In spite of his lack of formal education, he was wise enough to realize that the right associates could enhance his position, and he, therefore, developed a close relationship with Roy Williams, the president of the powerful Teamsters Union. This partnership flourished to the financial benefit of both men. With the enthusiastic aid of Williams, the union's money was made available to finance the purchase of the Las Vegas Tropicana Hotel and Casino in 1977. Civella couldn't possibly get licensed to run a casino in Nevada so he used straw man, Joseph Agosto, to front the property. Agosto was known as the entertainment director of the French topless revue called the Folies Bergere, which was the main stage production at the Tropicana for 49 years, establishing a record of 29,000 performances until the show was finally closed in March of 2009. Nevada gaming authorities were not aware that Agosto not only ran the Folies but the whole joint, and he controlled the skim as well. Justice caught up with him when he was arrested by Special Agent Michael Glass in Las Vegas on a Kansas City warrant accusing Agosto of skimming $280,000 out of the "Trop" from June 1978 to February 1979. Glass, a veteran of the Army and later an exceptional undercover agent who posed as a horse race fixer and insurance fraud co-conspirator, was also intimately involved in other straw men investigations. Other charges were pending against Agosto in addition to the skimming warrant, and determined survivor that he was, he rolled over and began cooperating with the Bureau. He provided volumes of sworn grand jury testimony regarding the Tropicana's hidden ownership by Nick Civella and how the Tropicana skim was carried out and transported to Kansas City, where it was shared with the Chicago Outfit.

Agosto had testified in the Tropicana (Trop) skim trial held in Kansas City in 1983, and I flew out to meet with him in August of that year. He was waiting to testify in another federal case so he was kept in an FBI safe house under 24-hour guard during his debriefing period. He was accompanied by a Las Vegas showgirl, a beautiful 6-foot-tall, shapely redhead who had been a topless dancer in the Folies. I arrived in the late afternoon, and when I was delivered to the house by Kansas City agents, Agosto was busy cooking marinara sauce. I could smell the sweet aroma as it simmered on the stove when I entered the condominium. After we were introduced, Agosto asked, "Are you hungry?" Not allowing me to answer, he continued in his Sicilian accent, "I'll fry up some pork chops, you like chops? Then you'll have some pasta and some nice Italian bread. How does that sound?"

I smiled. "Sounds good to me."

Then he asked, "What do you want to drink? I got Coke, beer, 7-Up, milk. I even got some wine."

I asked, "What is this, a fancy restaurant?"

He raised his hands, palms up, and smiled slyly. "I got nothin' else to do. I get bored. I cook for all you guys. It's the least I can do, since you're protecting me." He sat down with me at the small kitchen table as his girlfriend adjourned to the front room to watch TV. While I ate, Joe only munched on a thin slice of fresh unbuttered Italian bread. I asked the rotund man, "Aren't you going to eat?"

He gave me the same palms-up shrug. "My health's not that good. I got diabetes and I'm supposed to watch my weight. You know, my heart," he said, holding his right hand over his breast.

I found Agosto, mob associate and casino skimmer, to be charming and engaging as we talked at length about his past, his present and his future. He told me he was born in Sicily and had been in the construction business in the United States for many years before coming to Las Vegas. He said he had made and lost several fortunes, adding, "I moved to Vegas to do some building, but I met some people and got a job at the Trop, and before I knew it I was mixed up with the wrong guys. I thought I could work with them and not be affected but I was wrong. The slime always rubs off on you." He provided a great deal of insight into the mob's control in Las Vegas, including the hidden ownership of the Tropicana and Stardust casinos. He said, "We skimmed out of the joint and Nickie Civella got about 40 grand a month. He split it with the guys in Chicago."

Agosto also told me that former Nevada Gaming Board

Chairman Harry Reid, now Senate Majority Leader, was known as "Mr. Clean Face" by the Kansas City mobsters. I asked him what that meant, but he refused to say. Even when I pressed him, he just smiled and said, "I've got to hold something back so I won't be expendable when I finish testifying." Later, after learning of the derisive nickname, Senator Reid publicly stated that he was called Mr. Clean Face because he was clean, not corrupt.

I slept fitfully in the safe-house with a shotgun next to my bed, as a precaution in case the mob should find out where Agosto was hiding and come to kill him. The next morning Joe cooked breakfast for me: eggs, bacon, and hash browns seasoned with his secret Italian spices. His girlfriend joined us as we ate, but she only had orange juice and some fruit. She was very solicitous towards him and seemed sincerely concerned for his welfare. He discussed the Chicago mob and how they had decided that stealing from the casinos was like "living in heaven" because, for them, the skim money was "clean" in the sense that it wasn't taken by force. He said, "It was like sitting back and having bushels of money dumped at the bosses' feet. They didn't have to get their hands dirty." Agosto once mentioned to Civella that he was adding 100 slot machines in the casino and the greedy Civella responded, "You'll be minting money in there pretty soon. Just bring some of it my way." Agosto also said he worked directly under Civella, and while they became close, he never trusted the aging boss. He realized that he was just a tool for Civella, used to hide the real ownership of the Tropicana. Joe explained that once the FBI brought down the Trop, he knew he was expendable to the mob and his friendship with Civella would be considered a liability so, as he said, "I jumped ship and changed uniforms." I didn't know him well, but Agosto loved life: he lived heartily, loved heartily, stole heartily, and certainly understood what he had done. Three weeks later, on September 1, 1983, he died of a massive heart attack.

There are those who ask, "What's wrong with skimming casino profits? Don't the owners have a right to the money? Isn't it theirs?" The simple answer is that skimming is a form of embezzlement. In casinos that hide behind straw men, the hidden owners are members of a criminal enterprise, La Cosa Nostra, that acquires, maintains, and conducts its affairs through a pattern of racketeering activity by committing crimes. These people, the ones who really control the casino, have no right to any money. They are simply criminals siphoning off profits that should be going to shareholders or to legitimate owners. The hidden owners have invested nothing in the businesses they own, and if they do, the funds are derived from illegal activity. Furthermore, the state and the federal governments have the right to tax all the profits of the company, not just the profit that is made public. But the biggest danger of the skim is that it contributes heavily to the black cash that criminal gangs use to bribe politicians, cops, or anyone who can help the mob. On top of that, the mob's need to protect that lucrative source of funds often leads to murder. The under-the-table black cash also pays off union officials who arranged for the loans to purchase the properties. Skim is like pollution poured into a small stream that flows into a larger river. The toxin may not hurt the polluter, but the people downstream suffer the malignant consequences.

At the time, we in Milwaukee knew nothing about where the Kansas City connection would lead as we continued listening to the conversations of the Balistrieris. During the long, often tedious hours of wiretapping Frank Balistrieri and his crew, I left the office from time to time to shake off a form of cabin fever, and sometimes, if the surveillance team was unavailable, I would watch Fancy Pants on my own. On one such day, I followed him as he drove west, out of town. This was very unusual for him. He was a big city guy and seldom left Milwaukee's confines, so I lay back and continued tailing him on Watertown Plank Road. Frank was driving a brand new black Cadillac Eldorado that was registered to his son, Joseph, who drove a black Rolls Royce with maroon trim and the tag "JPB 1." Since he had no visible source of income, he needed ways of covering up his ownership of properties. Whether in his car or in the restaurants he frequented, Frankie Bal always hid behind the shield of his attorney sons. During my career as an FBI agent, I could never understand why the Criminal Division of the IRS would not look at guys like Balistrieri more aggressively. Certainly, a net worth investigation would be devastating to the bad guys, seeing as how they live large and yet have no legitimate source of income.

In any case, the drive was lovely. The rolling farm country, with its symmetrically furrowed fields and straight fence lines, brought order to the magnificent chaos of nature. As we left the city further behind, there were fewer and fewer cars on the road and I had to lay back all the more carefully so he wouldn't notice me, much the way we did during the Onalaska kidnapping surveillance. I couldn't conceive of what the guy was up to, as I had never known him to drive outside of Milwaukee. As Fancy Pants continued west, I realized something unique was happening and I didn't want to blow my chance. He continued through the farm country for a time, then stopped at a rural house and went inside. I wondered what he was doing in the house. Who could he be meeting with? Was he receiving some kind of payoff? There was no way of knowing, but I did know that he didn't come for the scenery or to pick apples. One other car was parked in front of the house, so I drove past and stopped about a quarter of a mile down the road and parked under some trees on the side of the road. I was far enough away from the house, in the open farm country, to remain hidden. As it was a clear day, I could view the license tag through binoculars and I called it in. It came back registered to Frank Ranney, a Milwaukee Teamster official. What this union connection meant was a mystery at that point in our investigation, although I was aware of the reputation of the Teamsters Union. I knew of the many convictions of Teamster officials in the past, as well as their association with mob guys, but I had no way of divining what the meeting with Ranney meant. At that point, the meeting was another piece of a very complex puzzle.

One evening, I believe it was in late 1978, I followed Balistrieri from his palatial home in Shorewood to the Centre Stage Dinner Playhouse, located in the downtown border area between the business district and the industrial section of Milwaukee. It was a dark evening and the place was shut down at that particular time, as business had dropped off. Fancy Pants went inside the large two-story brick building and stayed for about an hour. I couldn't see any internal lights from my outside position, so I assumed he was in some non-public area of the building.

Nighttime surveillances can be very lonely, but at the same time fascinating. I sat in my Bureau car in a dark alley, radio off, watching and waiting. I wondered if Balistrieri was meeting with someone or doing something else that I would love to know about. As I sat there, a homeless man dressed in dirty, shabby clothes wandered through the alley, moving from dumpster to dumpster, fishing with a bent coat hanger. He didn't even pay attention to me, he probably figured me for a cop or a john waiting for a hooker. About an hour later, Frank got in his car and drove off. I followed him to the La Scalla Restaurant, where I broke off the surveillance. It had been a long day and I was tired. This evening's activities, along with many others, left questions in my mind as to what he was up to. Realistically, only an informant or hidden microphones could answer these questions, and then only if Frank happened to mention his intentions. It was like putting a huge puzzle together with only a few pieces and trying to make out the picture. The puzzle pieces we had were: overhears concerning murders, informant information about Balistrieri "going back and forth to Chicago a lot," his connection to illegal bookmakers Sam and Dennis Librizzi and we had a union connection, but those pieces certainly didn't paint a clear picture.

Sometimes turf battles ignite between police agencies and the FBI or between FBI offices, but these problems are usually a result of personality conflicts or because of different goals. In this case, Milwaukee and Kansas City worked hand in hand as we became aware that both LCN families were dipping in the same well – Las Vegas casinos. We realized that attacking both families would wreak the most damage on the LCN, so phone calls and written communications regularly flowed between our offices sharing valuable information. In early 1979, before Milwaukee and Kansas City began to coordinate their investigations, and before the many pieces of our respective puzzles came tightly together, the Kansas City Division sent Milwaukee communication requesting information about an individual who had been overheard on one of their taps of mob boss Nick Civella. The phone conversation had been cryptic, but Kansas City believed it had to do with Las Vegas casinos. Civella had called a phone number in Milwaukee and the Kansas City agents had identified the number as the Centre Stage restaurant but, of course, they had no way of knowing who actually owned the dinner playhouse. As luck would have it, the call was made on exactly the night and time I had followed Balistrieri to the Centre Stage. Now I knew what he had been doing there that night. Luck can play a role in any investigation and, in this case, the good angels smiled on the persistent investigator.

The Kansas City FBI was monitoring the telephones of Nick Civella and his enforcer, Carl De Luna, plus several pay phones that the mobsters regularly used. They eventually inserted a microphone at one of Civella's relative's houses, where he often met with trusted associates. In late 1978, Kansas City caught a major break: Civella had a six hour meeting at the targeted residence with Carl Thomas, one of their Las Vegas straw men, in which they discussed the casino business, and Thomas laid out the process of skimming from the casino count rooms where the night's profits are counted. But the Kansas City mob's death blow was struck on February 14, 1979, with a search of Carl De Luna's residence. Search warrants are much easier to obtain than wiretap warrants as judges are usually inclined to approve such warrants with minimal proof. The search produced De Luna's personal phone books and hand-scribbled diaries kept in small notebooks.

De Luna was clearly obsessive about keeping records. The notebooks provided intricate, detailed accounts of meetings, telephone calls, and amounts of skim received. He used code names to identify participants in the scheme and referred to the skim as "sandwiches" or "packages," but Agent Bill Ouseley understood the Kansas City mobsters extremely well and was able to identify each of the people being described and interpret De Luna's codes. For example, "Berman" in De Luna's notes was a misspelled version of Beer man – code for Balistrieri. His records proved to be the fatal stake that we would drive into the heart of Civella's illegal empire. Once the evidence was reviewed and correlated, indictments were brought and arrests made, though legal dithering held up the trial for many months.

On March 4, 1980, a year after the Kansas City raids, it was our turn to strike at the heart of the beast in Milwaukee. We hit Sam Librizzi's house armed with a search warrant as a preamble to the major event that was to come the next day. Librizzi was an illegal bookmaker who worked for Balistrieri and had been the subject of a previous illegal gambling investigation that had sent him to jail. Surveillances indicated that Sam always sat at a small table in front of a large picture window where he could look out on Brady Street and his front yard to keep an eye out for a raid. This would give him time to dump his bookmaking records, which he wrote on rice paper, in a bucket of water near the table. The water would dissolve the paper within seconds, destroying the evidence, so we knew we had to come up with a plan to enter his house before he spotted us.

My co-case agent, Mike De Marco, and I decided to set Sam up by having Special Agent Betty Shober drive along the street in front of his house and fake a mechanical breakdown. She jerked the brakes a few times, then stopped and got out of the car. Acting disgusted, she opened the hood and began looking inside. Betty continued her charade for a while, ensuring that Librizzi saw her plight, and then she walked casually to his door and rang the bell. It was cold and crisp, and dirty snow lay in patches along the curb and in shaded areas of Librizzi's lawn. I could see De Marco's breath in the chill as he exhaled, crouched out of view near some shrubbery to the right of the picture window, waiting to make his move to the door. I was crouched to the left of the window, up against the house, while the remainder of the search team anxiously waited around the corner of the block ready to move in when I gave the go signal over my hand-held radio. As Shober stood ringing the doorbell, Mike and I crept along the front of the house from opposite directions. When Sam opened the door to ask what she wanted, we moved quickly and pushed our way into the house, catching him completely off guard. I put out the call and the other agents then joined us to begin the search.

Our first job was to clear the house. We went from room to room making sure no one else was there. When I opened the door to a large closet, I was startled to find an elderly man, dressed in a suit, on all fours, eating out of a dog dish. Librizzi, somewhat embarrassed, explained that his wife's father, Cono, was senile and thought he was a dog. I admit I had to suppress a laugh, though it was a sad sight. You never know what you'll find during a search, and I can assure you, I have found some very strange things. I have been in a home with a fully equipped sado-masochistic dungeon and another that was a witch's residence equipped with an altar decorated with a ram's skull and multiple signs of blood from sacrificed animals. In another house, photos of nude men and women covered every wall, and a wooden stock stood at the center of the living room complete with hand and head holes and chains.

Cono the human dog wasn't all we found in Sam's house, however. We seized Librizzi's betting records at the window table as a start, but there were other older records throughout the house. Librizzi's phones were ringing off the hook, so Mike answered one of them and posed as Librizzi's assistant. "It was very funny," Mike told me later. "They gave me the bets. I read them back to them. I asked them if that was right. When the callers asked who I was, I told them, 'Mike Foolaroundo.'" Sam was very cooperative and asked if he could call his attorney, which we allowed, and about thirty minutes later Joseph Balistrieri arrived, all smiles. The raid was no skin off his nose, or so he thought, and he expected to earn a good fee. Joe had no way of knowing that this was only the warm-up, and I had no way of knowing that, from that point forward, my career would be tangled up in an all-out war against the mob's hidden ownership of Las Vegas casinos.

We had previously briefed seven search teams, so the next day everyone had their assignments and was ready to go. There is nothing more impressive than a well staged FBI operation of the magnitude we were about to carry out. Seven search teams with no less than five agents on each team had been instructed as to the exact type of evidence that could be expected at each location. The searches were to be coordinated so that each location would be hit at the same time, and everyone was reminded of the necessity for properly documenting each piece of evidence seized, as we knew the seizures would be attacked by defense attorneys at a later date. Additionally, we were searching the offices of two attorneys, so extraordinary care was required by agents who were also attorneys to protect the rights of innocent clients whose files would be present in those offices.

It had been a long, uphill climb but we were now at the summit and ready to savor the fruits of our efforts. This event was near the top tier of my FBI experiences and I was looking forward to it with great anticipation. We had search warrants for Frank Balistrieri's house, son Joseph's law office, son John's office, the business office in the Shorecrest Residence Hotel, as well as Leonardo's and La Scalla Restaurants and Alioto Vending. We began the operation at 9:00 a.m. on March 5, 1980. Fred Thorne remained at the office to handle any problems and coordinate the raids. Mike De Marco was the team leader for the search of the Shorecrest and John's office, and I led a team to Frank Balistrieri's house. There was palpable excitement in the air as we stood at Frankie Bal's front door with a feeble March sun rolling over Lake Michigan and warming our backs. My experience trying to serve Frankie Bal with a grand jury subpoena months earlier had taught me that he would not come to the door when we identified ourselves, so the plan was to knock several times, announce ourselves, and then have Fred Thorne call him on the phone and advise him of our intentions and their legality. I was convinced we would end up breaking down Frankie Bal's door to gain entry in time to keep the old man from destroying evidence. We knew his attorneys would fight the results of our search to the outer limits and we wanted to be on solid legal ground.

I had been on his trail so long and seen and heard so much on the tapes that I knew his arrogance wouldn't allow him to cooperate with us in any way. I was right. Balistrieri didn't answer the knock on his door, so I called Fred on my hand-held radio and told him to make the call. About one minute later Fred responded over the radio, "The jerk hung up on me. Go ahead!" The first sledgehammer blow hit the door just to the side of the ornate brass doorknob and the glass in the door shattered, spraying shards all over the entryway. The second blow was right on target and the door exploded open, splintering the door frame. I entered the house first, followed by the rest of the team. As I passed through the large foyer area of the mansion, Balistrieri came staggering down the spiral staircase dressed in his pajamas and robe. I would have given $100 for a camera at that moment because I saw a wide-eyed man in total disbelief of what had just happened to him and his castle. The shock and dismay actually put some life into his normally dead eyes. I handed him a copy of the warrant, and as he stood mesmerized trying to decipher the document, we began the systematic search. Soon Joseph and John Balistrieri arrived with another well known mob defense attorney and began to get in our way, obstructing the orderly search. We warned them that any further interference would result in their arrest for obstruction of justice.

They finally acknowledged the reality of the situation, and I can assure you, Joe was not smiling now as he had been the evening before at Sam Librizzi's house. John, as always, was silent, but glared hatefully at the horror we were wreaking in their lives. Things got worse for Joe when he received a phone call from his law office informing him that it was being searched, but before he had time to digest that disaster, another call came in telling him of the search at the Shorecrest Hotel office. For the first time, I could see fear in Joseph's eyes. He whispered something to John and his sullen stare deepened, suppressed anxiety shadowing both their faces. John left immediately. At that moment I didn't fully understand what we would uncover during the searches. They certainly did.

After two hours I received word over the Bureau radio that there was a problem at the Shorecrest and they had found something very interesting, so I left the completion of the task to the search team. When I arrived at the Shorecrest, I learned that the search of John's office had been completed but agents had found a small wall safe, approximately nine inches in diameter, hidden behind a benign photograph of a Wisconsin landscape in the business office. No one seemed to know the combination, and John, who had just arrived, feigned surprise about the existence of the safe, though of course he knew. We decided the safe had to be opened, and De Marco told him that if he didn't open it we would have it pealed. John didn't respond. He knew we would eventually open the secret vault by force, and all he could do was stare at us in disbelief. He must have realized it was the beginning of the end for him, his brother, and his mobster father.

We obtained a special search warrant for the safe and had a locksmith come and drill the safe door lock. De Marco eagerly reached in and withdrew a large manila envelope that had been folded in two. Mike opened the envelope as if it were a precious artifact from the tomb of a king. Within were four packets of $100 bills, each amounting to $50,000. But that wasn't all. Under the packets of money was a legal document entitled "Exclusive Option to Purchase Shares of Argent Corporation." This turned out to be an agreement Joseph and John Balistrieri had made with someone named Allen Glick. It had been signed on June 15, 1974, and gave the Balistrieri brothers the option to purchase 50% of Argent Corporation, on demand, for $25,000. We wondered, who was Allen Glick? What was Argent?

By this time, Frankie Bal and Joe had both arrived at the Shorecrest and settled into John's comfortable office. I watched John walk the short distance across the hall from the business office to his personal office. He reminded me of a zombie, half alive and half dead. He joined his father and brother and, of course, they had no idea of the microphone in the office or that agents were monitoring their conversations. Although search raids are intended to obtain evidence to be presented to a grand jury, they often have a bonus: generating incriminating conversations from the targets of our investigation. That was exactly what happened.

The sons were beside themselves, so upset and frustrated that they babbled on about their world coming apart. The three discussed possible responses to our search when Frankie Bal blurted desperately, "Let's go get some guys with guns and shoot the bastards up." The sons responded, "Dad, are you crazy?" (At that point, as a precaution, we posted two agents in the vicinity but out of sight of the office to keep the Balistrieris contained.) The sons were bemoaning their plight when Joseph whispered to his brother, "You know, the sum and substance of it is, Brother John, that you and I are now . . . I mean, any hope of being legitimate is gonna be automatically erased. You might as well get that into your mind now. Time to make our move was in 1975 when we were absolutely clean." I believe this was a reference to their arrangement with Allen Glick in 1975 when they could have quietly become partners with Glick in his casino operations, but their father had insisted on pulling skim out of the casinos. Later Joe said, "I mean, we listened to him, we did it his way and we were absolutely corrupted. There's no way in the world now that we're gonna be legitimate. I hope you understand that." John responded in a hushed voice, as if the wind had been completely knocked out of him, "I know that."

As with many of the monitored conversations in the office, the subject often changed frequently as if their minds raced from thought to thought, and each participant added his opinion. Joe was the legal counsel, while John was the financial expert. Frank was like loose cannon, his mind bouncing around like a rubber ball. Joseph then jumped in, speaking about Kansas City, as if he instinctively knew they would be tied to the mob there. "No, there's only one guy, of all the Kansas City guys that I know of, Carl Thomas . . .."

Frank responded, "Let me tell you something else, I guarantee you, Carl Thomas'll talk." At this point, we had no idea who Carl Thomas was, though we would find out that he was overheard on the Kansas tapes.

Joseph went on, "I met him once in Allen Glick's office. I never met him again."

John, ever the pragmatist, brought the conversation back to their immediate problem of what was in the safe. "And all the money, all the money in the safe . . ."

"Yeah," Frank grunted.

" . . . was in sealed envelopes."

"What about it?" Frank demanded. "Is there any chance of us saying that it belongs to us, our family?"

"Yeah, so far as I'm concerned." John was willing to grasp at the straw Frank offered.

Joseph interjected, "It's our goddamn money. It was earned during the year 1979. I have not yet filed my 1979 tax returns."

"No, no, no," Frank said, "part of that . . . wait, listen to me now, listen to me. We had a big, big wedding attended by 1,000 people." Cathy Balistrieri, Frank's daughter, had indeed been married that year, and, of course, traditionally the bride and groom received large cash gifts.

" John began. "Part of it is Cathy's."

"No, wait a minute . . . Frank demanded.

An exasperated John interrupted. "Dad, Dad. We're involving people we don't have to involve," he protested.

Frank was having none of that. "No, we gonna do that, because--"

John tired to get his Dad's attention, "Dad."

"Now you listen to me," ordered Frank. "Because they can't refute that."

"The most," John worried, "the most you're gonna be able to cover is $50,000." "How much?" Frank questioned. Frank had no visible source of income, so they couldn't attribute the money to him and had to find another solution.

John, the financial counsel, reiterated his advice. "Fifty thousand. Now, because I can take fifty thou, if he, if Joseph declares $200,000 in income, by the time I'm done filing the tax return, I'll take off more than you can take off by taking $50,000."

Frank paused. "Let's think a little bit."

John continued, "Dad, this is a better way to do it. This way it's all declared. Catherine's not involved, her husband's not involved, there's nobody involved."

"Your son-in-law's a doctor," Joe added.

Joe said, "Bad enough you gotta do what you gotta do -- let's not involve anybody else."

Frank was still not happy. "I mean, I'm not bringing our money . . ."

"But I'll tell you something," John interrupted. "It'll be better this way. Then you can shelter it this way and we'll carry it forward and carry it back. His loss, Snugs, chapter S tax." (Snugs was a restaurant located inside the Shorecrest Hotel.)

Frank asked, "What about, what about, say they made it . . . "

John finished for him. "It will disappear."

I believe John was referring to the sober business decision to claim the $200,000 as income for Joseph Balistrieri's law practice, where it could be covered up as phony income from the restaurant, hotel and client billings and the like. Unfortunately for them, their scheming didn't look so clever when it was introduced as evidence.

Our search raids had been successful overall. We had seized records tying Frankie Bal to Librizzi's bookmaking operation and proving his control and enrichment from the proceeds. We had also seized volumes of records showing hidden ownership of numerous businesses and, of course, the smoking gun of $200,000 in hidden cash and the option agreement proving subtle control over the Argent Corporation. Now we just had to find out what Argent was.

CHAPTER 5

The "G" Cleans Up Milwaukee

"That's the fear. See, that's the respect I have in this town."

-- Frank Balistrieri

Several unanswered questions loomed as a result of our search raids that required answers, and our trio of case agents set about the process of answering those questions. As Fred and I watched, Mike laid the option to purchase document down on his desk. We read it carefully again and Fred commented, "I can't figure out what this option to purchase means. We have to get more information about Allen Glick and Argent and find out if this has any relevance to our case." I agreed "I'll run the names through our indices and see what we come up with." The answers came quickly as I determined that Allen Glick was the owner of Argent Corporation and was a major casino operator in Las Vegas. I called our Las Vegas office and spoke with the supervisor of the OC squad, and he informed me that Glick's casinos had been purchased with millions of dollars borrowed from the Central States, Teamsters Union Pension Fund. The Teamster connection caused me to recall my surveillance of Frank Balistrieri as he drove to the country home and met with Frank Ranney, a Teamster Union official. After returning to Mike's desk, I asked, "Remember how Ranney's Teamster money had been fronted to allow Balistrieri to purchase the Shorecrest Hotel?" Mike and Fred nodded. I continued, "Allen Glick owns four Las Vegas casinos and bought them with Teamster money." Mike piped in, "I wonder, could all this be somehow connected? If Glick is such a wealthy, big shot, how could the Balistrieri boys have an agreement to buy multi-million dollar properties for $25,000? It doesn't make sense." Fred added, "We need more specific information about the Teamster loan and how Glick got the money. This thing stinks."

We subsequently learned that Allen Glick had obtained a loan in the amount of $62,750,000 from the Central States Pension Fund of the Teamsters Union in 1974. This remarkable achievement by a virtual nobody caused many in Las Vegas to scratch their heads in amazement. The casinos were: the Fremont, the Marina, the Hacienda, and the Stardust. Las Vegas authorities couldn't figure it out, but we had a key piece of the puzzle that no one was yet aware of. The mysterious document we had recovered from the wall safe was dated June of 1974, the same year as his huge loan acquisition. This could not have been a coincidence.

The Kansas City connection came up in a monitored conversation between Balistrieri and his sons in John's office on November 15, 1979, in which Frank discussed his trip to Kansas City and a wedding he attended there where he met with the "Kansas City guys." Mike, Fred, and I reviewed the tape several times. Mike, when we heard the conversation commented, "This thing is spreading. I wonder where it will lead? We have the Teamsters, Las Vegas, and now Kansas City." We continued listening to the tape, and Frank was heard to say, "You know, I thought, too, that maybe somebody should approach the Genius instead of you . . ." He then told Joseph, "Get Frank when you've got him out there and concentrate on nailing this big Jew down. He's gonna need our help. He's dealt with us anyway, you gotta make him go up front. I'm counting the days until my license is granted. And it will be granted!" This portion of the monitored conversation didn't make much sense to us at the time. Fred questioned, "Who is the 'Genius?' And who is this 'Frank' he mentioned? And Bal mentions 'my license.' What license could he be talking about?" Mike remembered a recent communication from our Kansas City office that informed us about the De Luna search and information contained in his notebooks. Mike went to the case file then returned to his desk and read from the report. "Here it is. According to Kansas City, the Genius is Allen Glick, and let's see, a guy named Frank Rosenthal is referred to as the 'Crazy Guy.' We need to find out who Rosenthal is and if he could be the Frank they refer to." We subsequently determined that Rosenthal was Glick's number one man at Argent. Fred was troubled by the mention of Bal's license and asked, "How can Frank Balistrieri get any license associated with Las Vegas casinos? He's never been up front for any of his holdings. It must mean a license that Frank is supposed to get. What kind of license could that be?"

We continued listening to the tape, and heard Fancy Pants say, "And I figure it's about just the right for the time of the month . . . By Monday or Tuesday, I'll, I'll get my transfusion again." This seemed to be another strange choice of words. I questioned, "Is he sick? Do we have any information that he has a blood problem or something?" Mike and Fred shrugged their shoulders. We clearly had another mystery that needed solving. We eventually learned that "transfusion" was Balistrieri's code for his portion of the Las Vegas skim money, just as De Luna had used the term "sandwiches" for the skim. In another conversation, the self absorbed but delusional Balistrieri bragged, referring to the FBI, "Because they're gonna show I'm more lethal than Al Capone, cuz Al Capone just took care of his own and I'm surrounded with a battery of brains, with lawyers, accountants, and I infiltrate legitimate businesses."

Electronic surveillance isn't always a passive exercise. Sometimes it's necessary to cast a lure into the water to see if we can cause the bad guys to bite – in other words, prime the pump. We had obtained a court order requiring Sam Librizzi to write the names of murdered Milwaukee mobsters hoping they would come up in our target's conversations. To our great surprise and pleasure, they did exactly that during a conversation in which Joe discussed our court ordered demand that Librizzi provide handwriting samples to be compared with the handwritten bookmaking records seized from Librizzi and Frankie Bal's residences. We were pleased to hear Joe tell his father, "They made Sam Librizzi write the following names: Louis Fazio, Augie Maniaci, Augie Palmisano, Vincent Maniaci. What's this, the hit list?" and they chuckled.

On another occasion, we monitored the following conversation in John's office where Frankie Bal again discussed the FBI. "I have another worry. The 'G' wants to trap me and they, ah, they're doing things that, ah, they know that I'm gonna do something one of these days." He often used the term the "G" to designate government G-men [FBI]. The same general conversation continued on April 28,1980, when Frank brought up the attempted bombing of Vince Maniaci. "That's what aggravates 'em. They were in on it. On day number one because they got pictures of it, pictures of Skully [Montos]. They took pictures of Nick driving John's car." This was a reference to

Chuck Nicoletti being seen by surveillance agents while driving a car rented by John Balistrieri in the vicinity of Vince Maniaci's house. Joseph Balistrieri, always his father's consiglieri, was then overheard saying, "They can't make a case unless you make it against yourself by talking to somebody and they record you, or you do business with a stool pigeon." I had to smile when I first reviewed this conversation. Joe's counsel was good, but it would be some time before he realized how true his warning would be.

Sometimes we were so busy we didn't have time to leave the office for lunch, so we would send someone around to take orders for pizza or burgers and collect money. On such occassions we would sit around and relax for a while as we ate. Other times, we had to get out of the confined office space to keep from exploding. Mike would say, "Mugsy, let's go get a bite at Cousins or someplace. I've gotta get out of here for a while." We would take an hour or so, sucking in the fresh air and taking our mind off the case for a time. None of us could go on vacation or other extended trips because if we did, we would cause additional work for each other. The pressure was oppressive at times, but a brief lunch respite was the best we could do under the circumstances.

After learning of Allen Glick and Argent, we subpoenaed records from the Stardust Casino and copies of checks written to Joseph Balistrieri were obtained. They were dated: August of 1974 for $7,500, and again in August of 1976 for $10,800 and $7,500, and in October of 1976 for $27,500, and finally in January of 1977 for $26,700. All the checks were for services rendered as Argent corporate counsel, but we could find no record of actual work performed by Joseph, so this was an ideal means of skimming money out of the casino. I busied myself preparing a comprehensive prosecutive report setting out all the evidence we had gathered for the use of the Strike Force Attorney, and our Milwaukee team continued the daunting task of preparing the Bellwether case for grand jury action.

Before I was transferred to Las Vegas, a going away party was held at the historic Turner's Hall, an old refurbished athletic club converted to a restaurant in downtown Milwaukee. Since so many agents had been involved in the Bellwether case, every attendee felt a part of our remarkable achievement and recounted personal stories of interesting and humorous episodes they had experienced during the course of the investigation. Rick Prokop recounted, "When we were in Leonardo's installing the mic, a huge rat the size of a cat jumped up on the bar and ate maraschino cherries out of a bowl as if it was its personal feeding trough. That place was a real rat hole. I wonder how the customers would feel about that?" Another agent told me, "You know how the mob guys use the term 'stool pigeon' to refer to informers? I wondered how that phrase got started, so I looked it up." He asked, "Do you know what the origin is?" I answered, "I've never really thought about it. Tell me." He smiled and said, "It goes back to old England when pigeon hunting was popular. The hunters tethered pigeons to stools as decoys to draw other pigeons in so they could shoot them." I nodded "Thank you, professor." Another surveillance agent informed me, "I was following Bal one night. He went into a video rental store. I followed him in, and guess what movie he rented?" I sarcastically answered, "Little Red Riding Hood." He said, "No. He rented *The Godfather*. I guess he was trying to learn something about being an LCN boss."

I told the assembled crowd, "You can all mark this case down as a great achievement. I know many of you worked your butts off and often missed family events to monitor the wires or mics. Others of you sat in ice cold cars as you followed Frankie Bal. Some of you pored through thousands of pages of documents, correlating the information and making sense of it, and those of you who are clerical employees were absolutely vital to our success. We could never have done it without you. All I can say is, thank you from the bottom of my heart."

In October of 1980, I was transferred to the Las Vegas Division to continue the FBI's attack on the Outfit. I had every confidence in Fred and Mike, as I knew they were more than capable of carrying the case to a victorious conclusion by lining up witnesses, correlating the evidence, and all the other countless tasks that are required, and they did so in exemplary fashion. One year after leaving Milwaukee, on October 1, 1981, Fred called and informed me that indictments were brought against Frank Balistrieri, his sons, John and Joseph, Steve DiSalvo, Sam and Dennis Librizzi and others. They were charged with extortion in the threats to undercover agent Ty Cobb, as well as illegal gambling, as we had proven that Balistrieiri had contol over the Librizzi operation.

De Marco and Thorne continued seeking pertinent witnesses for the upcoming trial of Frank Balistrieri and they found a good one named Barbara Bertram. She admitted to being Frank Balistrieri's paramour and testified that she had accompanied Fancy Pants to Chicago on several occasions. She said that there was one specific time that caused her to wonder what he was up to. She said, "Frank met with some guy in Chicago, and then he and I went to the Ambassador Hotel and had dinner in the Pump

Room Restaurant. He was always treated like a king there. Frank had too much Dom Perignon, so he couldn't drive home. I took the wheel, and because of the treacherous weather and icy roads, I slid his Cadillac into a snow bank. Frank was unconscious in the passenger's seat, so I went to the trunk to see if there was a shovel or something I could use to get us out of the snow. There was no shovel, but there was a bag, and I discovered it was full of $100 bills."

United States Strike Force Attorney John Franke was the prosecuting attorney and did a great job in bringing the case. As much of our case hinged on electronic eavesdropping, the several defense attorneys turned their attention to having the Title III evidence excluded for various reasons during a motion to suppress evidence hearing. This is standard operating procedure in such cases because pertinent monitored overhears prove to be absolutely devastating to defendants. De Marco's affidavits withstood the test of defense claims that they contained insufficient probable cause, so they settled for a second round of attacks on the government's case by challenging the overhears based on claims of improper monitoring and sloppy minimization procedures.

If defense attorneys can get the tape evidence thrown out, the case is realistically over. I was called back to Milwaukee to testify in two separate hearings held to challenge our procedures in the defenses effort to suppress the overheard evidence. The many attorneys came at me with everything they had, but our procedures and practices were sound and we withstood the challenges. During the hearing I was asked by defense attorney Tucker: "You were in charge of whatever activities were engaged in with respect to wiretaps, correct?"

Magnesen: "Yes."

Tucker: "Prior to the time that the wiretaps or bugs, a bug, a wiretap is on the telephone and the bug is a microphone?"

Magnesen: "You can say that."

Tucker: "And wiretaps and mics were placed in the Shorecrest Hotel, right?"

Magnesen: "Yes."

Tucker: "Did you make any of the surreptitious entries in the Shorecrest yourself?"

Magnesen: "On one occasion."

Tucker: "How did you get in?"

Magnesen: "Through the door."

Tucker: "Did this door lead to the basement?"

Magnesen: "Yes."

Tucker: "Do you have knowledge, sir, how long prior to the entry you have been testifying to, the key was in existence?"

Magnesen: "Approximately, it would have been in existence after we obtained the first court order, in October, 1979."

The defense was trying to prove we made the key to the Shorecrest before we had judicial authorization to do so. If they could prove that, then all the tapes would be thrown out as fruit of a poisonous tree, but we were on firm legal ground, so they inevitably failed. Then they played tape after tape of recorded conversations and asked me to explain why they had been monitored - and so it went, hour after hour. In the end, the tapes were ruled to be proper and therefore admissible in trial. The FBI's electronic monitoring procedures were so well grounded that of the ten separate cases in which I was case agent during my career, and obtained Title III, court ordered electronic surveillance authorization, I never lost any evidence as a result of insufficient affidavits or poor monitoring procedures. Those cases often ended in plea bargains because it is nearly impossible to fight a case where the defendant's own recorded words doom him.

Sweeping indictments were brought against the Kansas City gangsters, including charges of skimming from the Tropicana Casino, and the trial was held in 1983. The boss, Nick Civella, age 75, was sentenced to 35 years in Leavenworth prison. His brother, Corky, age 73, received 30 years. Carl De Luna, age 57, was represented by attorney Oscar Goodman and received 30 years, and skimming mastermind Carl Thomas received 15 years. Nick Civella was released early for health reasons, unbelievably, as a result of the submission of over 800 signatures of sympathetic citizens asking for his humanitarian release. He died without being able to speak as a result of the spread of throat and lung cancer soon thereafter. Not long after Carl Thomas was convicted in the Tropicana case, I visited him in the federal correctional facility located in Tucson, Arizona, along with Supervisory Special Agent Jim Perry. He was brought to a room by guards, and when he saw us he literally panicked. I don't recall seeing anyone that frightened, not of us personally, but because we were there asking for him. He said, "What are you trying to do to me, get me killed? They'll know I talked to you and I'll just be a piece of dead meat." He then pounded on the door and demanded to guards that he be let out of the room. He was panicked, but I felt no pity for the man. He had chosen sides, he had chosen his life, and now he had to live with that choice.

After several postponements, legal wrangling, and desperate

measures by the defense, the Bellwether case went to trial. During the trial, Frankie Bal stayed at the Pfister Hotel, conveniently located across the street from the courthouse. One morning, Mike and Fred saw him walking across the street with two pieces of toilet paper clinging to his cheek, an attempt to stop the bleeding from razor cuts received while shaving. Perhaps the minor bleeding was a premonition of his slow and steady decline. Fred told me, "He looked so ridiculous; Mike and I couldn't stop chuckling." Everyone charged in the Milwaukee case was found guilty and sentenced in 1984. Street enforcer Steve DiSalvo was sentenced to eight years. He was released early for medical reasons and died of a brain tumor shortly thereafter. The Librizzi brothers were sentenced to one year and a day plus three years probation, and Sam died of a massive brain hemorrhage as he sat on a bar stool after his release from prison. Frank, during his sentencing and ever delusional, told the judge, "Hell cannot be any worse for me. But I will never know, for I am judged by the judge of judges and the worst sentence I can get is purgatory." The judge wasn't swayed and Balistrieri was hammered with 13 years for violation of nine counts of extortion and illegal gambling. The judge stated that if he had been younger and in better health, the sentence would have been substantially heavier. Frank was released in 1991 for medical and humanitarian reasons and died of a heart attack two years later at the age of 74.

The Balistrieri sons were sentenced to eight years and were disbarred, but they appealed their sentence to the judge and duplicitously turned on their father, blaming him for their legal ills. John submitted a letter stating, "We were dragged kicking and screaming into this mess. We didn't know what Frank was up to and didn't ask." John didn't happen to mention how he manipulated Joe's taxes and covered up the $200,000 found in the safe with the option to purchase signed by him and his brother. Joe also presented a letter saying, "I have always known Frank to be an inveterate liar and hopeless braggart." He went on, "Frank delights in portraying us to others in his image." Then he wrote, ". . . if the three of us were to stand side by side, no angry god need send any serpent to devour us; the real snake stands in our midst." The sons had turned the corner, it was their father's fault, or as they referred to him, it was Frank's fault. In other words, the devil made them do it. The judge was swayed somewhat and reduced their sentences to five years. They were both disbarred and released from prison in 1989. We had torn the heart out of the Milwaukee mob and it had been reduced to a pitiful, impotent shell.

An inteersting aside to the demise of the Balistrieri crime family is a challenge to Joe and John by their sister, Bennedetta (Benny.) She was once married to Johnny "The Kid" Contardo, a member of the retro rock and roll group Sha Na Na. In an interview with Kurt Chandler, senior editor of Milwaukee Magazine, she is quoted as saying, "I know my father wasn't an altar boy but he was my father and I loved him." Then she turned her wrath on her brothers, speaking of their duplicity by throwing their father under the bus, "Joe and John, they're like Milwaukee's answer to the Menendez brothers . . . These guys chewed off my dad's arm and hit him over the head with the bloody stump. . . . they wanted him in prison. They sold his Cadillac within 24 hours after his being taken to jail."

Sally Papia didn't buy the Balistrieri boys' lamentations,

either. After hearing of their protestations, she told Milwaukee Sentinel reporter Bill Janz, "I babysat for them when they were growing up. I changed their diapers . . . they had silver spoons in their mouths when my family never had a spoon. Touch their hands, they're like silk." In January of 2000, Sally left this world as a result of an automobile crash while a passenger in her daughter's car when it slid off an icy road.

The FBI was rolling to a perfect storm, a hurricane, crushing two of the Midwestern mobs. Now it was time to shift gears and attack the heart of the skimming operation, the source of the mob's lifeblood - Las Vegas.

PART TWO

It Ends in Las Vegas

CHAPTER 6

A Legend is Born

"Frank Rosenthal, one of the two pure geniuses I encountered in my entire Las Vegas career."

--Oscar Goodman

The third city in our story was built on the southeast bank of Lake Erie. Pre Cleveland, Ohio was a fertile area prized by early Native Americans. The city was incorporated in 1814 and is named after General Moses Cleveland. The city is located adjacent to swampy lowlands and wasn't considered inhabitable by white settlers until the lowlands were filled in and, as a result, the city eventually prospered. The dubious advent of Prohibition led to the spread of organized crime in Cleveland, as it did in many other cities. Elliot Ness, after jailing Al Capone in Chicago, was appointed Safety Director of Cleveland, resulting in the cleanup of the corrupt police department.

Viruses are extremely potent infectious agents that invade the cells of other organisms by penetrating all possible entry routes. This scourge is difficult to treat and, as such, only the symptoms can be effectively combated. The medical consensus is that the best defense against the deadly disease carrier is immunization. Unfortunately, the virus that is organized crime was allowed to multiply and infect much of the nation. Strike one on the Government was allowing immigrant members of organized crime to remain in the United States. Strike two was allowing the spread of the disease, but, thankfully, there would be no strike three for the FBI.

Inaction by immigration authorities allowed the virus of organized crime to enter the bloodstream of America. Congress compounded the infection in its zeal to solve all imaginable problems by legislation and passed the Eighteenth Amendment prohibiting the sale and consumption of alcohol in May of 1919. Think of it - amending the Constitution of the United States for such a foolish purpose. What happened to individual rights and "the pursuit of happiness?" Of course, the intent of the amendment was to eliminate the evils of liquor and drunkenness, but the law opened the door to clever and vicious entrepreneurs who stepped in to fill the public's desire for booze. The Volstead Act, meant to penalize illegal bootleggers, had little effect on the illegal liquor purveyors as various organized gangs fought for supremacy of the illegal business. The unwise constitutional amendment resulted in one of the most devastating, unintended consequences in American history – the ascension of the power and wealth of organized crime.

Morris Barney "Moe" Dalitz was 20 years old when Prohibition kicked in. He was one of the cunning men who stepped in to become a bootlegging racketeer. He was born in Boston and raised in Detroit, but later his family operated a large laundry business in Cleveland, Ohio, and he took advantage of the once-in-a-lifetime opportunity handed to him, as if it were a gift from the government. The young man cleverly used his family's laundry delivery trucks to hide and move the banned hooch. Dalitz, one of the founders of the notorious "Purple Gang," a predominantly Jewish crime group, was a very talented man and used his formidable gift for mediation to the gang's advantage.

He was able to negotiate an alliance between Cleveland's Italian "Mayfield Road Gang" and the Purple Gang. As a result, Dalitz, a virtual genius when it came to organizational criminal enterprises, became very wealthy.

The fourth city in our tale isn't anything like the cities of the Midwest. In the early days, the city was dry, hot, sun parched, and fit only for rattlesnakes and desert tortoises. For centuries, the local natives, the Paiutes, barely scraped by through tedious hunting and gathering. The Spanish explorers were the first white men to find "the meadows," for which the city of Las Vegas was named in Spanish. The explorers located small, widely spread springs and seeps providing life giving water that nurtured pockets of grass, shrub brush, and sparse trees. In the valley of scattered meadows, a few hardy ranchers and farmers, like the native Paiutes, eked out a dusty existence until the railroad extended its tracks to pass through the fledgling town. This event brought a limited boom to the fledgling settlement that was incorporated in 1911. Small, smoky gambling halls known as "saw-dust-joints" thrived, as did brothels and quickie divorces, but the hallmark completion of Hoover Dam changed everything for the parched community. Now water was no longer scarce, and the hydroelectric generators inside the dam produced enough electricity to power all the lights and air conditioners in Clark County. With the defeat of the stifling heat, the desert was embraced by forward looking entrepreneurs. The early crime problem in Las Vegas consisted of cowboy-type crooks and visitors from elsewhere looking to have a good time on their stolen money. Then a huge paradigm shift occurred in the railroad stopover when, with the urging of forward thinking Majer Suchowlinski, known as Meyer Lansky, convinced Benjamin "Bugsy" Siegel, former member of New York's "Murder Incorporated," to move to Vegas and set up shop. Lansky went on to develop organized crime controlled gambling casinos in Cuba and nurtured several New York City organized crime figures, convincing them to expand from the traditional hard-nosed, violent street rackets to the softer crimes of casino skimming and hidden ownership. He was a true visionary, but unfortunately his vision was one of power, greed, and dark deeds. Siegel was a ruthless killer who decided to expand his interests in Las Vegas with the aid of New York City organized crime funds and built the Flamingo Hotel-Casino far south on the Las Vegas Strip. Sin City was coming of age.

My first experience with Las Vegas happened on my honeymoon in 1969 when my bride and I stayed at the Flamingo Hotel-Casino for a few days. Like so many citizens, I knew nothing about Siegel, the founder of the resort, nor was I remotely aware of Las Vegas' history or the mob's influence in the neon city. Many years later, after being assigned to the Las Vegas Division, our OC squad was given a tour of Siegel's Flamingo presidential suite, an opulently furnished bungalow fitted with a 500-foot secret passageway used by Siegel as a quick escape route. He always had a car and driver waiting to whisk him away from his many enemies, should it be necessary. Siegel's paranoia proved to be well founded, as two days after the Flamingo's grand opening in 1947, he was murdered in the home of his mistress in Beverly Hills. He was sitting next to an underworld associate on a couch when an unknown person fired several shots through a picture window from a .30 caliber military M1 carbine rifle. Siegel was hit in the torso and twice in the head. One bullet entered his right cheek and passed out through his left eye killing him instantly. This was the first in a long series of murders associated with the mob's acquisition and control of Las Vegas casinos.

Moe Dalitz, Cleveland's premier underworld's negotiator, moved to Las Vegas and brought Teamsters pension fund money with him and left the running of the Cleveland mob to Jewish mobster Milton "Maishe" Rockman and the LCN. With his ill-gotten funds and using his umbrella company, Paradise Development Company, he bought out the original builder of the prime property called the Desert Inn Hotel-Casino and allowed the builder, Wilbur Clark, to run the place after the casino was finished in 1950. Clark was but one of the straw men used as fronts by mob controlled properties, but Dalitz was the real power behind the public throne. Earlier, the Flamingo Casino had been organized in the same way by Bugsy Siegel, as had Caesar's Palace, Circus Circus, the Dunes, and the Tropicana. Like many robber barons, Dalitz became a philanthropist and built the Las Vegas Country Club, Sunrise Hospital and several other Vegas institutions. He had a good heart and essentially bought his good reputation in the entertainment capital of the world.

Mobster Jimmy "Blue Eyes" Alo, a close friend of Meyer Lansky and a New York City LCN member, once discussed Moe Dalitz. He said, "You've got to give the Jews credit. They started out as fronts for the Italians and now they've got millions they made through the Italians. They were smart and declared some of that money to the government. See, a Jew makes a million, he declares two, three-hundred grand. An Italian makes a million, he declares a grand. The Jew in Cleveland – Dalitz . . . they were running all the gambling joints . . . .. That's how guys like Dalitz got wealthy and respectable. That's when they can invest in Vegas." I once interviewed Dalitz regarding a case I was investigating and found him to be a pleasant, gregarious man who skillfully navigated the interview like a slalom skier and provided nothing of value.

Emilio Muscelli, a former Las Vegas maitre d' and old time Las Vegan, was reported in John Smith's *Las Vegas Review Journal* column on March 29, 2009, to have said, "I want to tell the truth about the history of Las Vegas. They should be giving credit to those guys, not hiding them. Meyer was in the Flamingo from '46 to '67... Meyer's friend was Jimmy Blue Eyes [Alo]. When Meyer and his wife would come to town, I used to take them around. I would escort them. ...Meyer Lansky built Las Vegas, Nevada. If it wasn't for Meyer Lansky, Las Vegas would not be much. He is the one responsible."

As I explain in my book, *The Investigation – A Former FBI Agent Uncovers the Truth Behind Howard Hughes, Melvin Dummar, and the Most-Contested Will in American History,* Howard Hughes quietly moved to Las Vegas in the early morning hours of Thanksgiving of 1966. His men registered him at the Desert Inn under the name of Jack Trent and they took over the entire ninth floor of luxury suites, as well as several suites on the eighth floor. After a time, Dalitz realized that his most luxurious suites were not available to his high roller customers, otherwise known as "whales," and he became concerned. Each casino caters to these whales as they pour millions of dollars into the coffers of the casinos by way of gambling losses. Dalitz had a major problem on his hands, so he approached Robert Maheu, a former FBI agent and close confidant of Hughes, and asked him to approach Hughes and ask him to please move out. Maheu told me that Hughes was not the move out type. He liked his suite, and besides, he had nowhere else to go. This tug of war went on for a time, but the problem was reaching critical mass when Dalitz made a demand that the Hughes party leave or be evicted. When Maheu delivered the ultimatum to his boss, Hughes was quoted as saying, "I'm not moving. You tell Dalitz I'll buy this place."

Hughes, the wealthiest man in America at the time, had acquired his fortune through the Hughes Tool Company, Hughes Aircraft, Western Airlines, and the sale of his share of Transworld Airlines. He solved Dalitz's problem by purchasing the Desert Inn Hotel – Casino in March of 1967 for $13.25 million in cash, a huge sum at the time. The purchase of the "DI" was nothing more than an appetizer; the main course turned out to be thousands of acres of raw desert land west of the city, the KLAS Television station, two huge ranches, Alamo Airway, and the North Las Vegas Airport. Then between October of 1967 and mid- 1968, Hughes bought the Castaways Casino, the Frontier Hotel-Casino, the Silver Slipper, the Landmark Hotel-Casino and Harold's Club in Lake Tahoe. The political powers brokers in Las Vegas were ecstatic. They had always known many of the casino properties had shadow owners, and now they were rid of at least one of them, and probably more. At the time, their secret wish was that Hughes would buy all the questionable properties in town.

The Hughes properties ran at their own pace under the direction of Maheu, as Hughes bumped around the world in search of a sanctuary after leaving Las Vegas in November of 1970. In late March and early April 1976, Hughes fell seriously ill. He hadn't eaten in days, he was addicted to codeine, he and was totally emaciated. His kidneys shut down and his other organs had had enough abuse. His body was worn out. Aides finally flew him from Acapulco, Mexico, but he died on the 5th of April en route to a hospital in Houston, Texas. His death was the result of maltreatment, poor medical care and drug addiction. When the Hughes estate was settled, the executor sold off the casino properties and the mob settled back in to some of them, again with Teamster money.

Admittedly, the FBI was asleep at the wheel, or at the least, reticent to commit resources to combat the virus of organized crime for many years during the LCN's American ascension as Director J. Edgar Hoover publicly denied its existence. Prior to 1957, Hoover stated, "No single individual or coalition of racketeers dominates organized crime across the country." At the time of this statement, the Bureau was deeply engaged in an all-out fight with roving gangs of bank robbers and communist operations within the United States, but street agents knew that organized crime was a nationwide problem. Hoover's abdication was short sighted and foolish. Actually, Hoover didn't want to commit manpower to a cause that might lead to the corruption of his agents, as he was aware of the phenomenal amounts of money held by organized crime. He had seen police corruption and wanted none of it in "His Bureau." Hoover also realized that the FBI had few federal laws to combat the scourge of a nationwide criminal conspiracy. But, denying the existence of a problem of such magnitude will inevitably surface and cause a pandemic of unwanted consequences.

Hoover's opinion changed on a cold November day in 1957 when an assembly of organized crime figures were discovered meeting in the tiny village of Appalachian, New York. It was learned that the very select group of mobsters met there to plan the continued proliferation of the LCN throughout America and to determine how the expansion would be organized. The fortuitous roust of the assembled hoods by the New York State Police accomplished two important things. First, the mob went deeper underground and second, law enforcement's eyes were opened as to the LCN's existence as a national threat. Fortunately, the sleeping giant that is the FBI had been awakened from its slumber, but it took some years before an all-out, no-holds-barred battle was joined. Once the FBI was fully committed, things would never be the same for the mob.

In the late 1970's and early 80s, federal law enforcement authorities were viewed with deep suspicion by "good old boy" Nevada authorities. The two Las Vegas federal judges were particularly antagonistic toward the FBI and the U.S. Justice Department's Organized Crime Strike Force. They saw these agencies as threats to their practice of dispensing "Las Vegas justice." The FBI was working in extremely hostile territory during this time period. For example, one of the judges, Harry Claiborne, a former mob defense attorney, once flew into a rage on the bench regarding federal authorities as he yelled, "They are rotten bastards and crooks and liars." The other federal judge, the late Roger Foley, once learned that the Department of Justice – Organized Crime Strike Force had derogatory newspaper statements and cartoons about him posted on one of their office doors and, in a rage, he ordered the U.S. Marshals to seize the entire door and bring it to him. The Marshals were embarrassed, but they had their orders. They actually removed the door from its hinges and carried it to the judge's chambers. One wonders what state of paranoia beset the judge. At the same time, Las Vegas SAC Joseph Yablonsky said, "Las Vegas is no safe harbor for criminals. We have every intention of planting the flag in Nevada." But authorities, including Nevada Gaming officials, told him, "We're doing our own thing here. We don't need anyone else, and we sure don't need the FBI." What very few people knew was that with the resurrection of Atlantic City, New Jersey, as a gambling destination, a ranking representative of the Chicago Outfit had flown to New York City and met with the five heads of the New York City families as well as the New Jersey and Philadelphia families in 1977. This secret pact was known as "the Treaty of 1977." After some give and take, the bosses agreed that Chicago could have the Las Vegas casinos and the eastern cities would have free reign in Atlantic City. Simply put, a nationwide conspiracy required a nationwide response, and the only organization with sufficient national jurisdiction is the FBI.

The gambling control structure of the state of Nevada, or "gaming control" as they have more gently designated it to soften its vice ramifications, is set up in two bodies. The Nevada Gaming Control Board is the investigative and regulatory arm headed by a three member board and has many gaming control agents appointed to enforce gaming laws and regulations. The second tier of regulators is the five member Nevada Gaming Control Commission appointed by the governor and tasked with holding hearings and making policy.

The fifth city in our tale of five cities is Chicago. It was incorporated in August of 1833. Originally built on a patch of swamp land situated between the Des Plaines and the Chicago Rivers, on the southern tip of Lake Michigan, the city soon blossomed into a major metropolis of commerce. Like all the Great Lake cities, the Native Americans initially hunted and fished the area and French explorers were the first white men to settle there. The city was named using the French version of the Illinois Indian tribe's word for wild leek, "shikaakwa, that grew profusely in the region." Political wrangling is a trademark of the city, and Chicago soon became known as the "Windy City," not because of its constant wind gusts, but because of all the long-winded politicians, full of hot air, that controlled the political machine that is Chicago politics.

An infamous underworld icon whose persona has been blown all over the media was Alphonse Gabriel "Al" Capone, who was born in January of 1899 in the slums of Brooklyn, New York, to Italian immigrant parents. He was the fourth of nine children and often helped his father in the barber shop or his mother as a seamstress, but that didn't last. Little Al didn't have any desire to be schooled and was expelled because of exceptionally bad behavior at the age of 14. His nature was that of a street tough, and soon he joined the "Five Points Gang" in Brooklyn. He needed to earn his way, so he got a job as a bouncer at a Coney Island dance hall and after a verbal altercation, he got in a fight with a surly patron who slashed the left side of Capone's face three times with a switch blade knife, leaving permanent marks. He would thereafter be known as "Scar Face," a moniker he was proud of. Eight years later, the Capone family moved to the Windy City and settled on the northwest side of the city in an area known as the "Patch." Like his newly adopted city, Capone flourished in the environment of prohibition and soon became a major player in the underworld of bootlegging. Because of ethnic jealousy and huge profits, turf wars naturally broke out between various competing groups. Organized crime does not allow for competition in the open market. It abhors publicity and it vies for market supremacy through intimidation and violence. A major war broke out between the forces of Capone and an Irish group called the "North Side Gang." The war was vicious and wide open and resulted in the death of 200 men on both sides. Capone was cold, calculating, and ruthless, and he was able to set up seven leaders of the rival Irish gang on Saint Valentine's Day of 1929. The rival leaders were lined up by Capone's men who were dressed as police officers, and literally blown apart by bullets fired from fully automatic Thompson Sub Machine guns.

As was often the case in the rough and tumble days of Prohibition, the police had little interest in solving the notorious massacre, as it was felt the murders merely eliminated a bunch of bad guys, and good riddance to them. The police refer to this phenomenon as "a self cleaning oven." Capone moved in on Cicero, Illinois, and essentially took over the town. He used his wealth derived from prostitution, gambling, and bootleg liquor to bribe politicians, judges, and police officers liberally. Capone, always the rebel, chose to call his organization the "Outfit," as opposed to the LCN.

Elliot Ness entered the enforcement vacuum that was Chicago in 1929. He was a Prohibition Bureau Agent assigned under the U.S. Treasury Department, established as a result of the Volstead Act. He attacked Capone in a frontal assault on his bootlegging empire by raiding warehouse after warehouse and destroying the liquor and profits of the Outfit. At this time, it is believed that Capone was raking in $10 million a year in profits. Ness confiscated Capone's trucks and eventually charged him with tax evasion. The scar-faced boss, once untouchable, was sentenced to 11 years in federal prison. While incarcerated in island prison of Alcatraz, Capone was stabbed several times by a man who wanted to prove he was tougher than the boss of the Chicago Outfit. The once invincible gangster began to loose his health and was released from prison in late 1946. Capone, referred to by other prison inmates as the derisive "Wop with a mop" because his prison job was mopping the floor, contracted pneumonia and suffered a deadly heart attack, possibly exacerbated by stage three syphilis, not long after being released from the harsh, inhospitable prison.

The mob universe has many planets of varying sizes. Most families are small, secondary planets, but there is a massive Jupiter that, by its sheer size of membership, dominates everything west of New York City. The Chicago Outfit is the eight-hundred pound gorilla in the system, not that it controls the other families, but that it has the power and capacity to wipe out all the others in order to get its way. With the death of Capone, one of his most trusted enforcers rose to power in Chicago. Anthony Joseph "Tony" Accardo was a man known for his penchant for no holds-barred violence. He was often referred to by close friends as "Joey Batters" because of his reputation for mercilessly battering his victims. Accardo had the muscle but not the finesse of leadership so he enlisted the aid of Joseph "Doves" Aiuppa of Cicero, Illinois, and made him co-leader of the Outfit. Aiuppa, a pudgy man who wore eyeglasses, was a grandfatherly type, but that facade was nowhere near the truth. He was a quiet man or enormous ability who believed in developing strong connections with the Teamsters Union, but he could be a murderous leader who took whatever action was necessary to solve a problem. It was said by Chicago mob guys that "he had been boss so long that he had gray nose hair." The moniker of "Doves "was attached to him because he was once arrested for possessing hundreds of dead doves stacked in the trunk of his car after a very successful hunting trip. The number of doves far exceeded the legal limit and he was charged with a hunting violation.

From time to time, nature introduces a genius into the world of organized crime. One such man was Meyer Lansky; another was Frank Rosenthal. Rosenthal was born on June 12, 1921, just after the onslaught of the Prohibition era. He was a lowly Chicago boy who would evolve to become the premier sports handicapper in the nation. His early years are somewhat of a mystery, but a close associate was once asked about Rosenthal's ethnicity and he explained, "Frank was born in Sweden, adopted at six months by a family living in Tel Aviv. He moved to Chicago at the age of two with his parents. He's not really certain about his ethnic background-most likely mixed." The Rosenthal family settled into Chicago's West Side, an ethnically diverse neighborhood, where young Frank grew and developed his very unique skills. The nuances of the sport of kings appealed to him. The horse races themselves were exciting, but the chance of winning his bets by overcoming the nearly insurmountable odds was a narcotic, something he needed, something he craved above all else.

It is well known in Las Vegas betting circles that horse bettors are the most degenerate and easily the most frequent losers. I once met a Las Vegas cab driver who had the horse bug and would take his fare money and lay it on his favorite pony, only to loose again and again. To make up for his lost money, he got hooked into a loan shark and soon was on a virtual treadmill, picking up fares, running to the race book, then scrambling at the end of the month to pay the juice on his loans. I asked the cab driver, "Why do you do it? You have to know it's a losing proposition." He responded, "Yeah, I know, but I can't help myself. I'm addicted. It's as bad as being hooked on heroin." Frank Rosenthal was certainly not that kind of sick bettor. He used his hours of study, contacts with jockeys, horse trainers and sometimes race fixers to increase his edge. In the real world of horse racing, it isn't that uncommon for race horses to be juiced up to run faster or slower by unscrupulous trainers who secretly inject various drugs into the helpless animals, thereby eliminating the element of chance in the outcome.

The mob feeds on human vice. It caters to the weaknesses of the flesh by providing liquor during Prohibition, it provides drugs to all who want them, it takes kickbacks from prostitution operations, and with the passing of the 21ˢᵗ Amendment nullifying prohibition in December of 1933, illegal gambling became the major earner for the LCN. Rosenthal was only 12 when the liquor bane ended so he had no distractions to becoming an expert in the art of prognosticating sporting events, and as he aged, his reputation soared through the bookmaking community. Any edge uncovered by him was used to his advantage and inside bettors clambered to his side to receive his wisdom. LCN members are often notorious gamblers. They'll bet on anything, card games, table games, sporting events and horse races. Rosenthal's word was gold and his tips, often given to highly placed mobsters, made him very well respected and gave these insiders "locks" on many sporting events.

When the up and coming handicapper was a young man he learned that people were willing to bet on anything. This is known as proposition betting, or "props." Money can be bet on an endless variety of possibilities: the number of strikes pitched to a particular player, the number of double plays in a game, the number of times the manager walks to the mount, the number of interceptions made during a football game, the number of field goals kicked in a football game, and, of course, any conceivable prop on basketball. He saw this type of betting as absolute idiocy, but it opened a new door to him. If bettors were willing to place proposition bets, then he would be glad to book them. Rosenthal savored odds-making the most. He had scouts all over the country reporting on player's injuries, suspensions, and how particular players played against certain other players.

Rosenthal was a master odds maker. The odds, or "line," on a sporting event is vital. The Las Vegas sports books subscribe to handicapping experts who establish the line or point spread between teams. This equalizes the contest so that, at its worst outcome, the book doesn't loose a great deal of money. The book always has the advantage, as it takes a 10% piece of the action, win or lose. This is called "vig" or "juice." Sometimes the bookies set an over and under line which predicts the total, combined score of both teams in a game, and the bettor can place a wager on whether the total score will be over or under the total number set by the book. The Las Vegas betting line is quickly passed on to illegal bookies all over the nation by runners employed by the bookies. More often than not, the Las Vegas line is remarkably accurate, but a gifted odds-maker like Rosenthal can beat the Las Vegas line, thereby realizing an advantage.

In the late 1990s, I had the pleasure of having lunch with author Nicholas Pileggi, along with Agent Dennis Arnoldy, when he was visiting Las Vegas during the filming of the movie *Casino*, which is based on his book *Casino, Love and Honor in Las Vegas*. We talked about the movie and his interviews with Frank Rosenthal and former mobster Frank Cullotta, whom I knew well. He personally signed a copy of his book for me and, realizing my organized crime background, wrote, "For Gary Magnesen. You'll learn nothing in this book. Best, Nick Pileggi." Contrary to his statement, I did learn some things from his book. Pileggi also provided me with a copy of his research notes for his book.

Rosenthal is quoted by Pileggi as saying, "My dad was a produce wholesaler. An administrative type. Good with numbers. Smart. Successful. My mother was a housewife. I grew up reading the racing form. I used to tear it apart. I knew everything there was to know about the form. I used to read it in class. I was a tall, skinny, shy kid. I was six foot one when I was a teenager and I was kind of withdrawn. I was sort of a loner, and horse racing was my challenge. I got some resistance at home when I started getting into sports betting. My mother knew I was gambling and she didn't like it, but I was very strong headed. I wouldn't listen to anyone. I loved going over the charts, the past performances, jockeys, post positions. I used to copy all the material onto my own eight-by-ten-inch file cards in my room late into the night." The development of the gifted odds-maker and gambler continued for many years, but he had one personality flaw, an Achilles heel as he, himself, explained. "I wouldn't listen to anyone." This flaw, this chink in his otherwise impenetrable armor, would seal his fate and eventually lead to his downfall. Rosenthal didn't care for nine to five employment. As with most mobsters, a regular job was considered too mundane, too everyday. With the exception of serving for a time as a military policeman during the Korean War, a result of being drafted, he never worked at a legitimate job until his old age. His chosen calling was living on the edge, tossing the dice, relying on his wits and expertise as a handicapper and bettor.

Sports Illustrated once pronounced, "Frank Rosenthal is the best living expert on sports betting," and one of the beneficiaries of Rosenthal's winning picks was Fiori "Fifi" Buccieri, who FBI agents once named "The Lord High Executioner." Fifi Buccieri was the brother of Frank Buccieri, who was the boyfriend of Milwaukee restaurateur Sally Papia. Fifi had been a gunman for Al Capone in the 20's and was a feared enforcer. He was a notorious loan shark and grew to be wealthy from his hard-nosed lending practices. He ran a wholesale produce business and, because of his association with Rosenthal's father, he grew to know the young Rosenthal. Even though the young Rosenthal savored the excitement of the hunt for an edge, he was a realist and, certainly, a man who wanted insurance that he could pursue his chosen vocation without mob interference, so he took out an insurance policy by siding up to members of the Outfit

Fifi's produce business was a front and he certainly would never have allowed a competitor to exist without requiring some sort of street tax or protection money from competitors. If the owner refused to pay the "fire insurance," he would soon find his business burned to the ground. Everyone in the Chicago wholesale produce business knew this was just another necessary business expense. Buccieri was a brute. On one occasion, he and others ritualistically tortured William "Action" Jackson because he was suspected of stealing Outfit money and being an FBI informant. When the charge of "rat" or "snitch" is attached to someone who has the capacity to harm the mob, action is usually quickly taken in the absence of any strong evidence to the contrary. The organization can't afford to take a chance. The 300 pound Jackson was hung up on a meat hook and brutalized with ice picks, ball bats, and a blow torch for three days before he finally succumbed. One of the ruthless butchers, Fifi, was the man who befriended the neophyte Rosenthal and took him under his protective wing. Rosenthal was frequently observed by the FBI riding around Chicago with Buccieri in his car, providing a glimpse into the fledgling, blossoming relationship.

Rosenthal married briefly, but his lifestyle and obsessive compulsion for gambling led to a divorce. He was arrested a couple of times in Chicago for bookmaking and spent a few uncomfortable nights in jail, a small price to pay for the big money he was bringing in. In the late 50s, the FBI had determined that the goose that laid the golden egg for the mob was bookmaking, and an all out attack was launched throughout the country. The illegal gambling business statue was already in effect, but new laws were added to the Bureau's arsenal making it illegal to transmit wagering information in interstate commerce, as was interstate travel in aid of racketeering, and the new legal weapons were used effectively.

The law enforcement heat in Chicago pushed Rosenthal out of the city to Miami at the age of 30. He settled there and took up his vocation in earnest as he continued to rake in the money. Miami, Florida, is known as an "open city" by the mob.

This simply means that any LCN member can travel there and set up shop if he desires. If a dispute arises between members of different families, it is negotiated between the relevant capos of each family, and if the result isn't satisfactory then the bosses get involved. Most LCN members travel to Miami as ordinary tourists and spend their time there in opulent rest and relaxation, and Rosenthal was often visited by old pals from the Windy City, including his protector, Fifi. Not long after arriving in the city that was made home to hundreds of thousands of Cuban expatriates and exiles, Rosenthal was arrested again for illegal bookmaking and sports bribery. He decided that he was forever stuck on the treadmill of living the life he had chosen and the law that didn't like his life's choice.

During the time of Rosenthal's stay in Miami, the CIA was toying with the possibility of enlisting Cuban exiles and organized crime figures in a plot to eliminate the communist dictator of Cuba, Fidel Castro. A small, nondescript store called the Tamiami Gun Store became a supplier of weapons to deep undercover CIA operatives, but the operators of the store were more than willing to provide guns to others as well. A number of guns described as .22 caliber semi-automatic pistols were somehow obtained by members of the Outfit. The owner of the Tamiami and two employees were working both sides of the street and were eventually convicted of illegal gun running. It has never been determined exactly how many guns were obtained, nor is it known if the weapons were purchased or stolen, but the net effect was that any trace of the mob guns was frustrated at the dead end of the Tamiami Gun Store as there were no records kept by the operators on the disposition of the pistols. It is known that the guns were of high quality, but who obtained the guns is in question. Was Rosenthal involved? Was Buccieri behind it? It was rumored that the man who obtained the guns from Tamiami shipped them to Chicago in a box via Greyhound bus then sped north in his car to arrive in time to retrieve the guns in Chicago. They were then delivered to someone to be used as needed. It's also believed that a south side Chicago mobster named Ronnie Jerrett may have manufactured and fitted silencers for the Tamiami guns in his mother-in-law's garage. Ironically, he was shot dead in front of her house in December of 1999. After his murder, Jerrett's son stated that he found a bag full of guns in the garage.

The .22 caliber is a unique bullet. It's a small diameter round meant for target shooting and varmint hunting. It can be shot from a rifle or a hand gun and has a relatively quiet report, so when a pistol is fitted with a tube-like silencer, it is virtually noiseless. The .22 bullet, shot into the head of a victim, penetrates the skull but doesn't have enough velocity to exit the thick bones of the head. Instead, it bounces around inside the cranium, chopping through the brain and causing extreme damage. In 1977 there were at least 20 nationwide mob murders by use of .22 caliber weapons. Frank Bompensiero, a Los Angeles mob boss, was shot with one of the guns while he stood in a phone booth, as was Jack Molinas, a master basketball fixer associated with Frank Rosenthal. As a matter of fact, Rosenthal and Molinas were charged in the same college basketball bribery case in 1963, but Molinas was eliminated before the trial. Rosenthal pleaded no contest to the bribery charge and was sentenced to a few months in jail.

In the meantime, things were changing in the Outfit. Sam Giancana moved in to take over when Tony Accardo stepped aside as the boss in 1952. "Momo" Giancana was a different type of mobster. He was a high profile, high living man who publicly dated Phyllis McGuire, the lead singer of the once famous McGuire Sisters. He also dated Judith Campbell Exner, an actress who also happened to have had an affair with then President John F. Kennedy. Furthermore, Giancana was a contact of Robert Maheu, a former FBI agent and CIA operative and right hand man of Howard Hughes. It is strongly suspected that Giancana assisted the CIA, through his contacts in Cuba, in efforts to assassinate Castro.

On a warm June evening in 1975, Momo Giancana was frying sausages and his special recipe marinara sauce was simmering on the stove when he was shot in the back of the head. He slumped to the floor of his kitchen, and as he lay dying he was finished off with a shot through his chin. It's my contention that the shot to the chin was actually meant to penetrate his mouth – an old mafia sign that the victim was a snitch, probably due to his cooperation with the CIA. The murder weapon, a .22 caliber High Standard semi automatic pistol, was recovered several days later, discarded along the weed covered shoulder of a road not far from Giancana's house. Ironically, Momo had been the first victim of one of the Tamiami guns. Investigators determined that the volume of the simmering food cooking on the stove was more than one man could eat, so it was assumed that Momo was preparing dinner for himself and someone else. He was the boss of the Outfit-he wouldn't be preparing dinner for just anyone. The guest had to have been someone of stature and highly trusted in the Outfit. Furthermore, you can't kill a boss without some sort of authorization. One man who fits this restricted template was Joey "Doves" Aiuppa, and he benefited the most from the demise of Momo, as he ascended to the Outfit throne after the death of the high profile Momo. It was later learned that Anthony Accardo and Angelo La Pietra had assisted in the hit and, of course, with the participation of Accardo and La Pietra, two heavy hitters, the authorization was evident. Another of the Tamiami victims was Augie Maniaci, who was shot in Milwaukee as he knelt beside his car.

In the late 1960s, Robert Kennedy, Attorney General of the United States and brother of the president, had a running battle with J. Edgar Hoover over organized crime investigations. He felt the Bureau was not doing all it could in what he wanted to be an all-out war on the mob. His ardor may have been due, in part, to a reaction to his brother's relationship with mob girlfriend Judith Exner. Kennedy pushed Congress for an investigation of organized crime, and the McClelland Sub-Committee on Organized Crime was established. Committee transcripts show that Frank Rosenthal was one of the many witnesses who refused to provide testimony before the committee by pleading the 5th Amendment. Rosenthal was asked numerous questions and, frustratingly, he answered each by taking the 5th. Realistically, how could he possibly testify against himself and expose his tight connections to the Chicago Outfit? It would have resulted in a death sentence for him. In exasperation, Rosenthal was asked, jokingly, by one of the committee inquisitors, "Are you left handed?" Rosenthal smiled and responded, "I respectfully decline to answer the question, as I honestly believe my answer might tend to incriminate me." From that point forward, he would forever be known as "Lefty" Rosenthal.

In 1967, Lefty had had enough of South Florida and returned to Chicago. In an effort to circumvent the gambling laws, he was placing bets with the assistance of a runner at the Churchill Downs and Santa Anita sports books in Las Vegas, but this proved to be unwieldy, as the betting line often changed, thereby nullifying his tight picks. At the time, Las Vegas didn't allow sports betting in casinos, and only a limited number of small "mom and pop" sports books existed in the city. Every major bookmaker in the country had runners hanging around these properties, passing on the line and laying off bets. I have personally observed the runners, a motley swarm running back and forth between the books and pay phones outside.

Lefty was 38 years old when he made the decision of his life. He would move to Las Vegas and deal directly with the sports books there. Pileggi quotes Lefty in his book *Casino*, " . . . I'd have to go to Las Vegas. Take all my stuff and move out there, where I could sit down and watch the numbers until I was ready to pounce." Pileggi goes on to write that Rosenthal told him that Chicago mobster and hitman Tony Spilotro drove him to the summer home of Fifi Buccieri, located at Lake Geneva, Wisconsin, the day he was to leave for Vegas. The large house sat on a huge estate with horses, riding trails, and a rifle and skeet shooting range. The last minute visit to Buccieri's place speaks volumes about the two men's relationship and the influence this stone cold killer had on Lefty. Fifi hugged Rosenthal like a father saying goodbye, then Tony drove him to O'Hare Airport.

Unbeknownst to Lefty, a call from the Chicago Crime Commission to the Clark County Sheriff had preceded his arrival in the desert oasis, thereby setting him up for a very unpleasant

experience for the new arriver. Lefty told the story of his Las
Vegas experience in his own words on his website in 1998. "I can
remember the day as if it were yesterday! The weather was perfect;
the afternoon flight from Chicago to Las Vegas was smooth and
relaxing. I was on my way, prepared to settle into a paradise for
gamblers. Freedom, no more hassling with anti vice squads. You
can play as much as you weigh and you don't have to look over
your shoulder . . . Looked as though this was going to be easy as
picking cherries off a tree. Somewhere within the airport complex
I noticed two signs I would never forget. One read 'Welcome to
Las Vegas' the other read 'Clark County Sheriff – Ralph Lamb.'"

Ralph Lamb was first and foremost a cowboy. He was one
of 11 children born in Alamo, Nevada, to a dry land ranching
family. His grandfather was killed as a result of being bucked off a
horse and his father died after a horse rolled on him when Ralph
was only 11 years old. Lefty bet on horses, Lamb lived on them.
Lamb served in World War II as an Army intelligence officer and
then was hired on as a deputy with the Clark County Sheriff's
Department in 1948. He was elected sheriff in 1961. A *Las Vegas
Review Journal* article written by A.D. Hopkins attributes the
following quote to Lamb as he described a wanted man he tried
to apprehend. "A man shot at me three or four times and I wasn't
as far as from here to that door and he didn't hit me once. I hit the
concrete and shot at him a couple of times and I didn't hit him
once. Then he was running away and I would have had to shoot
him in the back, so I run down and tackled him." For the veteran
steer wrestler, pinning a man was a cakewalk.

Lamb's tough, hard-nosed approach to law enforcement was
highlighted when a pack of Hells Angels was reported traveling to

Las Vegas from the Los Angeles area. As the Harley hogs roared north, Lamb and several deputies drove south. The sheriff and his men set up on the Nevada state line and waited for the pack to arrive. When the gang arrived, they were met with loaded shotguns and ordered to turn around or die in the desert. The leather clad Angels turned and retreated, showing their colors as they rode off. Lamb once described his job and his wild-west approach to enforcing the law as a deputy to reporter Hopkins, "It was pretty exciting work. You were out there on the strip all the time, and mostly you dealt with guys coming here on the run. They had pulled bank robberies, for instance, and they would come here thinking it was an exciting place to spend their money, to kind of launder it. So we'd catch a lot of those guys." Lamb treated mob guys no differently than he treated street criminals. They were all the same to his way of thinking. On one occasion, mobster Johnny Rosselli, a close associate of Sam Giancana, was sitting in a booth at the Desert Inn with Moe Dalitz when Lamb sent a rookie cop in to order Rosselli off the premises. Nevada law requires convicted felons to register with the sheriff within 24 hours of their arrival in the city, and Rosselli had neglected to register, so he would soon learn how tough Lamb was. Rosselli laughed at the rookie and told him to get lost. This was part of the plan Lamb had laid, so he marched in and confronted Rosselli. Lamb explained that he grabbed the hood "by his necktie, dragged him across the table, and slapped him around for a while . . ." Then Lamb threw Rosselli into the back-seat of the rookie's waiting cruiser and I sent him to jail, ordering the extra touch of delousing."

After arriving in what he thought would be his paradise,

Lefty settled into a room at the Tropicana Hotel-Casino on his first day in Vegas. He provided the following description of his accommodations in his website. "Beautiful suite, fresh fruit, cut flowers, and a tray of hot and cold appetizers, compliments of the casino." He explained that he was, "all freshened up and ready to visit friends and top executives of Caesar's Palace, when there was a knock on his door." The official welcoming committee had arrived. "Two plain clothes detectives with the department advised me that I'm under arrest. 'Put your hands behind your back. You're under arrest for breaking and entering.' Bullshit, you got the wrong man. I just checked in and haven't even finished unpacking." They responded, "Don't bother, you won't be staying very long." Lefty was taken to headquarters and introduced to a man described by Lefty as "a well known enforcer for the sheriff's intelligence division." The enforcer, Gene Clark, chief of detectives, grabbed Rosenthal by the throat with "hands that looked like hams. His grip around my throat felt like a steel vise. I was a struggling, just hoping to remain conscious. No doubt in my mind. I'm dealing with an unpredictable cop who may not be playing with a full deck." Rosenthal was ordered to hit the road because "you and your Chicago friends aren't welcome here."

Rosenthal was eventually released from jail, and he then drove to Caesar's Palace to visit friends. He explained, a "short ride down the strip and I'm keeping one eye on my rear view mirror. I couldn't detect a surveillance . . . I'm sitting with the Creme De La Creme of the Palace. The Chairman of the Board and several casino executives including Dean Shendal, better known as the 'Cowboy. He loved steer wrestling, calf roping and the whole aura of the modern day rodeo cowboy . . . I noticed the chief of detectives and his two bloodhounds entering the casino. The chief began eyeballing our table with an expression of indecision. His eyes focused my way like a laser beam.... the chief asked me what I was doing at Caesar's.... You must have a short memory or a hard head . . . I have my orders, were taking him downtown." There were protests by the executives, and Dean Shendal, a man with a short fuse, jumped into the verbal fray. He said, "He's our guest and not about to cause any problems." The chief exploded, "You ought to mind your own business, Dean." Shendal was furious! He had been embarrassed by the detective and impetuously invited the cop for a back parking lot meeting of fists. Lefty stated, "What a natural match, a double tough cowboy and a deranged copper who hadn't been known to back away from anyone." Everyone realized that emotions had ruled the moment, and professional gamblers are realists if nothing else, so Lefty tossed in the towel and was taken downtown and booked again. Lefty continued his story. "Same basic routine, strip searched, photographed, fingerprinted and placed in a holding cell with a bunch of winos and weirdoes. The odor was nauseating but I was feeling okay." Lefty had gotten the message. He was many things, but he was never known to be stupid. The next day he returned to Chicago.

Let's engage in some analysis of Lefty's behavior in Las Vegas. Why did he stay at the Tropicana? The simple answer is that it was a mobbed up property at the time, first by New York interests and later by the Kansas City LCN. Something Rosenthal neglected to mention in his descriptive narrative is the reason he had received cut flowers, fresh fruit, and hot and cold appetizers in his room. These are not commonly provided to ordinary guests. These specials are only provided to big casino gamblers or to connected guests. There was no sports book at the Tropicana at the time, so it wasn't as if he was a big gambler there. Also, interestingly, this outsider from Chicago could come in from out of town and on his first day in the city, sit down with the creme de la creme of Caesar's casino hierarchy. How did that happen? The clear answer is because Caesar's was a mob joint back then. Is it possible that Lefty's "rabbi," Fifi Buccieri, had made some calls to friends and set things up for his genius student?

After returning to Chicago, Rosenthal waited impatiently to hear fro Las Vegas and finally received a call from Dean Shendal about a week after being chased from the city. Shendal told him he had met with his cowboy friend, the sheriff, and Lamb had relented and said he would allow Lefty to return to Vegas as long as he kept "his nose clean." This relenting of Lamb's long standing policy proved to be a major mistake.

This was a time of change in the world of Las Vegas policing. The Clark County Sheriff's Office and the Las Vegas Police Department were folded together and became the Las Vegas Metropolitan Police Department (Metro) even though it is actually a sheriff's department. Lamb was selected to head up the new agency, but scandal tarnished his legacy. He was charged and was found not guilty of tax evasion but his department suffered persistent claims of corruption.

Las Vegas Organized Crime Squad

Allen Glick

Frank Rosenthal

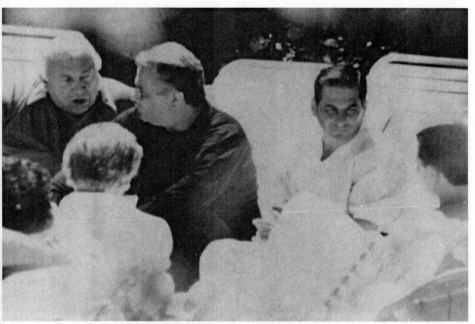

Natali Richichi (left) and John Gotti (center)

Joseph Aiuppa

Nick Civella

Sally Papia (right)

Tony Spilotro (left) and Oscar Goodman (right)

Frank Balistrieri

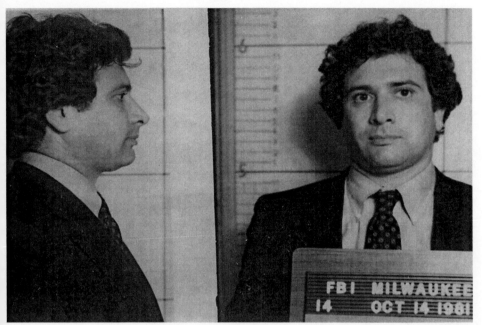

John Balistrieri

Joseph Balistrieri

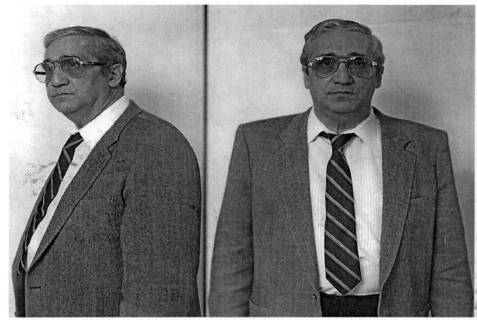

John Fecarotta

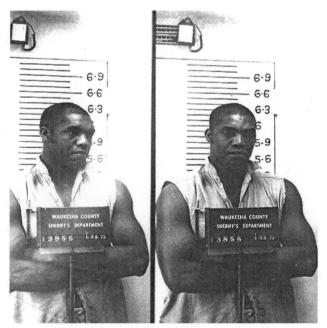

Willie Davis

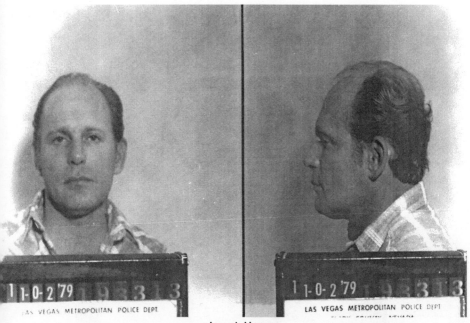

Joseph Hansen

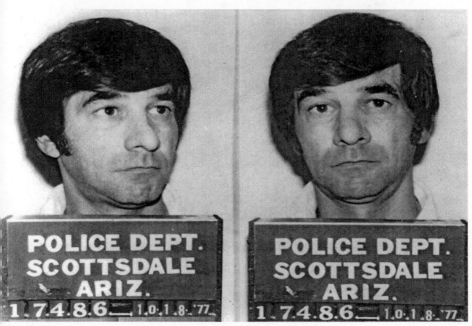

Paul Schiro

GARY MAGNESEN

Tony Spilotro - Age 16 (left) and Joseph Hansen - Age 16 (right)

158

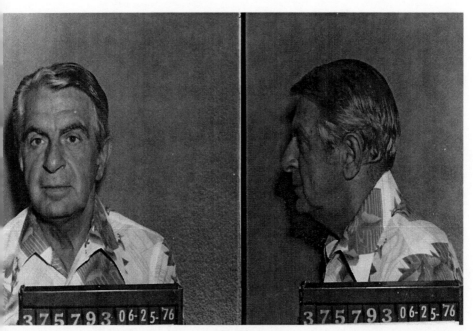

Mel Vaci

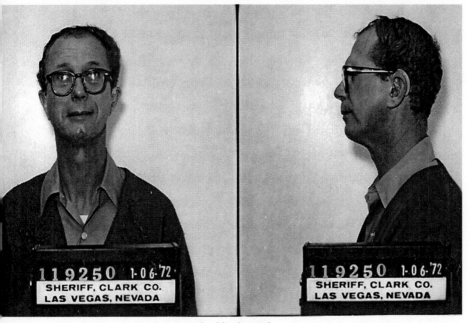

Jay Vandermark

CHAPTER 7
The Pot of Gold

"Frank Rosenthal happens to be a very competent executive."
--Allen Glick

Lefty, who had returned to Las Vegas through the intervention of Cowboy Shendal, once described his plans for a life in the gambler's paradise on his website. "Originally, my goals and professional aspirations were basic to my background - booking and betting. Within our stable we had contracted with the super scouts from designated conference, throughout the country. With over 50 outs bookmakers from coast to coast, we had an excellent arsenal at our disposal . . .. We were consistently successful, perhaps a little bit lucky. Our win percentage on single bets were close to 60% . . .. Our primary targets were the Churchill Downs and Santa Anita." Lefty was happy; he was doing what he was born to do. Then he made one of the biggest mistakes of his life.

In his book *Casino*, Nicholas Pileggi, quotes Lefty as saying, "Meanwhile, I'd met Geri. She was a dancer at the Tropicana. She was the most beautiful girl I ever saw." He explained that it was Geri's nightly pattern to finish dancing in the Folies Bergere and then hit the casinos. Lefty told Pileggi that she earned between $300,000 and $500,000 a year hustling chips and partying with high rollers. On one occasion, late into the morning hours, Lefty observed her with a man playing craps. "Geri was tossing the dice and the guy was winning a great deal of money off her throws. She was grabbing black hundred dollar chips and slipping them into her purse, but when the guy wanted to cash out, Geri reminded him she had been his lady luck and he should tip her five or six grand. He laughed at her." Then Lefty described what happened next. "Geri leans over and grabs his chip racks and tosses them into the air as high as she can . . . Within seconds everybody in the casino is diving for chips. I mean players, dealers, pit bosses, security guards - everybody's fishing for the guy's chips on the floor . . . At that point I can't take my eyes off her. She's standing there like royalty. She and I are the only people in the whole casino who weren't on the floor. She looks over at me and I'm looking at her. 'You like that, huh?' she says, and walks out the door. That's when I realized I had fallen in love."

It's amazing that an intelligent, street-wise guy like Rosenthal was so mesmerized by Geri's beauty and feistiness that he overlooked the inevitable fact that the woman was absolutely uncontrollable and had no self-imposed boundaries. Nevertheless, Geri McGee and Rosenthal were married in 1969 by Justice of the Peace Joseph Pavlikowski and they threw a big, expensive reception party to celebrate the occasion, but Lefty admitted that he knew from the beginning that Geri didn't love him. He realized early on that he was nothing more to her than another promising mark.

Everyone believed Lefty was a gentle genius. His hands were softened by expensive, custom-made lotions, his fingernails were exquisitely manicured, and he dressed impeccably, but this was the facade of the external man. His upbringing in the trenches of Chicago had created another man, the internal man - the real Lefty was capable of anything. He may not have personally dirtied his hands often, but when there was trouble, he regressed to the man he had always been. A vivid example of Rosenthal's inner man, a man with a volatile personality, was displayed when he described that he once saw Geri dancing with a man at a club. The two began arguing and the man shoved her forcefully. Lefty, enraged by this act of disrespect, attacked the man on the dance floor. Lefty wasn't a fighter, but they both hit the floor and Lefty's face was scratched badly, causing him to bleed all over the place. Luckily, the fight was broken up by bystanders. Lefty recounted to author Pileggi, "I was crazy. I went back to the Trop, where I was living, and went into my bag and got a gun. I was going to find the sonofabitch and kill him." Fortunately for his opponent, Lefty was stopped and talked out of his crazy plan by friends.

Geri, after some cajoling, convinced Lefty to get a legitimate job in a casino, probably because she wanted to know where he was so she could continue her extra- curricular activities unhampered by her husband's nighttime interventions. In 1971 the Stardust Hotel-Casino was owned by Recrion Corporation, with Al Sachs as president and Robert "Bobby" Stella as the casino manager. Rosenthal approached Stella, an old Chicago associate, and applied for a job. Stella, knowing who he was, immediately hired him as a floorman. It's unusual for a man who has had no casino experience to be appointed floorman, since the applicant is normally required to be a dealer, then a pit boss for some time prior to being elevated to the floorman position.

The floorman's job is to watch, keep an eye on players and dealers, to be on the lookout for purposeful distractions that may accompany attempts at cheating or stealing, and to make players comfortable. Lefty had walked into a big job. This tells me that he had inside help. In other words, someone from Chicago had juiced him into the job. As a result, Lefty was resented by many of the other employees because he had jumped them in seniority, and this caused dissention on the floor.

When the Gaming Control Board learned of Lefty's hire, they moved in and demanded that he submit to a background investigation before he could obtain a gaming license as a floorman. This is standard operating procedure in the industry, and as his reputation had preceded him to Las Vegas, they were sure their efforts would ban him from the casino industry, thereby eliminating him as they had done to many other applicants who didn't qualify for employment. Gaming didn't foresee that their efforts would lead to a continuing war between Rosenthal and Nevada Gaming authorities when he refused to give up. Al Sachs didn't need this kind of trouble, so he suggested that Rosenthal quietly step aside, but Lefty Rosenthal never stepped aside for anything. He responded by calling in his sponsor, and a few days later Fifi Buccieri appeared at the Stardust under an assumed name. A meeting between Sachs and Fifi took place in the rear of the closed Auku Auku restaurant. Pileggi quotes Rosenthal as overhearing part of the conversation between the two men. Lefty heard Sachs say, "I know he's just like a son to you." Buccieri retorted impatiently, "You're wrong," Sachs was surprised at the response, until Buccieri explained, "No, he's not like a son; he is my son." Clearly, the real power behind the Stardust had spoken and Sachs, realizing the consequences of not keeping Lefty in place, got his mind right and Rosenthal was kept on in his position, gaming authorities be damned.

Allen R. Glick, before sweeping into Las Vegas, had been a nobody. He was born in Pittsburgh, Pennsylvania, in 1942. His father was an iron scrap dealer, and his mother was a housewife. He had been drafted into the Army as a helicopter pilot during the

Vietnam War and was awarded the bronze star for gallantry. He attended college and after graduating with a BA degree he went on to Case Western University and obtained a law degree. Glick, only 32 years of age, was a short, balding man who wore owl-like eyeglasses. After graduating, he moved to San Diego where he, like so many others, became involved in the real estate development business. He may have been a nobody in the beginning, but he was a genius when it came to thin-ice financing of projects. Over time, Glick wanted to be a player in Las Vegas and began flirting with the possibility of buying the King's Castle in Lake Tahoe as an entry point into the gaming business. There he met a blackjack dealer named Marty Buccieri who said he could introduce Glick to Teamster officials who could come up with large sums of money. It isn't known if Buccieri actually made the introductions to these people or not.

In 1974 Allen Glick was rewarded beyond his wildest dreams, and with the stroke of a pen he became a multimillionaire player in the land of wondrous casinos as $62,750,000 was deposited into the account of Argent Corporation by the Central States Pension Fund of the Teamsters Union. The financial magician used the money to buy four Las Vegas Casinos: the Freemont, the Marina, the Hacienda, and the flagship of the four, the Stardust. This remarkable and unprecedented achievement caused many to scratch their heads in amazement, including Las Vegas authorities. At the time, no one knew that the secret to his achievement was hidden away inside the dark wall safe in the Shorecrest office in Milwaukee.

Public as well as governmrntal exuberance over this clean-cut, 32-year-old neophyte casino mogal was electric. Harry Reid, the current Senate Majority Leader, had been appointed chairman of the Nevada Gaming Control Commision and served in that capacity from 1977 to 1981. During his tenure, he wondered about Glick's meteoric ascension and questioned, "We couldn't understand how somebody could get that kind of money from the Teamsters. I don't know if we'll ever know." The gamers in 1974 weren't aware that the Teamsters Pension Fund was referred to as the "money store" by Midwest mobsters and didn't know that with the right OC connections, all kinds of questionable deals could be finessed through the mob's control of the pension fund trustees. If gaming officials were concerned with the loan, why wasn't it looked into more deeply? An investigation into the Teamster pension fund trustees as financiers could have answered Reid's wonderment about the loan. Additionally, the trustees could have been asked to testify before the Gaming Board and provide loan application documents.

It was well known and a matter of public record that the International Brotherhood of Teamsters had, in the past, been a breeding ground for corruption. The union was first organized in 1906 and has had mob ties since the time of Al Capone. Ron Carey, its president, was removed for corruption and in 1948, and as a result James "Jimmy" Hoffa took control. Hoffa was convicted of corruption in 1964 and imprisoned. Hoffa returned in an effort to regain control, but he disappeared on July 30, 1975. He was snatched mobster-style after having lunch in a Detroit restaurant. There is much speculation as to his fate, but FBI informants have stated that he was killed because other forces didn't want him to return as head of the union. His successor, Roy Williams, was also convicted of corruption in 1982, and his replacement, Jackie

Presser, followed his example as well. This unquestionable pattern of corruption and deal making, and the fact that the union pension funds hold countless millions of dollars for investment, made the system ripe for corruption in the 1970s.

With his multiple acquisitions, Glick became the second largest owner of casino properties in Las Vegas, behind the absent Howard Hughes. The corporate umbrella for his properties was named Argent Corporation, an acronym for Allen R. Glick Enterprises. The new man in town delighted gaming authorities, and after a less than complete due diligence investigation, they found him to be clean and acceptable for key employee licensing. Glick moved ahead expeditiously and set up his headquarters in the Stardust, where he ordered major renovations, including the building of a plush office for himself. He also refurbished his home in La Jolla, California, just north of San Diego on the Pacific coast. The palatial spread had tennis courts, a pool, a sauna, cabanas, and fountains. He also bought an airplane and had several expensive cars at his disposal. Not long after his acquisitions, he threw a house warming party and invited 400 guests to the lavish affair. Then, out of the blue, Glick did the unthinkable. He promoted Lefty Rosenthal from floorman to the number two position in his corporation. This caused ripples to spread throughout the Stardust, and certainly in law enforcement circles, and Gaming would have none of it. They wondered, "Why him? He has too much dirty laundry." The answer was slow in coming but it eventually became clear.

In the meantime, Lefty moved quickly and turned the casino upside down. He fired anyone not up to his high standards or those he couldn't trust and pulled management of the three other

Argent casinos under his direct control. He also hired some very questionable characters to key position within the casinos. From the outside, Glick appeared to be a laissez fare owner, content to allow others to run his show while he lived the high life.

From that point forward, Frank Rosenthal was gripped in a monumental struggle with Nevada Gaming authorities, and at the same time was fighting another battle at home with Geri. He once said, "She was an extremely complex individual, far beyond my ability to describe. Our marriage was doomed from day one. Geri's addictions were not compatible for a successful marriage or any form of a lasting relationship. That is not intended to demean or degrade her. She was one tough cookie, so was I." With his promotion, Rosenthal purchased a lavish home inside the gates of the Las Vegas Country Club Estates, but this residence became the gates of hell as far as Lefty and Geri were concerned.

With regard to his licensing battle Lefty once rationalized, "I drew more attention than one might expect for two basic reasons. One, beginners luck, two, my association with fellows that were not looked upon as model citizens. Winners attract a crowd, and sometimes a penalty." At another time he surmised, "I've been a professional gambler for most of my lifetime, consequently Sin City seemed to be the logical destination. Unfortunately, I ran into some rough and tough dudes within the power structure of the gaming structure of the gaming establishment and just wasn't able to sustain my career. The Nevada Gaming Control Board and the Commission acted arbitrarily without standards or obligation to due process of law. Like the saying goes, they can indict a 'ham sandwich' without bating an eyelash." His hatred for Nevada Gaming officials was made clear when he vented in his blog after years of being away from Las Vegas, "Remember the Saint Valentines Massacre that took place many years ago inside a Chicago garage? I wish those 10 bandits disguised as safe keepers for the state would have accidentally lost their direction and wandered into the massacre."

Rosenthal had filed all the required paperwork for the gaming board and the required vetting had been completed, so his application was scheduled for a hearing before the Gaming Control Board in Carson City, Nevada, in June of 1978. His attorneys were Oscar Goodman, defender of mobster Tony Spilotro and numerous other mob figures, and Harry Claiborne who was later to become a federal judge. As an aside, a few days after my arrival in Las Vegas in October of 1980, I was scheduled to work on a Saturday afternoon. I had been issued a key to the Federal Court House, where the FBI had its office on the second floor at the time. I was at the back door unlocking it when a man came up from behind and startled me when he said, "I'm glad you have a key, I forgot mine." I showed him my credentials and told him I couldn't let him in unless he had some kind of official identification. He said he didn't have his ID on him, but he was U.S. District Court Judge Harry Claiborne. I was apologetic when I told him I was new to the city and didn't know him, therefore, I wouldn't let him in. He was remarkably understanding and said, "Welcome to Las Vegas agent Magnesen. You did the right thing." He then turned around and walked away.

The Nevada Gaming Control Board unanimously voted against Rosenthal and it appeared his fight was over, but Lefty and Oscar Goodman didn't like to lose, so they appealed to the Nevada courts. In the meantime, Lefty changed his official title at the Stardust from operations manager to food and beverage manager. Food and beverage didn't require licensing, as the position, in a perfect world, had nothing to do with gaming. Lefty's job description changed, but his responsibilities didn't. Lefty continued running the casino operations out of his plush office and, to the continuous frustration of Glick, Lefty excluded him from most of his decisions. Lefty once described Allen Glick as " . . . a highly intelligent individual... when I originally met Allen Glick he was unmistakably a neophyte in hotel and casino gaming, he was however a Johnny Come Lately to finance and administration and the ability to perform and execute the difficult and challenging day to day responsibilities that encompass a chairman of a publicly traded company."

Not only did he run Argent's casinos, but Rosenthal took credit for being the first executive to bring women into the casinos as dealers. He explained, "I felt it was in the company's best interest to offer an opportunity for women to become equally eligible for employment, not just for maid service or food and beverage . . .. The plan was to gradually integrate the gals so long as they are qualified." This was a certainly a positive move by Rosenthal, but he only brought women dealers in to spice up the casino and draw more players, as the male gamblers enjoyed flirting with the ladies and not because of some anti-misogynous zeal. Rosenthal had definite female tastes. He once said, "It is true that blonds do catch my attention, however, dizzy and dumb blonds are a dime a dozen and I'm not a dime store customer." Lefty also took credit for signing Siegfried and Roy and their marvelous animal illusion act for the Stardust. His crowning achievement was bringing sports books into the casinos – admittedly a brilliant move.

A little more than a year after being soundly rejected by Gaming officials, Judge Pavlikowski, the same judge who, coincidently, had married Lefty and Geri, ruled the Gaming Board's decision to exclude Lefty was in violation of Rosenthal's constitutional rights and was "arbitrary, capricious and void of responsible due process." The victor was jubilant and was immediately reinstated as Chief Executive Officer of Argent Corporation, and he moved back into his plush office and pushed forward at a hectic pace. His executive office, much larger than Glick's, was extravagantly furnished by any standard, and Lefty was especially proud of a sign hanging on the wall that read "NO" in very large letters and "yes" in tiny, barely visible letters. Everyone knew the sign reflected his management philosophy. It was business as usual for Lefty.

The casino industry caters to two classes of clientele; the everyday Joe who comes with a modest amount of money which he is willing to throw into the gambling coffers, and the "whales," who are incredibly wealthy and, who, with the play of only one hand, may fill the coffers with half a million dollars or more. These whales, otherwise known as high rollers, are catered to and pampered by the casinos. Jamiel "Jimmy" Chagra was known as a "whale" in casino circles. He was a major El Paso drug lord who was charged with drug trafficking in 1978. He believed he had no chance of avoiding a life sentence before Federal Judge "Maximum" John Wood, so he hired Charles Harrelson, father of actor Woody Harrelson, to kill the judge for the fee of $250,000. He also tried to assassinate the prosecutor in the case. Chagra was convicted in spite of a proper defense by attorney Oscar Goodman, and in a plea agreement, Chagra admitted to the murder conspiracy.

I visited Chagra in a federal medical prison in upstate New

York sometime around 1984. There was a special cell block in the prison appointed for federally protected witnesses, and they lived like retirees, among their own kind. They did their own cooking, played cards, read, and played checkers all day. I debriefed Chagra regarding his knowledge of Las Vegas, and he informed me that when he was trafficking, he loved to play poker. He played at Caesar's Palace and the Stardust, where he was treated as a king. He told me he would travel from Texas to Las Vegas two or three times per month and would bring suitcases full of cash with him. He would be met at the valet parking area by armed security guards who would take his suitcases to the casino cage where the money would be credited to his account. I asked him if he was ever asked about the origin of all the cash. He smiled mischievously and answered, "I was a high roller. No one cared where I got the money." He informed me that he was making so much cash he had no way of hiding it. "I couldn't put it in a bank, and you can only stash so much of it. Besides, I got a rush playing a million dollars on one poker hand." When asked about Rosenthal, he responded, "He loved me. In one night I could make his bottom line skyrocket. Lefty was a gem. He loved taking my dirty money."

The Chicago Outfit's tentacles reached to any place where problems arose that posed a threat to its gold mine in Las Vegas. One such problem occurred when the St. Louis mob's Morris "Moe" Shenker, the straw man owner of the Dunes Casino owed money to Allen Dorfman. Dorfman owned Amalgamated Insurance Services, which provided insurance to the Teamsters. His office was located above Teamster president Roy Williams,' and they were very close. Dorfman had assisted the St. Louis mob and Shenker in obtaining a Teamster loan to purchase the Dunes Casino, and Dorfman wanted his piece of the money, so he went to the Outfit and complained. Giuseppe Patrick "Joey The Clown" Lombardi, who changed his last name to Lombardo, met with Shenker in Dorfman's office in 1979. Lombardo, one of 11 children born to Italian immigrants worked in his father's butcher shop for a time then dropped out of high school to become a full time criminal. He was once convicted in an attempt to bribe former Senator Howard Cannon of Nevada. He received 15 years in prison, but when he was released, The Clown, placed the following ad in the Chicago Tribune: "I never took a secret oath, with guns and daggers, pricked my finger, drew blood or burned paper to join a criminal organization. If anyone hears my name used in connection with any criminal activity, please notify the FBI, the local police, and my parole officer."

The conversation between Lombardo and Shenker was overheard on an FBI microphone. Lombardo told Shenker, "Allen belongs to us in Chicago. Now, you know what I mean when he belongs to Chicago? I was sent here to find out what the story is. When they talk to Allen, he says he don't get this, he don't get this, he got this, he got this coming. Allen's not that type of guy. But the people that got a piece of him are that type of guy. Allen is meek and Allen is harmless. But the people behind him are not meek and harmless. Do you know what I mean?" Lombardo presented Shenker with a not-so-subtle threat to pay Dorman his piece. It's clear from this conversation that the Chicago Outfit could tell the St. Louis mob what to do. Dorfman had outlived his usefulness to the Outfit and was assassinated as he walked through a parking lot in Chicago in 1983, after being indicted along with Lombardo. Dorfman had been the Teamsters Central States Pension Fund trustee, and after his death the fund was reorganized.

Meanwhile, in Chicago, Allen Glick had some self inflicted skeletons in his closet that came back to haunt him. One such skeleton was Edward "Marty" Buccieri, a distant cousin of Fifi and the same man he had met at King's Castle in Lake Tahoe. Buccieri claimed he had introduced Glick to Al Baron and Frank Ranney, both Teamsters officials, and Glick's massive pension loan had resulted from the introduction. Buccieri felt he was entitled to a $25,000 finder's fee but Glick kissed him off and told him he hadn't been that much help, which he may or may not have been. A desperate Buccieri, in a fit of uncontrolled anger, grabbed Glick by the throat and threatened him. Glick broke free and returned to the Stardust in a storm of fury. Glick prided himself on his complete self control, but the confrontation with the Caesar's Palace blackjack dealer had shaken him to his core. His anger spilled out as he described the incident to Lefty, who was somewhat amused but understood the implications of a possible lawsuit or other unneeded problems from Buccieri, which could have opened the Teamsters Pandora's box. Later it was learned that Frank Balistrieri, in an effort to protect his golden goose, had ordered the murder of Buccieri after clearing it with the Outfit's Joey Aiuppa.

Not long after, on a hot Las Vegas afternoon in June of 1975, Marty Buccieri was leaving work after a long day of standing behind a blackjack table. He was tired and was anxious to get home, where he could sit down and relax. As he approached his car, two men came up from behind and pumped several bullets into his tired brain. Joey Hansen and Paul Schiro, two trusted members of Tony Spilotro's hit crew, had taken care of the bloody business while Spilotro looked on from a distance. Buccieri died face down on the hot asphalt surface of the Caesar's Palace parking lot, his blood pouring out of five bullet wounds in his head. No charges were ever brought for the murder because of lack of evidence.

About six months later, on November 9, 1975, a 55-year old businesswoman named Florence Tamara Rand was drinking a cup of tea in the kitchen of her upscale home located in the Mission Hills section of San Diego. It isn't known if she heard her attackers enter the house or if she was totally ambushed without hearing the shots that took her life. The innocent victim died from five bullets to her head on an otherwise peaceful Sunday afternoon. About two hours after the murder, her husband, Dr. Philip Rand, returned home and found his wife sprawled dead on the kitchen floor, her cup of tea spilled out as a witness of her last living act. The murder weapon was determined to be a High Standard .22 caliber semi automatic, a Tamiami gun. It was later learned that the murder was to have been set up to look like an accident but the shooters didn't do as they had been instructed. It isn't known why. The assassins, believed to be Schiro, Hansen, and possibly Harry Aleman, had somehow made entry through an unlocked door, and for some reason the plan went awry. The cowardly killing of Rand may be the only known Outfit-sanctioned murder target who was a woman. This sort of ruthlessness towards innocents who may cause potential problems should forever take the fascination out of fanciful views of organized crime.

It was learned that Rand had previously entered into a

business deal with Allen Glick and claimed she had given Glick money for an investment in a land deal and he refused to repay the loan, so she had traveled to Las Vegas and engaged the head of Argent in a heated argument and threatened to push a lawsuit against Argent. All she wanted was her part of the legitimate profits from her investment in one of Glick's land deals. Lefty was present for part of the confrontation and had harsh words for Rand, who foolishly disregarded his warning. This turned out to be a deadly mistake. No charges were ever brought in her murder for lack of evidence.

Glick, according to author Pileggi, responded to the Rand murder by writing an open letter to the media. Part of the letter stated, "Two weeks ago a woman was found dead in her home in San Diego. Mrs. Rand was a past business associate of mine and most recently party to a lawsuit filed against a company I was active in, as well as me personally . . . To associate me or any department or employee of my company with so-called 'organized crime' is false. The truth is that I have never been convicted or guilty of a crime greater than a traffic violation. The truth is that Argent operates three Las Vegas hotels and four casinos. The truth is that I was unanimously approved for licensing to operate these hotel casinos after an exhaustive and extensive investigation . . .." Glick failed to mention his association with Frank Balistrieri whom he knew to be an organized crime figure.

The powers in the Outfit saw no purpose in sending someone to talk with Buccieri or Rand, as they were regular citizens who may have reported the threats to authorities. There was but one option left, the ultimate sanction, the final solution for those who could hurt members of the secret organization – death.

CHAPTER 8

A Mobster Reveals All

*"I would rather have my daughter date
Tony Spilotro than an FBI agent."*

--Oscar Goodman

Lefty Rosenthal, described by some as a wizard of sports betting and by others as arrogant, narcissistic, and self-serving, was in an all out war with Nevada Gaming officials and was beginning to attract negative attention back home among the dark powers of the Outfit. They abhorred any kind of publicity, fearing the spotlight could easily fall on them and negatively affect their nefarious activities. Amazingly, in the midst of the unwanted publicity, Lefty, as the Stardust entertainment director, did the unthinkable. He started a television program called the Frank Rosenthal Show in April of 1977. He hosted dancers and other entertainers and interviewed celebrity guests, such as Frank Sinatra, Robert Conrad, and O.J. Simpson. The show was a B-grade version of the Tonight Show, but it put him and the Stardust up front and in the public eye every week. Lefty once explained the geneses of the program, "I was asked if I was willing to do the show by our advertising department." This explanation was ridiculous on its face – his ego was driving him.

At the same time, Lefty's attorney, Oscar Goodman, fought a high profile battle in the courts and in the media, pushing for Lefty's civil rights as a man who had been driven from his chosen occupation by evil regulators. Protected witness, Joe Agosto had told me that he reported to Nick Civella in late 1977 and early 1978, about the pending problem of "that crazy sonofabitch, Lefty. He's getting out of hand. He's stirring up dirt all over Vegas. He's dangerous. He could cause us big problems with his big mouth and his T.V. show." He went on to tell Civella, "This guy is trouble and he's had people killed to protect himself." Agosto said that Civella listened intently, but didn't respond. The boss would never discuss killing someone with anyone who wasn't made.

Outside the view of Lefty, his troubles deepened. On one occasion, the FBI surveillance team watched Geri Rosenthal meet with Tony Spilotro in a trailer located in the desert, which he used for various encounters with women. It was clear that there was trouble in Lefty's marriage, and things would soon escalate to the point of no return. Spilotro realized he had broken a cardinal rule by sleeping with Lefty's wife, Geri, but he rationalized his actions and turned on his old friend. He complained to Cullotta, "That Jew ran back to Chicago and cried. I gotta do something about it." Tony knew the dye had been cast as to his future, but Tony, besides being viscous was also pragmatic. Rosenthal soon learned of his wife's indiscretions and reacted as any husband would, even though he had dallied with countless showgirls himself. He was also very concerned that Tony would try to kill him, as Geri had told the hitman about the affair in a fit of violent temper.

From time to time, circumstances arise that cause a change in a criminal's allegiances. Sometimes, hardened career criminals, even mobsters, roll over and come to the side of law enforcement. I have had the good fortune of causing this to occur, and I have also had the opportunity to interview many of these men who decided, for whatever reason, to turn their backs on their old life and past associates. The unparalleled insights and first hand evidence they provide to law enforcement is incalculable. One such man is Frank "Brahma" Cullotta. He had been arrested by the Las Vegas FBI in a major case, and he, as Joe Agosto would say, decided to changed uniforms.*

I remember very clearly the day Frank Cullotta was released from federal prison.

As the mob guys would say, "He'd been away." To the best of my recollection, it occurred sometime in 1984. Special Agent Dennis Arnoldy and I traveled to Miami to welcome Frank to a life of freedom. Arnoldy, a former Military Police officer and Vietnam veteran and respected polygrapher, had developed a close relationship with Cullotta and wanted to see him before the rehabilitated mobster entered the witness protection program. Frank had lost some weight, but otherwise looked good. Of course, it wasn't the first time he'd been in stir so it hadn't been a life-altering shock to him. We took him to a fancy dinner and he talked about his prison experiences and how good it felt to be out. He was to meet federal marshals later that evening and was scheduled to fly to parts unknown as a result of being placed in the federal witness protection program. In the meantime, it began to rain. It was as if the heavens had been torn open and all its waters poured out on Miami. We sought refuge in a nearby lounge as the water rose in the parking lot and began to seep under the front door of the bar. Dennis and I were somewhat anxious about having Frank in such a public place filled with all kinds of people. Dennis mused, "We don't know any of these people. For all we know, an Outfit guy could be here and recognize Frank." I responded, "Yeah, let's keep an eye out for anyone who uses the

* The arrest of Cullotta will be covered in chapter 10.

pay phone, just in case he's calling to tip somebody off. I doubt that anyone is going to leave the bar in this weather." Dennis agreed. "Let's sit over there in the corner near the emergency exit where we can see the whole place and duck out the door if we need to." In spite of our concern, we could see Frank was having a great time. He hadn't been in the company of women for many months and a flirting cocktail waitress brought a huge smile to his face. Finally, the rain relented and it was time to put him on the plane where he would fly off to begin a new life.

Some months later, Dennis and I met with Cullotta again in Oklahoma City and debriefed him regarding some details of investigations we were working on. The last time I met Frank was on a bright, clear Las Vegas day in March of 2009, 13 years after my retirement. The temperature had already climbed to 80 degrees when I met with the 70- year-old, along with Dennis Arnoldy. Frank is, without a doubt, a man with a dirty past who has made every effort to cleanse himself of his old life by cooperating with the FBI, and although there is still a murder contract out on him, he has melted into normal society. Frank was in a good mood and, of course, was wearing his trademark designer eyeglasses as he settled into an overstuffed chair that seemed to envelop him. We talked of old times and we had a few laughs, but then it was time to get down to business. I began questioning him about his personal history, and he willingly responded by explaining, "I grew up in the Patch, an area around Grand and Desplaines Avenue on the Northwest end of Chicago. It was a rough neighborhood and you learned to be tough or you got beat all the time." He said that his father, Joe Cullotta, was a hard nosed armed robber who had been killed while attempting to elude a police chase. He was driving 70 miles an hour as the police closed in and he hit another car head on, ending his long criminal career instantly. Frank continued, "When I was 14 years old, I was earning nickels and dimes shining shoes on Grand Avenue when this kid, about the same age as me, came across the street and threatened me to get out of his territory. I was bigger than him, so I says, 'Screw you.' I got this side, you stay over there! I could see he was mad, but he walked away." Frank later learned that the competing shoeshine boy was Anthony "Tony" Spilotro. He was later told by Tony that he had gone home from their confrontation and asked his brothers if they knew a kid named Frank Cullotta. They didn't, but Tony's father knew who he was and told Tony, "That kid's father saved my life, you leave him alone – be his friend." After that, Frank and Tony became very close friends as they grew up together in their rough world.

Anthony John "Tony" Spilotro was born in Chicago's Patch. He was the 4th of six children born to Italian immigrant parents. He was sometimes disparagingly referred to as "The Little Guy," and later by various law enforcement and newspaper reporters as "The Ant." Cullotta told me, "You know, people think Tony was called 'The Ant' because he was little, you know like an ant, but he was called Ant because it was a shortened version of Anthony. People made a big deal out of the Ant name, but it was just a chance to take a cheap shot at him." Spilotro was only 5'5" tall but had a barrel chest and heavy shoulders. When Tony was required to appear in court he had to buy a large suit coat to fit his torso, then have inches cut off the sleeves and trousers so it would fit properly. Whatever he was called, he was a man of ambition and a man who washed his hands in the blood of others.

According to Cullotta, growing up in the Patch was different than what most people consider coming of age. Growing up on Grand Avenue for Cullotta was learning how to rob, strong arm, and burgle. After a time, Frank and Tony realized they had to make a decision. Would they develop a reputation within the Outfit and curry favor with mobbed- up guys, or would they merely freelance in their criminal careers? Tony wanted to be made more than anything but Frank was content with doing his own thing. He said, "I didn't want no controls on me. You have to answer to somebody, and I didn't want to answer to nobody."

As time passed, both men were in and out of jail. They were career criminals, and inevitably, the law caught up with them from time to time. Cullotta had his own crew and began to specialize in high end burglaries. He told me, "One of my crew members was Paul 'Paulie the Indian' Schiro," a thin, pockmarked tough guy who eventually shifted to Tony's crew. Frank added, "Tony's goal was to be noticed by mob guys, so his crew did hits and real heavy stuff like that." The guys in Tony's crew were Schiro, Joseph "Joey" Hansen, and Frank "The German" Schweihs. Hansen, of Norwegian ancestry, was a trouble maker. Cullotta told me "Hansen was a scary guy. There was something about him, his eyes, and he was uncontrollable. Hansen would fight anybody. He was in the Colony House Restaurant one time. It was owned by Jackie Cerone, one of the Outfit bosses and Hansen got in a fight with one of Cerone's guys, so Joe Gaglione, Cerone's enforcer, told Hansen, 'I hear your name all the time. Next time I hear your name there's gonna be a loud noise but you won't hear it.' Hansen was tough but he wasn't stupid, so he left Chicago for Los Angeles, where he sold cars for his brother-in-law, but he was still part of Tony's crew." Frankie Schweihs was of German decent, and he killed without a second thought. He left for Florida, but moved back and forth between there and Chicago. "Paulie Schiro moved to Arizona and pulled high end burglaries while Tony stayed in Chicago, but they were still a crew, even though they were spread around the country."

Cullotta believes that Tony finally achieved his dream and was made sometime in 1972 or just prior to that time. "Tony got made with Joey Lombardo. Jack "Turk" Torello proposed both of 'em. Torello was up there with the boss, Joey Aiuppa. Tony had developed a reputation, you know, whatever you wanted done, he would do it."

Cullotta explained that Joey Lombardo eventually rose within the Outfit and worked directly under Jackie Cerone and Joey Aiuppa. Cullotta told me Lombardo was called "the clown" because he was always joking around, usually at the expense of others. Jackie Cerone, whose true name was John "Jackie the Lacky" Cerone, was a balding man of immense ability and a cold blooded killer who had participated in the torture-murder of Action Jackson, a Chicago loan-shark. He was arrested 20 times and rose through the ranks to run Cicero, Illinois, and served as underboss to Joey Aiuppa.

Cullotta went on to say that the Chicago mob didn't care much for the old Italian word Mafia or the New York mob's term La Cosa Nostra, so they referred to themselves as "Our Own Outfit." They didn't like the terms capo or soldier, either, so they refer to these positions as made guys and bosses and, of course, one top boss or "Old Man." The crews are divided by geographical area, for example: the North Side, the West Side, the East Side, China

Town, and the Suburbs, and each crew has various made guys working out of those areas. I asked Cullotta how a contract would come to Tony and how it would be carried out by his crew. He explained, "It would come down, usually from Sam 'Mad Sam' De Stefano, and Tony would pull his crew in to do the job. It didn't matter where it was, he would take it." Frank scoffed at the idea of professional hitmen in the mob who were paid for carrying out murders. He reminded me, "Money never goes downhill inside the Outfit, but money can go for expenses, to cops, judges, and union guys to pay for their help. If you're on the inside, you do it to get a reputation, you know, as a tough guy. If you're made, you don't have no choice. You pay your own way – you do the hit – that's it. If you don't do it, you don't last long. That's part of the deal you made when you came in." Cullotta also explained that even if someone wasn't made, he was required to kick back part of large scores to mob guys who learned of his success, just to stay alive. He added, "I did some favors for 'em, broke a few heads – you know, get recognition so they can trust you."

Frank went on to explain that when Allen Glick had a problem at the Stardust, such as the one with Marty Buccieri, he would have told Lefty, "You know, this and that. Lefty could reach farther than he could, so Lefty would see flags goin' up and he would talk to Tony. Then Tony would talk to the people in Chicago and get an okay to, you know, or maybe he didn't get the okay, and it was done by Tony's crew anyway." In the mid 70s, when Cullotta was in Chicago on a visit, Lombardo approached him and asked, "Who the hell is whacking all these people out there?" [Referring to Las Vegas]. "He asked in all sincerity – he wanted to find out. I don't think he knew it was Tony, at the time." Frank went on, "Glick may not have known about the planned whacks but he sure knew about the results." Frank continued, "Lefty Rosenthal had a reputation as a big time bookie and odds-maker but he wasn't made, plus he was a Jew, so any Outfit boss could control him. He had to answer to all of 'em, but Fifi Buccieri was his guy, and he answered to Jackie Cerone, and Cerone answered to Tony Accardo and, after he stepped down, to Joey Aiuppa." Lefty benefited from his mob connections, but the connections also carried a price. Business with the mob always comes with a ball and chain. Cullotta told me he had known Frank Rosenthal only slightly. They weren't friends, but they came from the same general neighborhood and they were aware of one another. Frank recalls meeting Rosenthal in the 1950s at Tony Spilotro's house in Chicago while they were playing cards. Frank walked in and was introduced to Rosenthal, but he, arrogantly, didn't respond. Tony had Rosenthal down by $60,000 and Rosenthal was upset. Some time later, Cullotta asked Tony if "the Jew had paid him." Tony responded, "Oh, yeah, he paid me."

Frank told me an interesting story that showed the kind of man Spilotro was. In 1962, Frank had two members of his crew named Billy McCarthy and Jimmy Miraglia. They were referred to as the "M and M Boys." Both men were hot tempered and easily provoked and were constantly getting into trouble with Outfit members. Frank warned them of their stupidity, but they wouldn't listen to him. McCarthy was bar hopping one night and had a run in with some guys at the Black Door Saloon in Rosemont, Illinois. The place was run by the Scalvo brothers, and the event erupted into a fist fight in which McCarthy was beaten up. Furious, he came back later with Miraglia, but the result was the same. They came to Frank and asked for his help in killing the brothers because they were obsessed with getting revenge. Frank told them they were nuts, as the Scalvo brothers were connected, but the M and Ms persisted in their demand and Frank told them they were on their own. One night, Frank was listening to the radio and heard a report of a triple murder where two men and a woman had been shot to death while sitting in a car in Elmhurst Park. This was a suburb where it was forbidden to commit any crimes because Joey Aiuppa lived there and he had made it known that no one was to bring any heat on him. Frank later learned that the two male victims were the Scalvo brothers and the female victim was their waitress. Frank knew immediately who had done the killings, and this caused him to worry as they were members of his crew and he was responsible for them.

His concerns were well founded when, a few days later, Tony showed up and questioned Cullotta about the murders. Tony accused the M and M Boys, along with Frank, of the unauthorized murders, but Frank protested, "I didn't do it, Tony." Tony understood and responded, "Look, I'm on your side. I told them you didn't do it, but you gotta prove yourself now. You've gotta give up Billy and Jimmy. If you don't, I can't save you." Cullotta found himself in a trap. He had no choice but to set up his crew members. Some days later, Tony returned. This time he told Frank he had to make Billy available because "they want to talk to him." Cullotta called Billy and told him to come to a certain location where, unbeknownst to Billy, Tony was waiting for him. Later that night, Billy's wife called Cullotta and asked if he had heard from her husband, but Frank lied to her. "I don't know where he is. I haven't seen him." Cullotta didn't know exactly what had occurred until later, when Tony said that Billy and Jimmy had been taken care of and had been dumped in the trunk of a car. Tony confided, "Billy was one tough Irishman. We beat him with everything, but he wouldn't tell us he did the killings or who was with him. We finally got so pissed at him that we put his head in a vise and turned it. The kid's eye popped out, then he begged to be killed. He finally gave up Jimmy just before we killed him. When we got Jimmy, he asked to be strangled and not tortured so we did." An autopsy of McCarthy determined that he had been viciously tortured with ice picks and blunt objects and his cranium had been crushed, resulting in the dislodging of his right eye from its socket. He died from a slit throat. Frank told me that Chuck Nicoletti, one of the hit-men seen in Milwaukee before the murder of Augie Maniaci, once described the M & M murders to Cullotta. Nicoletti had participated in the killing and characterized Tony Spilotro's demeanor during the torture. Nicoletti said, "He's cold. He was eating a ham sandwich when we were beating the guy." Frank also told me that Nicoletti was at Frank's restaurant just before he was killed on March 30, 1977, but Nicoletti gave no indication that he had any problems at that time. After he left, Chuck was seen by witnesses trying to evade a pursuing car, but was forced off the road in suburban North Lake, Illinois, by two unidentified men who jumped out and shot him multiple times. Nicoletti had clearly done something wrong, as he was eliminated in permanent LCN fashion.

Tony Spilotro arrived in the open city of Las Vegas sometime in the spring of 1971 and moved into an apartment. Before long, he opened a jewelry store as a front to work out of inside Circus Circus under his wife's maiden name, Anthony Stuart Limited.

Spilotro was the new kid on the block, so he went to someone who knew the town intimately, his old pal, Lefty Rosenthal. According to Cullotta, Lefty warned Tony that "Vegas was like a big fishbowl, the cops are always watchin', and the cops will come down hard on you if you step out of line." Spilotro couldn't imagine a hick town like Vegas being that threatening, as he had easily handled the big city of Chicago. He couldn't have been more wrong. Cullotta described Tony as "a Doctor Jeckyl and Mr. Hyde. He was unpredictable. He could be friendly and happy one minute, then something would set him off and he would become a monster. He was tough to deal with sometimes."

When Sheriff Lamb learned of Tony's presence, he ordered Spilotro's arrested, just as he had done with Lefty, and Tony was thrown in the drunk tank for a few days after his arrival and was given the message, "Get out of town." Tony was beside himself with burning anger when he was released from jail. He wanted to kill Lamb for what he had done to him. He knew he had broken no laws, so Lamb had no authority to push The Little Guy out of town. Needless to say, Tony stayed, and it was business as usual until he was arrested on a Chicago murder warrant. He was taken back to stand trial, but his co- defendant, Sam "Mad Sam" DiStefano, had chosen to defend himself in court and Outfit guys were afraid he might say or do something that would reflect on them, so he was unceremoniously shot gunned to death, probably by Tony. Additionally, Tony's sister-in-law provided alibi testimony for him in the murder case and, as a result, he was acquitted.

Spilotro's jewelry store was eventually thrown out of Circus Circus by Gaming authorities, so he opened another place on Sahara Avenue just west of the Strip. He called it the Gold Rush, and he surrounded himself with various guys including Joey Cusumano, and Herb Bliztstein who did his bidding. Unknown to Spilotro, Special Agent Bud Hall had been transferred to the Las Vegas Division from Milwaukee, and he set his sights on The Little Guy. Hall, a Marine Corps veteran, was a bulldog and may have had the best memory of anyone I have ever met. He had the uncanny ability to recall minute details and conversations that had occurred years before. Undercover agent Rick Bacon, using the name Rick Caliso, was enlisted to penetrate Spilotro's crew. Bacon, the son of an FBI agent, had the Bureau in his DNA and was fearless in his approach as a pseudo jewel thief, but Spilotro, a street wise veteran, was skeptical of the newcomer and unfortunately kept Bacon at arms length.

Eventually, microphones were secretly placed inside the Gold Rush and monitoring was begun. Special Agent Emmet Michaels, an ex marine and as tough as they come, had been transferred to Las Vegas and was assigned as the Surveillance Squad Supervisor. He assembled a group of agents who refined their skills as a first rate team specializing in surreptitiously following subjects and installing listening devises. Charlie Parsons was transferred to Las Vegas in 1979, and because he had worked organized crime investigations in New York City, he was put in charge of the Las Vegas OC Squad. He later became the SAC of San Antonio and Los Angeles and was promoted to Assistant Director. Charlie ran the OC squad artfully and had a sign in his office stating, "Little cases – little problems. Big cases – big problems." When he left Las Vegas I presented him with a commemorative plaque with gambling chips from the Argent properties prominently displayed. The chips were from the Stardust, the Freemont, the

Marina, and the Hacienda casinos. The plaque read, "To the best Capo in the Bureau."

I was sitting in Charlie's office one day when he received a phone call. He stiffened. "What! How did that happen?" He listened to the caller for a while then said, "Yeah, he is." He hung up, "Can you believe it? I sent (name withheld) over to Caesars Palace to serve a subpoena on heavyweight champion Mike Tyson, who's staying there for his big fight next week. Tyson is wanted as a witness in some New York case. (The unnamed agent) was stopped by Tyson's security people as he approached Tyson's room. They didn't believe he was an agent, even though he displayed his credentials. Metro was called in and they just called me." I was aware that the unnamed agent was somewhat strange and presented himself poorly. Charlie continued, "When (the unnamed agent) was assigned to the San Francisco office, he took a set of Bureau car keys off the board and went to the garage to pick up the car. All he knew was that it was Ford, so he wandered around for a while until he spotted a blue Ford and his key unlocked it and fit the ignition so he drove off. A short time later the real owner of the car, a private citizen, reported his car stolen. When the agent returned, the cops grabbed him for stealing the car. Eventually, everything was straightened out, as the key was found to work in the Bureau car and the citizen's car, but no one could figure out how the agent didn't notice that the car he took didn't have a Bureau radio or a red light." Charlie just shook his head in frustration. The agent eventually resigned under pressure for other missteps and indiscretions.

In 1979, Frank Cullotta followed Spilotro to Las Vegas. Cullotta told me, "Tony wanted me to put a crew together, you know, to do some strong arm stuff, burglaries, rip off dope dealers, stuff like that." Cullotta was told to call in his crew but not tell them he was working for Tony. "He only wanted to deal with me cause he wasn't suppose to being doin' jobs in Vegas, so he wanted to control who knew about it. If we made a good score, he was to get a piece of it. That was okay with me, so I went ahead and contacted my Chicago guys - Sal Romano, Larry Neumann, Wayne Matecki, Leo Guardino, and Ernie Davino." The newspapers dubbed the crew "The Hole in the Wall Gang" before the members were identified; as the gang specialized in breaking through the stucco walls of places they burglarized. Cullotta added, "Everybody in Vegas has alarm systems on the doors and windows. We got around that by goin' through the walls. We were getting tips from insurance guys, bellboys, hookers, even alarm guys. We even hit some bookmakers." Cullotta informed me that Tony had directed him to "put the arm" on bookie, Dominic Spinale and demand protection money from him. Cullotta sent "Lurch" Neumann to pay him a visit and explained, "He scared the hell out of the guy and he paid – no problem." Cullotta said that Neumann had once killed a bar owner and a female bartender in Illinois because of a slight to his ex-wife. Cullotta asked him why he had killed the woman, who had children, and Neumann merely responded, "They're probably better off without her."

Interestingly, some years later, Special Agent Jodie Petraci, a former gaming control agent with the New Jersey State Police, had developed an illegal bookmaking case on Spinale and requested my assistance in arresting him. Petraci and I went to Spinale's plush residence in the Las Vegas Country Club and got him out of bed. He was a small man, resourceful, as are all bookies, and pleasant to deal with, but he never mentioned being an unwilling partner of Cullotta. When he was to get dressed, I followed him into his walk-in closet and he held up two matching golf outfits, one was yellow and the other was pink. He asked me, "Which one should I wear?" I responded, "The yellow one. I don't think you want to go to jail wearing pink clothes." We both laughed.

Frank Cullotta had opened a pizza restaurant from some of his illicit earnings and called it The Upper Crust. It was located south of downtown Las Vegas, so Bud Hall turned his attention to that location, as Tony Spilotro spent a great deal of time there in the back room, even though he had his own bar nearby called My Place. Emmet Michael's team successfully installed a listening device and a video camera in the back room of the restaurant and agents settled down, ready to monitor incriminating conversations. Less than 24 hours later, one of Cullotta's crew climbed up on some appliances to take a nap. As he was staring at the ceiling he noticed something strange. There was a tiny hole in the suspended ceiling and a small device protruding ever so slightly through the hole. He was a professional burglar and was an expert in alarm systems, so he knew immediately what he had discovered. He called Cullotta and told him to come to The Upper Crust immediately. The monitoring agents wondered what was happening, as there was nothing but silence except for sounds of scraping and movement in the room. Then they saw Cullotta climbing up on a stool and the camera went dead. Cullotta had seized the micro- video camera. He took it to Spilotro and he called in Joe Blasko, a former Metropolitan Police Department intelligence officer who had been fired along with detective Phil Leone, for cooperating with Spilotro. Blasko opined that it was federal equipment, and Tony knew immediately who was behind it - the FBI. Soon after, Cullotta was visited by supervisors Michaels and Parsons and a tense negotiation resulted in the return of the devise. The mob's lucky ghosts had struck again and thwarted the Bureau's best laid plans. It was as if Tony and his crew of burglars would forever run free in Las Vegas. The FBI didn't stop its investigation of Spilotro, but the Bureau was now thrown into a full scale investigation of Argent Corporation.

Strange thinks often happen in the squad room of FBI offices. For example, Agent Jerry Doherty, often the target of practical jokes in retaliation for pranks he pulled on others, was a heavy smoker at one time, so I bought a small fan, which I aimed at his desk next to me. Each time he lit up, I would turn the fan on, blowing his second-hand smoke back on him. He was trying to quit, but was having difficulty breaking his addiction. Some of us in the office, "in the spirit of charity," decided to help him stop by planting small, harmless explosive charges in the tips of some of the cigarettes in his already opened cigarette packs, which were usually left on his desk. Every once in a while, when he lit up and took the first few drags, one of the loaded weeds would blow the end off his cigarette, startling him. He would yell out, "Damn it!" and throw the shredded cigarette into his ashtray. Naturally, practical jokes can often have unpleasant consequences. On one occasion, Jerry unthinkingly gave one of the loaded cigarettes to the ASAC and it blew. As Jerry left the ASAC's office, he heard a pop and a startled yell, and he got the blame. Eventually, the suspense got the best of him and he quit cold turkey. When the government initiated the policy banning all smoking inside federal buildings, I reminded Jerry, "You should be grateful to me for helping you quit. You don't have to stand outside in the heat, banished to the furthest reaches of the parking lot like some leper to take a smoke."

Sometimes good fortune plays an amusing role in the fight against the mob. Jerry Doherty and I were traveling to San Diego to attend an organized crime conference in 1986. Doherty, a former police sergeant with the West Covina, California, Police Department, was driving the Bureau car. As we turned a corner in San Diego's downtown district, we passed a known mob controlled strip joint. At that very moment, as if loosened by unknown hands, the left front hubcap came loose and rolled across the street, jumped the curb, and ended up at the feet of one of the hoods standing watch outside. It was a perfect hit, as if we had purposely lobbed a hand-grenade in his direction. We laughed ourselves silly.

I had a morning ritual when I arrived at the office. I would sit in my cubical at the rear of the squad room, having a full view of the famous Stratosphere Tower, and eat an old fashioned donut. I perused the *Las Vegas Review Journal* to keep current on the happenings in the city, and after that 15 minute custom, I was ready to go. It was office policy that agents had to be on standby on a rotating basis to handle walk-ins who came to the office. One of the regulars, a homeless woman, often came carrying shopping bags full of scraps of paper, newspaper clippings, and so on. She was a disheveled lady who complained about receiving telepathic messages from outer space. She wouldn't listen to logic or anything I had to say, so in desperation, I told her to wrap her eyeglass frames with aluminum foil, as this would deflect signals from outer space away from her. She looked at me, seeming to understand, and smiled broadly. Her schizoid symptoms had plagued her for who knows how long but she left satisfied. She very well may have developed other symptoms later but for a time she was free of the troubling voices from space.

Sometimes walk-ins surprised us by playing roles in solving crimes. For example, a guy walked into the Las Vegas office unannounced to report a crime. We later referred to him as "The Nose" because of his very large proboscis. He told the duty agent about a murder he had participated in, and the duty agent notified the OC squad. Dennis Arnoldy and I skeptically went up to meet with him to determine what he had to say. He told us that he and two others had invited a loan-shark to their apartment, as he was putting pressure on them to make their vig payments. When he arrived, he was hit with a nightstick with such force that it broke over his head. The man staggered but wouldn't go down so they stabbed him to death by thrusting the sharp end of the broken stick into his neck. His mutilated body was wrapped in a blanket, and dumped in the desert. Dennis and I were aware of the murder and asked The Nose to describe the blanket used to wrap the body, having seen police photographs of it and realizing this fact wasn't known by the public. He described the blanket perfectly. We called Metro Homicide and the investigation was on. The FBI portion of the case was handled by Special Agent George Togliatti, a former helicopter pilot in Vietnam and who later became the supervisor of the OC squad and, who, after his retirement, was selected as the head of the Nevada Department of Public Safety. We kept The Nose in a safe house as he participated in various investigations. One night when I was assigned to keep an eye on him, he approached me and asked, "I'm starved. Can you get me a pizza?" I said, "Sure, I'll just go down the street and pick one up." Then he boldly asked, "While you're at it, will you get me a hooker at the same time?" He was serious, and I just looked at him with disdain. "You know I can't do that." The murder case and several good dope cases were made as a result of The Nose's assistance and excellent investigative work by Togliatti.

The Las Vegas version of the Chicago Outfit investigation, code named Strawman, was pressing forward directed by other agents, so I had settled into my routine in Las Vegas. But for a couple of trips to Milwaukee and Kansas City, I focused on mobsters from New York City who had made Sin City their home. My first Las Vegas OC target was on Gaspare Anedetto "Jasper" Special, an elegant, amiable bookie and loan-shark who had the reputation of being easy going and low key. The problem was that he worked for the Genovese crime family, and they siphoned off a piece of his earnings. Jasper had operated for years out of his restaurant, The Tower of Pizza, and had been left alone, but when he moved his operation to the newly opened Jasper's Manhattan Florist on Las Vegas Boulevard, Tony Spilotro took an interest and contemplated moving in on him. He told Cullotta to look into the possibility of strong arming Jasper, but he found he was connected to New York City mobsters, so they backed off.

I did wiretaps on the florist, and he was immediately overheard taking action and, at the same time, taking orders for flowers. One call I remember clearly involved a man who said, "I want to order two dozen red roses for my girlfriend's birthday." Jasper asked, "Do you want the flowers delivered to your home or will you be picking them up?" The man interrupted, "Oh, no, don't deliver them to my house, my wife will find out. I'll pick them up." Then he paused for a moment. "While you're at it, I'll need a dozen for my wife, too," We frequently observed Jasper standing outside his shop's rear door and settling up with his bettors and lenders. After a time of successful intercepts, Jasper was arrested and charged with running an illegal gambling business. When we went to arrest him, he was terrified because he had recently been the victim of a home invasion robbery, and he thought we were there to rob him again. Even when I showed him my credentials, he wasn't completely convinced.

At the same time, there were rumblings in Chicago about The Little Guy, Tony Spilotro. He was making too many waves and may have violated their code by committing unauthorized killings, as well as having an affair with Rosenthal's wife. Lefty Rosenthal once said, "Anything Tony did in Las Vegas reflected on Frank Rosenthal. I didn't have a chance." The Crazy Guy clearly had developed hard feelings against his once friend. Adding to the mix, Geri had gone to Tony for solace and asked him to kill Lefty. At this same general time period, while on a trip to Chicago, Frank Cullotta was questioned by several mobsters, including Joey Lombardo, who asked, "Is Tony screwing around with that Jew's wife?" He lied and told Lombardo the rumor wasn't true in order to protect his friend, but he knew there was a problem with Geri and Tony and it would eventually bubble to the surface.

Agent Mark Kaspar, a Navy veteran and a son of Czech immigrants, had learned what hard work was as a child toiling in the cotton fields of southeast Texas. He was assigned to the Spilotro case after the transfer of Bud Hall. I assisted him in procuring a wiretap on Tony's home phone. We learned very little about The Little Guy's criminal activities, but we found out how absolutely addicted he was to sports betting and what a foul husband he was. Kaspar was relentless and eventually developed a friendly relationship with Tony's brother, John, and gained the begrudging respect of Tony. We even installed a microphone in the residence of Tony's friend and criminal associate, Joey Cusumano. He had refurbished his house so that his garage led directly into his living area and he could drive his Mercedes convertible right into his living room. I was able to obtain an automatic door opener that allowed us to open the garage door and the microphone was successfully installed. Unfortunately, it turned out to be a dry hole. Some years later, Cusumano was shot several times as he drove into his house, but he survived.

Las Vegas is two towns: One is the Strip, lined with casinos, lights, and glitter, a plastic world of make-believe. The other is the home of regular folks who have neighborhood parties, help each other, bring food to their sick neighbors, and baby sit one another's children. They take their kids to Cub Scout meetings, soccer games, and dance lessons. But like any city, I soon learned that there is a hidden underbelly beneath the glitz, plastic, and neon lights that can be very ugly.

Frank Cullotta described Jerry Lisner as a "loud mouth scam artist." When Frank was working the streets of Las Vegas, he met Lisner at a restaurant and Lisner approached him and "played the big shot." He told Frank about a scam he was pulling on a guy in Florida and asked if Frank wanted in on it. Frank decided to go along but the scam fell through and Frank was upset about the whole deal. Then Lisner told him about a dope dealer, and Cullotta strong armed the guy for $10,000 worth of Quaaludes. In July of 1979, Lisner was arrested by the FBI for Interstate

Transportation of Stolen Property in Maryland and Frank got a call notifying him that Lisner was getting ready to cooperate with authorities. Cullotta went to Tony Spilotro to discuss the problem, and Tony told him, "You worked with the guy. You gotta take care of it yourself if he can hurt you." Cullotta assumed that Tony had called Chicago for the okay for Frank to take care of the problem, but he later learned that Tony had done nothing.

Cullota informed me that on October 10, 1979, he went to Lisner's house while crew member Wayne Matecki remained in the get-away-car as a lookout. Lisner invited Frank in, and as they walked down the hall, Cullotta pulled a .32 caliber pistol and shot Lisner in the back of the head. Lisner staggered slightly and turned, yelling, "What the hell?" and began running from Frank as he emptied his gun into the fleeing victim. Lisner fell, but continued to scream uncontrollably. Matecki came running in with more ammunition and Frank reloaded his gun, then covered Lisner's head with a pillow and pumped 10 more rounds into him. They completed their merciless work by dumping the body in the backyard swimming pool. Frank said he was astounded at Lisner's capacity to take all the bullets before dying, but it was probably due to the fact that Cullotta had removed some of the gunpowder from the bullets to decrease the report from the shots. Frank, to this day, regrets the murder of Lisner, but when he carried out the murder, he was a different man.

CHAPTER 9

A Perfect Storm

"Lefty Rosenthal spoiled his own parade."

--Joseph Agosto

After nine fulfilling years in Milwaukee, I was transferred to the Las Vegas Division. The cold, endless winters of the Midwest had worn me down, and I wanted to return to the West, where I grew up. There was a need for an experienced OC agent in Las Vegas and I was immediately assigned to the organized crime squad. Eventually, I was promoted to principle relief supervisor for the squad, but I had no intention of proceeding any further up the administrative ladder. I liked Las Vegas and had no desire to ride a desk and become a bureaucrat, and I didn't want to put my family through moves from place to place in pursuit of my career. I knew my talents were better served on the street, making cases.

When I arrived in the city of glitz, the FBI was already in hot pursuit of Allen Glick and Frank Rosenthal. I learned that Nevada Gaming officials had been reluctant to pursue Glick and his properties, but had focused their attention on Lefty. Politics stifled an all out investigation of Argent, which caused dissension in the ranks of gaming investigators so Dennis Gomes, a young auditor for the Nevada Gaming Control Board, bravely decide to conduct an audit of the Stardust slot department in May of 1976, even though his superiors had little interest in the project. He had the gall to believe he could make a difference, so he took it upon himself to make the daring and unprecedented move. On his own initiative, he brought along an assistant named Richard Law, and the two walked into the Stardust unannounced. Law, an attorney and CPA, happened to live only a block away from me. He later became so disenchanted with the Gaming Control Board's lack of action against Argent and the entire system of gaming control that he dropped out of normal society and took his family far from Las Vegas in a converted, blue, hand painted school bus. I recall him working on the vehicle for months, installing beds and a kitchen in the mobile residence.

The duo of gaming crusaders began by attempting to decipher the slot records, and as they dug in the convoluted mess, they began seeing signs of fraud. They could see no justifiable reason for the four Argent slot departments and the entire slot drop being handled out of one casino, as it was unprecedented in all of Nevada's casino industry. Then they discovered the unauthorized floor banks, a startling violation of regulations, so they focused their attention on the records for those drop boxes. The slot operation reeked of fraud, and Gomes was about to do something about it, so later, he and other gaming agents went into the Stardust cashier's cage and locked it down. The cage employees, in a total state of panic, were literally frozen in place, not knowing how to respond to Gomes' inquiries. Gomes called slot department supervisor Jay Vandermark in his office and demanded that he come to the cage and bring his records and unlock an unauthorized file cabinet found in the cage area. Vandermark refused and the cabinet lock was drilled open, and piles of $100 bills were discovered. They had found the skim, at least a portion of the slot department skim. No one could show them corresponding records for the cash, so Gomes knew he was on to something big. Then the team discovered the miscalibrated coin scales in the hard count room and the jig was up. Word surreptitiously went out to the Freemont Casino from Vandermark, and employees there immediately dismantled the coin scales and removed the floor banks form that casino. The predictable cover up was on.

With the discovery of massive wrong doing, Allen Glick denied that the stolen money was skim and accused employees, including Vandermark, of embezzling from him. Gaming Control officials were concerned with political, as well as economic implications of Glick being involved and were reluctant to accuse the golden boy of any wrongdoing, as they had no direct evidence of his participation in the systematic theft. The Las Vegas economy is based on gambling. It's the city's life blood, and economics play a significant role in Gaming Control actions. The law is always weighed against economic impact and this is, naturally, a difficult tightrope for gamers to walk. Interestingly, Glick was once described by the Las Vegas media as the "Boy wonder of gaming," and "good for gaming." He was even cited as "Las Vegas man of the year" in 1975, so action against him was deemed imprudent. After the Gomes raid, a ranking gaming official stated, "We have discovered some discrepancies, but we do not know what kind of money we are talking about. We are not talking about skimming, because for that we would have to show management participated in the scheme. We are looking for the possibility of embezzlement." I ask the logical question - What about Frank Rosenthal's control over Vandermark? Could it be that his management was at the root of the theft of massive amounts of money? Of course, Rosenthal was out of the casino for the time being but he was second in control at Argent at the time of the discovered skim.

Carl Thomas, a highly respected casino operator who had developed his skills as a manager at Circus Circus casino and Slots of Fun, was appointed in Rosenthal's place. Thomas who had operated International Bookings from inside the Stardust, was pure as the new snow, according to gaming officials, and they were delighted with the change but, unbeknownst to anyone but the mob, Thomas was not all he appeared to be. During an FBI microphone overhear in Kansas City, Thomas had met with Nick Civella and laid out the most energetic and all-encompassing skim technique in the history of Las Vegas. He explained that all the various skims were unnecessary if you just focused on the soft count room. This is where the currency is counted, as opposed to the hard count room where the coins are weighed. He said a good count team, when uninhibited by gaming regulators, can steal a great deal of money in $100 bills by setting aside one for the casino and one for the mob. During the recorded conversation, Civella expressed that he was upset with employees who stole money for themselves while stealing for him. Thomas explained that Civella had to understand that the people involved in the skim would naturally take some money for themselves. This was part of the cost of skimming and made the skimmers more loyal because, with their direct participation, they had a great deal to lose should the skim be discovered.

Glick was in a tough spot, as he had relented to the mob again and hired Thomas at Civella's demand. Nick Civella, although he was in prison at this point in time, held a death grip on the skim operation, and his man, Thomas, followed his instructions to the letter. Thomas was old school, low profile, and efficient, just the kind of guy the mobsters needed, but Civella's dream was shattered when Lefty was reinstated by Judge Pavlikowski's court order. Lefty moved with the speed of light and literally pushed Thomas out of his office, saying gruffly, "Get out of my office, and take your stuff with you - I'm back." This was a slap in the face of the imprisoned boss of Kansas City, and he must have been furious. The Crazy Guy was going to ruin everything, so it is my contention that Civella communicated with Joey Aiuppa and presented his case against Lefty. This assumption was corroborated when Joe Agosto told me that he had once informed Carl "Tuffy" De Luna, Civella's enforcer that "Rosenthal is a rat and he will bite the hand that feeds him." He said that De Luna responded disgustingly, "The guy is dead!" He also said that De Luna hounded him about providing a detailed map of Allen Glick's La Jolla estate, but Agosto knew "he wanted it cause he was thinking about whacking the kid, so I stalled."

As the pieces of the skimming puzzle came together, Argent was under full assault by the FBI, Metro, and Gaming officials. Glick was treading water in an effort to maintain control of his casino empire while Lefty was out of the operation. Rosenthal's jubilation over the long shot court ruling allowing him to return to his job at the Stardust was short lived when the Nevada Supreme Court overruled the district court decision on February 4, 1977, and Lefty was again out of the casino.

During Lefty's final Gaming Control Board hearing held in June of 1978, Chairman Harry Reid informed Rosenthal he was finished in the gaming industry and would never be licensed. In addition, Lefty was added to the Nevada List of Excluded

Persons, along with Tony Spilotro. This list is better known as *The Black Book*, which banned the men forever from entering any Nevada casino. As a result of the Gaming Control Board ruling, Rosenthal struck out verbally against Reid, "This was predicable. You double crossed me . . . Mr. Chairman, didn't you ask me for a favor? Didn't you ask me through Jay Brown [Lefty's attorney] to stop a story? You had lunch with me at the Stardust. Isn't that true?" Harry Reid reluctantly answered, "Yes." Rosenthal must have expected some sort of quid pro quo from Reid for the favor of killing a story negative to Reid, but that didn't happen. Lefty, undeterred and tenacious as ever, told his casino executives that he would run the place from his house over the phone, and that's exactly what he did for a time.

Jay Brown is a former law partner of Oscar Goodman and is considered a political go-between and close friend of Reid. Lefty learned to have little respect for Brown because in 1999, Lefty wrote in his e-mail site, referring to his hearing before Nevada Gaming authorities, "I wasn't comfortable or confident in spite of the fact that I had met with a dime store attorney named Jay Brown who was considered to be politically well connected and an associate of Oscar Goodman. Jay Brown assured me that above all, I would receive a fair and impartial hearing in the unlikely event that one would be ordered. 'Fair and square, Frank, you have my word on that.' That was Jay Brown back then." Lefty tried to reach Brown after the decisive rebuff, but bitterly continued, "As for Jay Brown, he never returned my calls and continues to practice his style of bullshit." Brown continues to have a close association with Senator Reid to this day and has entered into some questionable land deals with the Senator that have been the subject of significant media attention in Las Vegas.

Interestingly, Reid, in his bid for reelection to the U.S. Senate in 2009 - 2010 used his service as a mob fighting member of the Gaming Board as a campaign topic. A side note to the Reid story occurred on July 28, 1981, when a potential incendiary device was discovered in one of Reid's cars by his wife. Police responded and found an "electrical device." The police report states, "The electrical device was a wire leading from the distributor to the fuel tank." The case was never solved. Reid, in his book *The Good Fight,* states that he suspected that bar owner Jack Gordon was behind the placement of the device.

Unbeknownst to most law enforcement authorities, a series of sit-downs were held in Chicago in 1978 in which Balistrieri, Aiuppa, and Carl De Luna, standing in for Civella, met to finalize their decision about what to do about the Genius, Allen Glick. Balistrieri proposed a replacement for Glick, but De Luna would have none of it. A furious argument resulted, and Aiuppa was so upset with Balistrieri that he threatened to kill Fancy Pants himself if he didn't shut up. Glick had become a festering problem as the FBI and gaming authorities were uncovering the rot at the Stardust, and they wanted him out of Las Vegas so they could make some changes and continue their skim quietly and undisturbed. Carl De Luna later made notes regarding the high level meetings. He wrote, "Talk was of who should see Genius. It was decided it would be me." Glick had to go; he was causing too many problems and Tuffy De Luna was assigned the task of giving the termination notice. There was discussion about killing Glick, but it was agreed that such an act would bring too much heat on them, so the first and best option was to scare him out of the Stardust. If that didn't work, the murder option would back on the table.

Nevada Gaming officials were finally becoming more and more suspicious of the strange happenings at the Stardust Casino. Glick seemed to be an absentee owner as he spent a great deal of time in La Jolla and elsewhere, while Lefty Rosenthal fought like a pit bull, never relenting in his pursuit of a license. Added to this mix was the spurious Jay Vandermark, a man who should never have been allowed to run the slot department. He was a known slot scammer whose bogus job title of "construction consultant" was ridiculous on its face. How could Argent possibly be running a clean operation with Vandermark having access to tons of coins? Rosenthal had hired Jay Vandermark in late 1974, not as a consultant but as his de facto casino slot department manager. Vandermark was an otherwise unremarkable, bespectacled, goofy looking guy who wore hearing aids in both ears and may have been the premier Las Vegas slot cheat. He had made a living beating slot machines and stealing directly out of the drop boxes. He was listed in the casino-wide publication, *Book of Slot Cheats*, but was hired anyway. Lefty gave Vandermark orders to consolidate all slot operations for the four Argent casinos, and he carried out the assignment with a vengeance. First, he manipulated the record keeping system and ordered that all slot proceeds from the Argent casinos be transferred to the Stardust for counting. Vandermark also brilliantly rigged the slots to register 1/3 more wins than actually occurred. Then when the coins were weighed, the calibration, of the scales were set to show 1/3 less than the actual weight of the coins. The problem was that the skim of 1/3 of the slot winnings was in heavy coins. The weighty treasure couldn't be secreted out of the casino in any realistic way so this required a system of exchanging the skimmed 1/3 in coins for soft currency. Vandermark solved that problem by setting up unauthorized auxiliary banks filled with $100 bills on the casino floor, but no one seemed to care or take particular notice of this gaming control violation. The floor banks were custom made and were to have only two keys, one for the auditing department and one for the count team, but a third key was made and provided to Vandermark.

Each morning, usually during the slow period when most gamblers have left the casino, crews empties each slot machine and the coins are taken to the count room for weighing. This occurs at 8:00 a.m., but the sly Vandermark made the switch from coins to bills at 4:00 a.m., so he had plenty of time to carry out his blatant theft. Vandermark, like a kid in a candy store, placed the 1/3 overage of the coins into the floor banks. Then with his personal key, he withdrew the corresponding amount in $100 bills, placing the cash in an envelope and taking the money to his office. Before long, he spent much more time stealing and counting than he did running the slot department. His actions became a joke around the casino, but everyone just gave it a wink and a nod and no one said anything to gaming officials. The Stardust was a closed shop. Most of the supervisors were Chicago guys or were afraid to say anything. Vandermark was a consummate thief - not only did he steal for the mob, but he took a piece for himself each day. The skimmed currency was then delivered to Bobby Stella, the casino manager.

With the May 1978 audit raid, Jay Vandermark realized he had a target on his back and slipped out of the casino and went to Bobby Stella's house to await the results of the raids. When he learned that Gaming was drilling the lock on the file cabinet in the cage, the arrogant slot man said, "Screw 'em." Let them drill it open. It gives us more time." He spent the night in Stella's house, and then disappeared from Las Vegas forever. He was, as mobsters say, "on his bicycle." The cockroaches were scurrying to their hiding crevices as the investigative spotlight illuminated them. Vandermark and 10 other employees were immediately terminated, and Allen Glick hung on by his fingertips. At this point, Glick willingly left the operation of his casinos to others. He must have known the end was coming, and he wanted no part of the consequences, realizing that the less he knew the better off he would be.

The money drop at the Argent casinos under Rosenthal was like pouring water into a barrel with holes punched in it. It's estimated the skim take was between $100,000 and $350,000 per month. It was a dream come true for the mob. They stole out of every conceivable department. Demands for kickbacks from various suppliers and vendors were answered positively, and if they said no, then they lost their business with Argent. The blackjack tables provided another tremendous source of skim by use of a clever scam called a fill slip hustle. Chips were brought from the cage to resupply all the dealers - blackjack, craps, poker, and roulette - but the fill slips were inaccurate and forged. These official casino documents were to be completed and signed by no less than four casino employees who confirmed the amount of chips delivered, thereby verifying the accuracy of the fill slips, but only one man completed the slips, forging the other signatures. The slips are supposed to indicate exactly how many of each denomination of chip is transferred to the gaming tables, but the slips over reported the number of chips delivered and the overage was skimmed out of the cage in cash.

In the meantime, Metro Police were in hot pursuit of Spilotro, and on a June afternoon in 1979, Frank Bluestein, the maitre' d at the Hacienda Casino show room, met with Spilotro and Cullotta at The Upper Crust and he complained endlessly about being followed by Metro. They told him to just play it cool and not do anything stupid, but he was a hothead, and after leaving the pizza place, he picked up the tail again. After driving for some time, often speeding erratically, Bluestein had had enough. He stopped and got out of his car holding a pistol. The detectives, Gene Smith and David Groover, were hard nosed cops, but they were fine veteran officers who were doing their jobs and were legitimately following someone who associated with known felons. The two detectives, thinking they were in danger, ordered him to drop the gun, then opened fire as they had been trained to do and he Bluestein was shot dead. When the news reached Cullotta and Spilotro they were both furious. Cullotta told me that he knew Bluestein carried a gun and had a short fuse, but he didn't think he would be stupid enough to make a move like he did. Spilotro was so consumed with burning rage that he said he would kill the two detectives who were assigned to the intelligence unit under the command of Kent Clifford.

Commander Clifford, a friend and a neighbor of mine, was every bit as tough as The Little Guy, and was very much like the fictional character Don Quixote, as he "would willingly march into hell for a heavenly cause." He is an Idaho farm boy who joined the army and won a bronze star and a silver star for gallantry in Vietnam. He then put himself through college and cleaned up the once-tainted Intelligence Unit of Metro. He was not one to sit and wait for the consequences, so he made a bold and unthinkable move. He flew to Chicago and visited the homes of Joey Lombardo and Joseph Aiuppa. Clifford told me he felt responsible for his men and would never let any harm come to them as long as he could somehow stop it. The two bosses weren't home, but he left word with Lombardo's attorney that "if any harm comes to my detectives, I will personally hold Lombardo and Aiuppa responsible," and in old west fashion, "I will come back to Chicago with my men and kill the two bosses." The attorney promised to pass the message along and would let Clifford know. The intelligence commander waited for several hours and, finally, received the phone call. The coded message was short and to the point, "Have a good trip."

The bosses, of course, would never admit that they had control over Spilotro, and they would never acknowledge that they had any power to stop The Little Guy from making a rash and fatal move, but the message had been received, and by giving the prearranged message they were telling Clifford that his demand would be honored. Spilotro's undisciplined, high profile life in Las Vegas had now come home to Chicago. He had done what the Outfit feared the most, he had brought heat on them and in my opinion, this pushed Spilotro to the very brink of the Outfit's patience.

The Las Vegas FBI surveillance team, under the direction of Supervisory Special Agent Emmett Michaels, had determined, with the help of an informant, how the skim was being secreted out of the Stardust Casino and delivered to Chicago. In May of 1981 the members of the team observed Bobby Stella, the Stardust Casino manager, leaving the casino carrying a paper grocery bag on a Tuesday afternoon. Stella drove to Von Tobel's Home Improvement store on Maryland Parkway, and there he met Phil Ponto, another Stardust Casino employee, in the parking lot. The paper bag was given to Ponto and he drove off. Inquiries in Chicago later determined that Ponto was an Outfit sleeper, in other words, a Chicago made member who operated totally under law enforcement radar screens. Ponto drove home and entered his apartment, located in a lower middle class area of town near the Country Club Estates, carrying the bag. A 24 hour surveillance of Ponto showed no unusual activity for days. The agents were afraid that they were chasing a red herring and couldn't be sure if Ponto was moving the money out in bits and pieces, perhaps hidden in his pockets, but Michaels held their feet to the fire and the surveillance continued. The following Sunday, their persistence paid off when the sleeper made his move. He came out carrying the grocery bag and put it in the trunk of his car. Then he drove to church. We don't know if he took communion to absolve himself of his sins or used the church as a means of throwing off any tail.

After church he drove around for some time, pulling in and out of parking lots, doubling back, and looking over his shoulder in a clear attempt to dry clean himself. This type of driving behavior heightened the anticipation of the pursuing agents and, of course, is very difficult to deal with, as the subject is on the lookout for any suspicious activity. He finally ended up at another Von Tobel's, located on east Tropicana Avenue, and he pulled into a parking space where another man was standing nearby waiting for him. Now the excitement level of the agents really escalated.

The two men talked for a time, then the bag was removed from Ponto's trunk and placed in the trunk of the unknown man's rental car and he drove off. The agents followed the package south on Interstate 15 until the driver pulled off into a rest area inside the California State line. He was observed opening the trunk and rummaging around for a while. One of the agents casually walked by and glimpsed money being taken out of the bag and placed inside a sports coat that was also in the trunk. It was later learned that the coat had several custom made pockets sewn into the lining. Then the man transferred an overnight bag from inside the car to the trunk. He dumped the paper bag in a trash can and continued his journey to the Los Angeles International Airport, where he, using an assumed name, boarded a plane destined for Chicago.

The Chicago Division was contacted and informed of the flight number and description of the courier, and they hustled to place the man under surveillance upon his arrival. The bag-man, identified by Chicago agents as Joseph Talerico, a Teamster official, drove around Chicago for a while, clearly trying to dry-clean himself, but it was only half- hearted as he was obviously tired and had done this many times without mishap. Then he was observed doing the unthinkable - he personally met with Outfit boss Joseph Aiuppa in a restaurant. The Boss' direct participation in the skim proved he was personally invested in the scheme. The men enjoyed a fine meal with wine then after dinner Aiuppa and Talerico met in the rear parking lot, where Aiuppa opened his car trunk, as did Talerico. Remarkably, the boss of the Chicago Outfit himself was the recipient of the skim money, a clear indication that he was in control of the whole operation. Suddenly, the

Chicago FBI developed an interest in the case.

The legal question causing our overriding consideration was if the FBI seized the money at the end of the line from Aiuppa, how could we prove that the money actually originated from casino skimmed funds? We could certainly prove it came from inside the casino, but how could we prove it was stolen from the casino? Organized Crime Squad Supervisor Charlie Parsons, Emmett Michaels and case agent Lynn Ferrin concluded that the only way to do this was to drop marked $100 bills at the Stardust and Freemont blackjack tables. Then, when the $100 bills were skimmed out of the count rooms, perhaps some of the marked bills would be included in the paper bag carrying the skim. This kind of special expenditure required Bureau headquarter authority, and, after some prodding, the approval was given to expend $5,000. The money was gambled at the blackjack tables on the weekend because the skim was removed by Stella on Tuesday, and this would give them time to steal the take from the count room. Of course, the idea was to lose the money and have it placed into the casino system, but sometimes the FBI gamblers won. This complicated things to a degree, so they had to play stupid so they could plant the marked seeds. Although the FBI was gambling at the tables, we were also gambling on the possibility of the dropped money being included in the skimmed funds. We would never know until the skim package was grabbed in Chicago, and what if none of the dropped bills were in the package?

Agent Lynn Ferrin, a veteran Utah Deputy Sheriff had been transferred to Las Vegas from the New York City Division and was immediately assigned as the case agent on the Argent skim matter in 1978. He was so assigned for five years without receiving any other cases - this was his full time case assignment. The skim transfer had been observed for several straight months, but FBI Headquarters held back any overt action because they wanted to be able to prove the bag contained skim money before they would authorize overt action. The battle between Las Vegas, Chicago, and the Bureau droned on while we were running out of options. Ferrin, frustrated, tried everything he could think of to prove the skim. He proposed receiving authorization to confront Talerico and seize the bag of money from him. This proposal was denied. He then brought in lip readers to attempt to read the silent words of Ponto and Talerico when they met at Von Tobel's. This proved to be unsuccessful. He even tried to monitor portions of their conversations by putting court ordered microphones near cars and in shopping carts in and around Von Toble' but without success.

Finally, as a last ditch effort, Ferrin prepared an affidavit in support of a request for electronic monitoring of a booth located inside the Aku Aku Restaurant at the Stardust. This was, according to informant intelligence, where Bobby Stella and others frequently met and discussed the skimming operation. The affidavit, necessarily, laid out all the probable cause the FBI had developed, including the method of skim, the participants in the skim, and the pattern of the process. Ferrin swore to the truthfulness of his affidavit, and a monitoring order was signed by U.S. District Court Judge Harry Claiborne in early October of 1981. Ferrin was greatly concerned that Claiborne was assigned as the authorizing judge because he knew of his defense of Rosenthal before the Gaming Board when he had been a practicing attorney, but there was no reasonable alternative. The FBI can't pick and choose judges. The installation of the microphone was expertly accomplished by agents posing as telephone repairmen during business hours. From that time forward, Stella and the others didn't once discuss the system of skim but, in fact, provided disinformation with such statements as, "We run this place on the up and up. Gaming thinks we're skimming, but we're not." This turn of events caused very serious suspicion that there had been a tip off about the microphone. The Stardust boys were playing off a script, clearly suggested by a cunning, sophisticated man. Otherwise, they would merely have stopped meeting in the restaurant booth. Furthermore, the skim pass changed its character somewhat. For example, Ponto discontinued going to church before meeting with Talerico after several months of attending church before the skim money pass. He must have felt the phony church attendance was no longer necessary, as the FBI was on to him, or perhaps he had been absolved of his many sins.

The agonizing decision was made to grab Ponto and Talerico as soon as possible before it was too late, but Chicago was adamant about waiting until the actual transfer of money to Aiuppa occurred. He was the boss; Chicago wanted him, but Las Vegas was extremely concerned that a protracted surveillance could cause harm to the investigation, if it hadn't already. FBI Headquarters made the decision in favor of Las Vegas, and finally the big day arrived on a brisk Sunday afternoon in January of 1982. I can remember the day as clearly as if it was yesterday. The arrest team was in place, as was the search team, as we waited for the meeting to occur. The excitement and anticipation was palpable as we waited in our cars parked in the Von Tobel's parking lot. The skimmers were a little late in arriving, but then Talerico, dressed in a white shirt and white ball cap, arrived and sat in his vehicle due to the chill in the air. Before long, Ponto, dressed in his trademark black shirt, pants, and ball cap, drove up. We watched as he got out of his car and opened the trunk and withdrew a cardboard box, not a bag. The plan was to grab the ebony and ivory dressed pair as soon as the package was in the hands of Talerico, so when the package was unceremoniously placed in the trunk of Talerico's rental car, we moved in. The two were placed under arrest and the box was seized. The first thought that entered my mind was, is something wrong here - why a box? They had previously always used a grocery bag. Had they merely changed the package, or was there more to it? A group of us stood peering into the trunk of Talerico's car as the box was carefully opened. We all wondered if we would find some of the dropped, FBI $100 bills in the package. But the contents of the package caused our eyes to bug out. We had seized a bag of home-baked cookies and a bottle of wine. There was no cash. We were stunned at our plight. How could this have happened?

Talerico and Ponto smugly looked on, but they refused to answer any questions and immediately asked for their attorneys. At this point, we had no prosecutable case against them. Later the two were subpoenaed before the Federal Grand Jury, but they refused to testify and were sent to jail for 18 months for contempt of court. We knew someone had sabotaged our investigation, and we wanted to know who it was. The only people who knew about the details of the investigation were those who were directly involved; a select number of FBI agents, Assistant United States Attorney Stan Hunterton, and Judge Harry Claiborne who had read the affidavit and signed the electronic surveillance order. Furthermore, the guile and sophistication of the setup perpetrated on us pointed to someone other than street hoods. If the Outfit had acted on its own, it would have immediately stopped the operation and probably killed everyone involved to silence potential witnesses. The elaborate "cookie caper," as it came to be known, was carried out for the express purpose of slapping the FBI in the face while at the same time showing that smarter people than those in the FBI were behind the setup. My guess is that Claiborne, or someone else, perhaps a double agent informant, had convinced the mobsters to pull off such an extravagant deception. As I reflect on it now, it seems that every time we were to make a significant move in the Strawman case, based on facts provided by a certain informant, we were thwarted in some way. Perhaps this was a result of that informant maintaining his credibility with his Outfit pals, while at the same time working with the Bureau - walking a careful tightrope between the two sides. Of course, I can't prove my theory but the unpleasant possibility sticks in my craw. Some years later, Judge Claiborne was charged with income tax evasion as a result of an extensive FBI and IRS investigation, and after being convicted, he was impeached by the U.S. Senate, removed from his federal judgeship, and sent to prison. After his release from prison, he practiced law for a time, then fell ill with cancer and ended his life by shooting himself in the head at the age of 84 in 2004.

In 1984, the Department of Justice, led by Chief Strike Force Attorney Michael De Feo, assembled extensive evidence of hidden control of casinos and skimming from the Bellwether Case in Milwaukee, the Civella case in Kansas City, the Rockman case in Cleveland, as well as evidence developed by the Chicago and Las Vegas Divisions. Indictments were brought charging racketeering against the mob bosses who had benefited from the Argent skimming conspiracy. The defendants in the case were: Joseph Aiuppa, Joseph Lombardo, Frank Balistrieri, Jack Cerone, Milton Rockman, Carl De Luna, and the Balistrieri brothers. Spilotro was also indicted, but his case was severed from the others and was scheduled to be tried separately at a later date.

Inexplicably, Rosenthal wasn't charged in the case, nor was he called as a witness. Besides all the wiretap and surveillance evidence, some unlikely characters, by varying means, were convinced to testify. Allen Glick told his compelling story, as did ex- Teamster's official Roy Williams, who was pushed into the courtroom in a wheelchair sucking on an oxygen tube. Another key witness was former Cleveland LCN boss Angelo Lonardo as well as, Carl Thomas, the proficient Las Vegas skimmer who was promised reconsideration on his Tropicana, 15 year sentence if he testified truthfully. As with many other agents, I was also subpoenaed back to Kansas City on three separate occasions to testify in the massive trial.

Roy Williams, suffering from the late stages of emphysema, was a somewhat sympathetic witness, even though he had been very much involved in setting up the Teamsters loan for Glick. The former head of the Teamsters Union laid out the process by which the huge loan had been presented and approved. He explained how the fix was in and how the various mob bosses had influence over Teamsters officials and how, once the skim was in operation, it came back to Chicago to be dispensed to the conspirators, including himself. His detailed testimony was devastating.

Angelo "Big Ange" Lonardo became the boss of the Cleveland

family in 1980. He was well mannered and a gifted negotiator, but he had the heavy handed mob side to him, as well. He was responsible for no less than 10 murders and was feared when he became angry. His father, Joseph "Big Joe" Lonardo, was a huge man known for his hard manner who had been the boss before he was killed in a gang land style execution while he sat in a barber shop. Big Ange got his nickname from the fact that he was big Joe's eldest son. After the murder of his father, Angelo, and unbelievably, his mother, Concetta, drove to the Porrello Sugar Company and asked for Salvatore Todaro, the man they knew had killed Big Joe. When Todaro came to the car, Angelo shot him five times, killing him. Both Angelo and his mother were convicted of murder, but an appeals court ordered a new trial and the only two witnesses to the crime had mysteriously disappeared. Charges were finally dropped, as there was no longer a case. Angelo married and his wife's sister married mobster Milton Rockman. This solidified their friendship and working relationship for years to come.

Lonardo ran the Highlander Restaurant and lived well, but he got involved in the illegal drug business to his eventual chagrin, and this led to a 1983 conviction. He was in failing health and missed his wife and son. While incarcerated, two FBI agents came to visit and left their business cards with him. After all his appeals were exhausted, he called the FBI from the public prison telephone and, using a prearranged code, asked, "Are you still there?" He was removed from the prison and began cooperating with the FBI. He also testified before a Senate sub-committee, where he made the following statement. "I became a member of the La Cosa Nostra in the late 1940s, but I had been associated with the organization since late 1920. My father, Joseph Lonardo, was the boss of the Cleveland family." Lonardo made the deal – to cooperate fully with the government with no exceptions or he would go back to general population in prison.

I flew to New York in 1993 where Lonardo was serving a life sentence in a witness security penitentiary and debriefed him regarding any Cleveland influence in Las Vegas. He told me about LCN control of the Tropicana and Stardust casinos and said he began receiving skim money in 1974 from Milton Rockman, a close friend of Moe Dalitz who was a Cleveland mobster and who had close Teamster Union ties through Bill Presser. Lonardo referred to Rockman and Dalitz as "The Jewish Boys." Lonardo stated he didn't know all the ins and outs of the skim but had been told by Rockman that Lefty Rosenthal ran the skim operation, and somehow the money came out of the casinos and was brought to Chicago. He said, "At first, when they were skimming out of the Trop, I got $2,000 a month but then with the Stardust I got boosted up to $6,000 or $7,000 a month. Not bad for doin nothin." Then he added, "I didn't really care how it came out of the joints as long as Rockman brought me my piece each month." I asked him why Rockman felt the need to share the skim with him. He smiled and answered, "Cause he was my friend and besides, he wanted to live." Then he chuckled. He said Cleveland received as much as $40,000 a month, and he, Rockman, Bill Presser, as well as Roy Williams and other Teamsters got their piece of the money, as they had set up the Teamster loans. He also told me, "We had a problem with Kansas City one time and I had to go to Jackie Cerone and Joey Aiuppa in Chicago to get things straightened out."

Lonardo testified in the Kansas City Argent trial and explained how Milton Rockman and others helped obtain the approval for the Argent loan to Glick through Bill Presser, a Teamster official who told Rockman, after being guaranteed a healthy kickback if the loan was approved, "Let's give it to that kid, what's his name." Lonardo also testified how he had received his piece of the skim each month because he was the Cleveland LCN boss. It was obvious that Lonardo was tired and worn out from the life he had been relegated to. I got the impression he wanted it all to end so he wouldn't be bothered any more, telling of his life, his sins, his regrets. He had broken the code of silence to make life easier for himself, but I couldn't help think he had turned his back on his father and all he believed in and this ate at him from the inside even though he knew he had done the right thing. The old man, in failing health, was released from federal protective prison just before he passed away in his sleep in 2006 at the age of 95. Then Carl Thomas testified and explained how he ran the skim while Lefty was out of the Stardust and how he was Nick Civella's man. He also explained how the various crime families received the skim. Joseph Agosto was to have testified in the trial, but he had passed away. He had told me before, however, that Roy Williams and other Teamsters were receiving secret kickbacks of 10% of the skimmed funds, and that the Chicago Outfit owned 25% of the casinos and, as such, received that percentage of the skim every month.

The key witness in the 1986 - 87 Kansas City Argent trial was Allen Glick, the Argent casino straw man. The balding, immaculately dressed, and always-in-control former Argent Chairman presented himself as the ultimate victim, scammed by people he trusted and placed in an impossible position by those who had originally entered into an agreement with him. He laid out the entire story, filling in gaps and telling his version of the story from the perspective of an innocent man entangled in an inescapable net. He testified that he dallied with various Las Vegas casino projects in the early 1970s and was able to maneuver and leverage himself into the Hacienda Hotel-Casino, causing him to be on very thin financial ice, and he was desperately shopping for help when he was introduced to Al Baron, manager of the Teamsters Union Central States Pension Fund. Recall that Marty Buccieri had claimed responsibility for the introduction to Baron, and his persistent demands for a finder's fee may have gotten him killed. Glick went on to testify that the Teamsters held the mortgage on the Stardust and Freemont properties, so he approached Teamster Al Baron for financial help. Baron, a gruff and harsh man, told him, "Listen to me. I'm giving you the best advice you've ever had. Walk away from this thing. "But Glick, ever confident in himself, didn't take the counsel and pressed on. Baron went on to explain that in order to get a Teamster loan he needed to have a Central States Pension Fund Trustee on his side, and the best way to do that was to deal with men who had influence with the trustees.

Glick continued to testify and explained that some time in early 1974, Frank Ranney had come to Chicago from Milwaukee, where he had had lunch with Frank Balistrieri that very day, and Baron informed Glick that Ranney was one of the three members of the executive committee of the pension fund who decided on the merits of investments west of the Mississippi River. Baron explained to Glick, "Mr. Balistrieri could be a link to Frank Ranney . . ." I find it interesting that Glick didn't deal directly with Ranney, but worked through someone that should never have been involved with the Teamsters Union. Baron didn't bother to tell Glick of Balistrieri's true identity, but he would eventually find that out for himself. Baron, through Ranney, set up a meeting between Balistrieri and Glick at the Teamsters office in Chicago; then, somewhat later, they met again at the Hacienda Casino in Las Vegas. Glick testified, "After I submitted the package [loan application] I went to Milwaukee, where I met Frank's two sons, John and Joseph. They were both attorneys. Balistrieri was very congenial and said he would like his sons involved in the casino operation in some way." Glick said he didn't make any commitments at the time, as he didn't want to lock himself into anything.

Just to be on the safe side and to find out who he was actually dealing with, Glick made some inquiries about Balistrieri that resulted in some very troubling news. He learned that Balistrieri was the mob boss of Milwaukee, but Glick testified, "On the other hand, I didn't feel there was anything I could do. What was I going to tell him? I know you're the head of the Mafia in Milwaukee, so don't help me get the loan?" Glick's overwhelming desire to own Las Vegas casinos overpowered his common sense and, as a result, he made a deal with the devil. As with all such arrangements, the devil always comes for his due. Glick was led to believe by Balistrieri that Bill Presser, the Cleveland representative on the executive board, had questions about the loan and was dragging his feet on the approval but it could be worked out if Balistrieri pushed Presser. Glick testified that Balistrieri was so excited about the pending deal that he wouldn't leave Glick alone. He invited Glick to come back to Milwaukee, but Glick was becoming nervous about meeting with the mobster. But as usual, his desires overpowered common sense and he relented, meeting with the sons in Joseph's law office, where they reminded him of his agreement to get them involved in the casino business, even though no such agreement had been made. Glick testified that "... Joe and John discussed an agreement, actually an option agreement, in which for twenty-five or thirty thousand dollars, they would have the right to buy fifty percent of the new company if and when I decided to sell." With his explanation, the option we had seized at the Shorecrest business office made all the sense in the world. The sons were using their subtle threat that Bill Presser wouldn't agree to the loan approval without their intercession as leverage to squeeze their way into the casino business because they wouldn't intercede without the signed option to purchase. The Balistrieris were essentially extorting Glick to sign the option. They were playing their own inside game, squeezing out as much financial blood from Glick as possible without the knowledge of Kansas City or the Chicago Outfit.

Glick testified that he signed the option agreement but worried about it, as he didn't want to jeopardize his Nevada licensing if authorities found out about the document and his tight connection to the Balistrieris. Later that night, fear crept over him and he called Joseph Balistrieri telling him that he was backing out of the agreement. Soon afterward, he received a call from old man Balistrieri, using the name "Uncle John," and was unequivocally informed, "You can't back out." They argued back and forth, not coming to any understanding. Joseph then called Glick and said he would tear up the option if it would help him decide to go forward with the loan. Glick informed him that he had already torn up his copy and wanted Joseph's copy sent to him so he could be sure that it was destroyed. Joseph promised he would send it, but he never did. This shows the level of Balistrieri's desperate efforts to seal the deal with Glick before any other mob family got their hooks into him. Meanwhile, the loan was approved and Glick received a cool $62,750,000 loan. He was elated, in spite of the odds. He had pulled it off; now he could press on with the acquisition of the Stardust, Freemont and Marina and add them to his Hacienda property. He immediately set the gears in motion to begin the operation as Argent Corporation in August of 1974.

The La Jolla Genius naively thought he was home free, but the devil had other plans and he came for his piece of the pie. Balistrieri wouldn't leave Glick alone. He wanted to meet with him again, so Glick flew to Chicago and they had dinner together at the Pump Room inside the Ambassador Hotel. Balistrieri informed Glick that he should only deal with him and no one else, no matter what, and if there were any problems he should contact Balistrieri or one of his sons. Then, satisfied that his fish had taken the bait, he set the hook when he solemnly added, "You've got to do me a favor, Allen. There's a guy living in Las Vegas, he's working for you now. It would be helpful if you give him more recognition. He can help you." It was time for Frank Rosenthal to rise from the Stardust floor to the executive suites. At this point, Chicago had obviously made a demand on Balistrieri - Lefty would run the casinos, end of story. Glick couldn't understand why Balistrieri would interfere with his Argent operations. He assumed that once the loan was approved he would be left alone to run the show and pay the mortgage to the Teamsters, but again, against his better judgment, he relented and Lefty was invited to Glick's home in

La Jolla to discuss the situation. Glick testified, "He told me there was a lot of potential in the company. He was very good . . .. He may be the devil – which I personally think he is – but he's very smart." The Outfit had obviously pressured Balistrieri to put their guy in a position of power inside the Argent organization, and Frankie Bal could do nothing but comply with the eight hundred pound gorilla's wishes.

A very interesting event occurred during one of Balistrieri's visits to San Diego to meet with Glick during a problem phase of the mob takeover. An anonymous telephone call was made on May 3, 1976, to the Scripps Clinic switchboard in La Jolla, California. This was obviously done to circumvent the need to call the San Diego Police Department directly. The caller said, "This is an emergency. Please call the San Diego Police Department Homicide Division. Tell them Mr. Balistrieri is in room 911 at the Sheraton Hotel and has guns and plans to kill a man gangland style. It's organized crime. He has a partner with him that also has guns. Please hurry." Scripps called the police and they went to the Sheraton and confronted Joseph, John, and Frank Balistrieri. The trio denied having any intention of killing anyone but wouldn't provide any other information to police. After the confrontation, the Balistrieris couldn't get out of town fast enough, so they drove directly to the airport and caught the next flight to Milwaukee. Hotel records showed that Balistrieri had made a call from his hotel room to Circus Circus Hotel-Casino in Las Vegas. Recall that Tony Spilotro had a jewelry store in the Circus Circus at the time. I subsequently learned that Spilotro had made the anonymous phone call to embarrass Frankie Bal, possibly at Chicago's prompting, in order to thwart any additional secret

Glick – Balistrieri deals.

There is a character flaw, actually, the driving force for mobsters - greed. This characteristic doesn't change when they are dealing with other mobsters, so there is constant back-room wheeling and dealing, backstabbing, and outright theft from one another. It has long been said, "There is no honor among thieves," and that is particularly true behind the facade of the 'men of honor" in the mob. Frankie Bal thought he had an inside deal and his sons would be his point men in the casino business, but that was not to be. Rosenthal was promoted from floorman to Glick's assistant. His salary was set at $150,000 a year, but before long he was negotiating a salary of $2.5 million to the great chagrin of Glick the fox was now in the henhouse, and Rosenthal took advantage in every conceivable way. Without Glick's approval or knowledge, Rosenthal began making major changes, and it was clear that the other casino executives had been told by Rosenthal that he ran the place. He even renovated his office, which was much larger than Glick's. It was as if he was announcing to all, I'm bigger than the chairman.

When the chairman learned of Rosenthal's actions, he called Rosenthal for a meeting of the minds. They met privately in one of the Stardust's closed restaurants and Glick upbraided the loose cannon. Glick testified that Rosenthal stiffened at the rebuke and announced, "It's about time I inform you of what is going on here and where I am coming from and where you should be. I was placed in this position, not for your benefit, but for the benefit of others, and I have been instructed not to tolerate any nonsense from you, nor do I have to listen to what you say, because you're not my boss!" With those demanding words, the Outfit had spoken and the rules had been set. Rosenthal then moved threateningly close to Glick and added, "If you interfere with any of the casino operations or try to undermine anything I want to do here, you will never leave this corporation alive." Although Glick was taken aback by the threats, he couldn't imagine that Lefty was serious, so he called Balistrieri, as he had been instructed to do, and discussed the problem with him. What he didn't know was that Balistrieri himself had been placed under the thumb of Chicago and he was no longer in the driver's seat. He had been relegated to being a secondary recipient of the stolen gifts from the Stardust.

Glick, as he had been instructed, ran to Fancy Pants for help and demanded, "I want him [Lefty] out of the hotel!" Balistrieri stalled for time; he couldn't go against his masters and he knew he couldn't tell his puppet the real score, but Glick wouldn't relent. He was desperately turning to his secret partner for help, so he continued, "I felt the appointment of your sons as corporate counsel was done in a businesslike manner, and I have no problems with that, but I do have problems with this." Balistrieri, not having any option, was forced to acknowledge that "What Mr. Rosenthal told you is accurate." The new reality was made clear, but Glick, even after all the direct messages to him, continued to believe he was the owner of Argent and he and Rosenthal locked horns constantly.

Dennis N. Griffin, author of *The Battle for Las Vegas, The Law vs. the Mob,* quotes a woman who he identifies as "Connie," who tells of Glick trying to undo her promotion given by Rosenthal's. She told Griffin that Lefty called Glick on the phone in her presence and she heard his side of the conversation, which went something like, "Good evening, Allen. I hear that you had Connie come to your office today on a matter that doesn't concern you. We need to get something straight, Allen. I run things around here; Connie works for me, not you. And if you ever approach her or threaten to fire her again, I'll break both your legs. Do you understand? That's good. Good evening, Allen." Lefty's words left no doubt as to who was in charge of Argent.

Glick continued his devastating testimony and swore Rosenthal had once told him there was an emergency and Glick would have to fly to Kansas City as soon as he could. Glick couldn't understand why he would need to travel to Kansas City and wondered what anyone in that city had to do with the situation. He complained, but Rosenthal was adamant so he complied. He landed in Kansas City and was met by Rosenthal and a driver identifying himself as Carl De Luna. Lefty referred to him as "Tuffy." They drove around downtown Kansas City for a time in an obvious effort to shake any tails and eventually ended up at a hotel, where he was shown to a suite of rooms by Rosenthal.

Glick described the chilling meeting for the jury. "The suite was pretty dark. As I walked in I was introduced to a white haired older man named Nick Civella. I had no idea who Nick Civella was. He turned out to be the Mafia boss of Kansas City. I put out my hand to shake and he said, 'I don't want to shake your hand.' . . . Civella called me every name under the sun and then he says, 'You don't know me, but if it was my choice you'd never leave this room alive. However, due to the circumstances, if you listen, you may." Then the mobster with years of experience on the toughest of streets added, "You reneged on your deal. You owe us one point two million dollars, and you're gonna let Lefty do what he wants!" Glick was dumbfounded. What had he gotten himself into with these creatures? Civella asked him about any deal he had with Balistrieri, as he didn't seem to know about the option to buy, and he said he had also helped with the Teamster loan deal as a result of his association with Roy Williams, so he deserved money as payment for his efforts. At this juncture, it was evident that Chicago had turned the Argent operation over to Civella, as long as they got their cut of the action. Civella had had experience with the skim through his hidden control of the Tropicana, and he was a hard taskmaster and demanded absolute loyalty and subservience to him. Then Civella, staring at Glick, demanded, "Get him outta here, then drive down to Milwaukee and yank that fancy pants sonofabitch out of bed and bring him here!" I believe that Balistrieri was threatened with his life at this point and was told that he would be allowed to live only if he took a substantial cut in skim payments and behaved himself.

Glick also testified about another meeting with De Luna that was held in Oscar Goodman's Las Vegas Valley Bank office building. Apparently, Lefty, who was also present during the meeting, had provided Tuffy with Glick's La Jolla address and the names and ages of his children. They met in the law office, as it was viewed as being a safe place to meet. Glick testified about the meeting that occurred on April 25, 1978. "I entered Mr. Goodman's office and behind Mr. Goodman's desk with his feet up on the desk was Mr. De Luna." Glick continued his testimony. " . . . Mr. De Luna, in a gruff voice, using graphic terms, told me to sit down. With that, he pulled out a piece of paper from his pocket – he was wearing a three piece suite . . . He said he and his partners were finally sick of having to deal with me and having me around and that I could no longer be tolerated." De Luna told

Glick, in no uncertain terms, that he was out whether he liked it or not and he would announce his desire to sell his casinos not long after leaving Goodman's office. Glick continued describing what De Luna demanded. "And he says that since I perhaps find my life expendable, he was certain I wouldn't find my children's life expendable." De Luna then read the names of Glick's children from the sheet of paper and told him that his children would be murdered if he didn't comply with his orders. Reality had finally struck home for Glick. He was shaken to his core, and within a short time, he notified the Gaming Control Commission of his plans to sell his casinos. Interestingly, Goodman denied knowing anything about the use of his office by De Luna. He explained the use of his office to John Smith, as recorded in his book, *Of Rats and Men.* "You had to be buzzed into the office. They couldn't have just walked in. They had to be buzzed in. I certainly didn't give these people permission to go in there, but obviously someone buzzed them in." His comment makes me wonder who gave Lefty permission to use the office. Could it have been one of Goodman's partners?

An undated letter, purported to have been written by Glick to Nick Civella or Joseph Aiuppa, states in part, "I am writing this letter to you with a great deal of mixed emotions. I only wish the circumstances and conditions under which this letter is being written were different… I have decided, after my conversation with Carl [De Luna] . . . I honestly believe it is the best solution for everyone concerned; I will step out. I have respected the partnership, even though many will tell you differently, and I did not act selfishly, dishonestly, or deceitfully during the relationship. My decision is to leave the operation and turn it over to whomever you so designate… I never stole, or have taken without open record, one penny from the company as has been claimed…. After my meeting in K.C., it was made clear that we had a 50/50 partnership… I have stood up to the roughest of probes and pressures without once flinching or acting in any manner other than that which the partners would expect of me. …I have a great deal of respect for FB [Frank Balistrieri] and his sons. I consider them friends and enjoyed a personal relationship with the attorneys. I did not fully understand or know the various partners when I became involved in Argent in 1974."

A perfect law enforcement storm was rising, and the Argent/Strawman trial came to an end in 1985. Two of the defendants in the Kansas City trial could see the writing on the wall and pleaded guilty. As a result, De Luna was sentenced to 16 years on top of his Tropicana time, and Balistrieri received 10 years to run concurrently with his Milwaukee sentence. He was released early for health reasons in 1991 and passed away from a heart attack in February of 1993. The Balistrieri sons were acquitted, but the other defendants were all found guilty. Joseph Aiuppa, age 77, the Outfit boss, received 28 years and died in prison in 1997. Jack Cerone, age 71, the underboss, received the same sentence. He is now dead. The other Outfit bosses, Joseph Lombardo and Angelo LaPietra, each received 16 years, and Milton Rockman, age 73, was sentenced to 24 years in prison. Lombardo is the only living defendant. Carl Thomas was rewarded for his cooperation by having his Tropicana sentence reduced to two years, but after being released, he died in an automobile wreck. The Midwest mobs had been dealt a crushing blow, but they weren't finished off. The virus remains.

CHAPTER 10
Some Leftover Pieces

"When the FBI gets on to you, you're in trouble."
--Frank Cullotta

There are certain pivotal plays that can change the outcome of a football game. A fumble or interception can upset a team's chance of victory in a split second. There are also such pivotal events in criminal investigations. In early 1981, agents Dennis Arnoldy and Joseph Gersky had been assigned as co-case agents in the murder of Jerry Lisner, and during the course of the investigation they developed information that tipped them off to a big score that was planned by Frank Cullotta and his the Hole in the Wall Gang. The target of the planned burglary was Bertha's Gift Store on Sahara Avenue in Las Vegas.

As a result, everything came tumbling down for the notorious gang on July 4, 1981, and, at the same time, the beginning of the end was at hand for Spilotro. An informant and a member of Cullotta's gang had been carefully cultivated by Arnoldy, and he told him that Cullotta and his crew were going to hit Bertha's. The informant, an expert in electronic alarm systems, had rolled over and was cooperating with the FBI to mitigate a charge against him in Phoenix. The burglary plot was laid out to the agents, and Dennis and Joe developed a brilliant plan to deal with the upcoming burglary. The plan was the best organized and executed FBI tactical arrest operation I have been part of.

According to the source, Cullotta's intention was for him

to cruise the area looking for police while gang member Larry Neuman did the same in his car. Wayne Matecki, Ernie Devino, and Leo Guardino were to climb up on the roof of Bertha's and cut a hole into the roof above the jewelry vault. Another participant, who the informant didn't know, was to monitor police radio traffic to insure that the burglars were safe from detection. This person was to sit undetected in the parking lot of the Commercial Center across from Bertha's in the back of a white carpet cleaning van with a Superman logo painted on its sides.

The FBI surveillance team, under the direction of Emmett Michaels, and using encoded radios, surreptitiously kept all the members of the gang in hand for several hours as they moved around the city prior to the zero hour, a truly remarkable feat. The typical sauna heat of the July desert was oppressing the agents on the surveillance squad almost beyond the limits of their physical endurance. One of the agents, Jack Salsbury, sitting in the oven of a non air conditioned van, was nearly overcome by heat stroke as he watched the home of Frank Cullotta, while other agents waited on the various members of the Hole in the Wall Gang to make their moves.

To his credit, organized crime squad supervisor Charlie Parsons knew his personnel well and left the planning and execution of the project to his trusted case agents, and the SAC, Joseph Yablonsky, realized that when you have good people, the best option is to allow those people to do their job without undue interference. After hearing the master plan, they both told Arnoldy, "We'll be available if there's a problem and you need us." Assignments were made for the various arrest teams, which included the Las Vegas Metropolitan Police Department, Intelligence Unit. The

Intelligence unit was headed by Commander Kent Clifford in whom the FBI had complete confidence.

I was assigned the task of arresting the unknown player in the white Superman cargo van, along with Detectives Cordell Pearson and Louis Di Tiberious, and the three of us met together and devised an arrest plan. We decided that since we didn't know who we were dealing with and since the van would be dark inside, we needed to light up the interior of the vehicle. It was determined that Di Tiberious and I would pull in front of the van and light up the inside with the bright headlights of our car. This would also blind the occupant so that he couldn't see us in the event he wanted to shoot at us. Pearson, dressed in full police uniform, would drive up to the van in a police cruiser from the rear with his red and blue lights flashing. This would notify the unknown man that he had no chance of escape.

The wait for nightfall was uncommonly long and brutally hot, and our emotions were on edge as the hours ticked slowly by. Arnoldy and Gersky, who was a former Border Patrol agent, took a position on the roof of a high rise building some distance away from Bertha's. They were to coordinate the entire operation from their vantage point that afforded them a full view of the roof of the target, and they were to call out the movements of the burglars. We were also informed by Strike Force Attorney Stan Hunterton that we should wait for the tool-carrying burglars to actually make a hole in the roof, thereby fulfilling the requirement for a solid burglary charge, before we moved in for the arrests.

The dazzling 4th of July fireworks sparkled brilliantly in the Las Vegas night sky as a fitting preamble to the fireworks that were to come when the three burglars pulled up behind Berthas. The burglars set a ladder against the wall and climbed up on the roof and made their way to the intended location, where they began cutting into the roof with a power saw and an ax. They were surely anticipating the one million dollar's worth of jewelry and antiques that would soon be theirs. We were psyching ourselves for the order to move when we were advised over the secure, scrambled FBI radio that the burglars had apparently missed the vault and had to move a distance and cut another hole. This reminded me of the microphone installation in John Balistrieri's office when we, too, had first missed the mark. Finally they broke through and we got the order to make the arrests. Arnoldy, along with two agents and two Metro detectives, climbed, unannounced, onto the roof of Bertha's, armed with shotguns and got the drop on the astonished burglars. At the same time, Cullotta was pulled over and placed in custody, as was Larry Neuman, a multiple murderer who had chosen a life of crime, even though he was the beneficiary of a wealthy trust established by his father. He was a pure sociopath who delighted in intimidating people. He had no limits and was always more than willing to kill.

It was so hot that the interior of my car was like a wood-fired pizza oven. As we prepared to make our move, I turned on the air conditioner full blast and left the front doors open to allow the hot air to be blown out. Then our three man team moved on the Superman van and ordered the occupant to come out with his hands held high above his head. We could see a figure moving inside the confines of the vehicle, and then he emerged through the driver's door. Detective Di Tiberious had a shotgun trained on him, and I had my .357 Magnum aimed at his heart, when the headlights illuminated his face. Di Tiberious was shocked when he recognized the man as Joe Blasko, the former intelligence detective who had been fired for cooperating with Tony Spilotro. For a brief moment I thought Di Tiberious might shoot the traitor. As Di Tiberius and I approached Blasko, he recognized the detective and belligerently asked, "What are you gonna do, rookie, shoot me?" Lou told me that he didn't personally know Blasko, but he worked the Hole in the Wall Gang case and Blasko would have known about him.

The Hole in the Wall Gang was finished, and each member knew it. They were taken to the Clark County Jail and we searched the van, finding three walkie-talkies. One was set to Metro's radio frequency, one was set to the same channel as Cullotta's hand-held radio, and the other was set to the same channel as the burglar's radio on the roof. The arrests were blasted all over the Las Vegas media, and that's how Tony Spilotro learned he had a very big problem.

Dennis Arnoldy told me that shortly after the Bertha's arrests, a Chicago confidential source learned that Tony Spilotro was going to have Cullotta whacked, as he was a major threat to Tony and was no longer trusted. The LCN vaunts its oath of honor, yet turning on a lifelong friend means nothing to these cheap men of dishonor. FBI policy requires the notification of potential victims of violence, so supervisor Charlie Parsons visited Cullotta in the jail and informed him very succinctly, "There's a contract on your life – good luck." A few days later, Cullotta, using the public telephone at the jail, called Parsons and, in an equally terse statement, said, "Come and see me." A new attorney was secured for Frank, and negotiations were instituted, and it was eventually agreed that Frank would "come over" and testify regarding absolutely every crime he had ever committed or known about.

Frank was removed from jail at night and placed in protective custody by the FBI and Metro. He was debriefed by Arnoldy, Gersky, and Metro detectives for days. He even accompanied the investigators all over Las Vegas, pointing out all the places his crew had hit. Most importantly, he provided evidence on Spilotro and other Outfit guys. Cullotta pled guilty to burglary charges and was sentenced to eight years in prison, but after a few years he was released on parole. That's when Arnoldy and I flew to Miami to meet him. Arnoldy told me he has seen a remarkable transformation of the once-cold blooded killer. He is now, according to Arnoldy, a new man. He said he considers Frank "a very good friend who has always told me the truth. We have developed a high level of trust."

Tony Spilotro was beginning to wear down. He was burdened with two separate federal cases included the Bertha's burglary, where many other crimes tied together under the umbrella of racketeering. During the trial, Frank Cullota was the star witness and laid out his soiled history for the whole world to see. He testified about every detail of the various burglaries and other crimes committed in Las Vegas by him and his crew. Of course, the pinnacle of his testimony was filling in all the details of Spilotro's hand in the various crimes and how The Little Guy had benefited financially from the pattern of racketeering and how he had participated in some of the crimes by setting them up. For example, Spilotro had asked Frank to include Blasko in the Bertha's job, as he needed money after being fired by Metro.

Strike Force Attorney Lawrence Leavitt expertly handled

the prosecution of the Bertha's case. Near the end of the trial, I was called to testify regarding the arrest of Blasko. Leavitt was in the process of walking me through my testimony when he unexpectedly asked me to leave the witness stand and point to an overhead photograph of the surrounding area of Bertha's and the Commercial Center. Usually, testimony is reviewed with the witness by the prosecutor prior to trail so that no surprises come up while the witness is on the stand, but in the turmoil of the trial we hadn't had that opportunity. Unbeknownst to Leavitt, I hadn't seen the photograph before that very moment, and as I walked toward it, I couldn't orient myself to where the van had been located on the night of July 4, 1981. There were dozens of streets and tops of buildings pictured, and, of course, there were no street signs visible on the photograph. I walked slowly to the photo, staring intently as I tried to figure it out, when, luckily, the defense objected and the judge sustained their objection to my pointing out the exact location of Blasko's arrest, as everyone already knew where it took place. For the only time in my career, I was grateful for a defense objection.

Unfortunately for the government and surprisingly for Spilotro, the jury couldn't come to a unanimous verdict. It was hopelessly deadlocked at 10 for guilty and 2 for acquittal. The two hold outs, according to other jurors, were completely uncooperative and refused to deliberate the evidence. It was as if they had totally disregarded the evidence and refused to vote guilty. The judge was dumbfounded, and after ordering a mistrial he requested an investigation to determine if there had been jury tampering. This was a difficult task and it was never determined if the fix was in or not. I have always believed that 12 person juries in criminal cases should only be required to vote for conviction with a minimum of 10 votes. This would eliminate the nut factor or the fixed jury factor. In any event, a retrial was scheduled for Tony and the others.

It was later learned that the Chicago Outfit had set a plan in motion to kill Spilotro during the Bertha's trial. Cullotta informed me that Joe Ferriola, one of the Chicago bosses, hated Spilotro for an affront he had committed against him, but Joey Lombardo stood up for Tony, as they had been made together. Lombardo was finally convinced and Cullotta told me that it was the final decision, and "Tony had to go, it was over for him." Fortuitously for Tony, he wasn't living at home during this general time frame. I'm not sure why that was the case, but it may have been as a result of domestic problems. Unbeknownst to anyone, including his attorney, Oscar Goodman, there was a team of Outfit hitters in Las Vegas looking to whack Spilotro during the Bertha's trial. The team consisted of John Fecarotta, Frank Schweihs (Tony's old crew member), and Nick Calabrese. Schweihs had an Uzi sub machine gun, and Calabrese had some C-2 explosive, so they were ready for anything. They had difficulty finding Tony's temporary residence, and realizing they couldn't get a clean kill while he was walking to and from court with his defense attorneys and his wife, who met him at Goodman's office each morning, they looked for other options. They even followed Oscar Goodman hoping he would lead them to his client. Schweihs suggested that they kill Tony as he walked out of the courthouse, but this was deemed to be unacceptable.

The team was staying in Bullhead City, Arizona, across the Colorado River from the resort town of Laughlin, Nevada.

Bullhead City received its name, not from a bull's head but from the name of a bottom-feeding catfish. Fecarotta, like the fool he was, had brought a girlfriend along and spent much of his time gambling in the Laughlin casinos. He won a $2,000 jackpot and, for income tax purposes, was required to show ID before getting his pay-out. He didn't have ID so he talked Calabrese into showing his ID and signing for the funds. The signed payout slip with Calabrese's name on it was evidence of his presence in Nevada, and he was furious because the team had carefully traveled under assumed names. As a result, the nefarious mission was aborted.

Unbelievably, the murderous Lurch Neumann was released on bond after the Bertha's mistrial, but the police knew of his volatile nature and wanted him back in jail where he belonged. They pulled him over to determine his bond status and found a gun in his possession. Dennis Arnoldy obtained an indictment against Neumann charging him with being a felon in possession of a firearm, a federal offense, so Arnoldy, Joe Gersky, and I went out to arrest him, hopefully for the last time. Lurch was staying at a low rent apartment complex on east Flamingo Avenue at the time, a place that suited him perfectly. Gersky obtained a room key from the management and we made our way to the room on the second floor. Neumann, a cold blooded murderer who had killed at least six people, was not a man to be trifled with, so we were very cautious. It was early in the morning and we hoped to catch him in bed. The door was unlocked and we quickly stepped into the studio apartment with weapons drawn and confronted Neumann, who was in bed with a prostitute. He smiled when he was awakened, but the woman screamed and jumped out of bed. She was naked and in a state of uncontrolled panic, but we were concentrating on Neumann, who we realized was capable of anything. We placed him under arrest and then had to turn our attention to the crazy woman. Finally, she got dressed and left. Neumann, a man with no soul, was never set free again.

When the new Bertha's trial was about to begin, Spilotro was nowhere to be found. Even Oscar Goodman, didn't know where he was. The second trial went on without Tony, and all the burglars were found guilty. Cullotta was sentenced to eight years. Blasko, the ex- cop, received five years, and after being released he went to work as a bartender for a Las Vegas topless joint. He died in complete disgrace in 2002. Larry Neumann pleaded guilty to an Illinois murder before the second trial and was sentenced to life. He died in prison in 2007. Wayne Matecki was sentenced to 10 years for racketeering, while Devino and Guarino also received time in the federal prison.

Tony Spilotro had mysteriously disappeared, and the manpower-draining Strawman investigation was over, but there were some serious unresolved loose ends left to be addressed. For one, there was George Jay Vandermark, the master slot skimmer who wasn't a man of violence and wanted no part of being put in a trick bag by Gaming authorities, the FBI, or by Rosenthal's pals because he knew so much about the slot skim. Arrest warrants had been filed against Vandermark in May 1976 for tax evasion and embezzlement, and he was the subject of an unlawful flight to avoid prosecution warrant, but nothing much had been done in an effort to find him. When gaming authorities raided the Stardust in 1976, Vandermark knew well that he had serious problems, so he escaped to Mazatlan, Mexico. He left his family with sufficient funds to more than survive, and he lived off some of his ill-gotten skim, which he had taken for his personal use. Ned Day, a newspaper investigative reporter for the *Las Vegas Review Journal* traveled to Mazatlan in an effort to find and interview him, but by then he had disappeared again.

I opened an investigation into the Vandermark disappearance in late 1985, almost ten years after he left Las Vegas. His ex-wife, as well as a close family friend, told me that they had last visited him in cottage #140, one of the bungalows on the ten acre spread of the Arizona Manor in Phoenix in late August of 1976. He was using the alias of George Skinner and was described as being terrified and very lonely. He also had $150,000 in cash in his possession and more of his money and jewelry was in the motel safe deposit box. They said he was seriously considering returning to Vegas on September 16, 1976. He told his wife that he wanted Oscar Goodman to negotiate a deal for his surrender and cooperation, a strange choice of an attorney, as Goodman had also represented Lefty, Carl De Luna, and Spilotro. When I interviewed Vandermark's wife she wouldn't speculate as to his fate, but she was sure he was dead and she had moved on with her life. After Vandermark's disappearance, Vandermark's son told authorities that his father was going to cooperate as soon as he returned to Las Vegas. Not long after, the son was found dead with his head bashed in and lying on his apartment floor, probably due to a drug deal gone bad. Metro's investigation concluded that his death had no connection to the Stardust situation, but we can't be sure.

Though the FBI didn't know it at the time, Vandermark had made contact with his old pal, Bobby Stella, and asked him for help. Stella told him about the Arizona Manor in Phoenix, which was run by Mel Vaci. Vandermark knew Vaci through their association at the Stardust, so, of course, it sounded like a perfect solution. Vandermark didn't want to live on the run for the rest of his life. Who would? But he was stuck and was wrestling with his very limited options. He had told associates before leaving Las Vegas that he would testify if he was granted immunity from prosecution, but he continued to struggle with his decision. Should he go to the authorities and try to make a deal, or should he try to live a life on the lamb, surreptitiously visiting his family from time to time? If he returned to Vegas, authorities would certainly jump him and want answers, and if the Chicago boys found him, he could end up sucking sand in the desert. He was a desperate man who had nowhere to turn. His life in the fast lane was over and he was now in survival mode, so he turned to those who he thought were his friends. Unfortunately for him, friendship in the mob is temporary at best – the only permanent mob characteristic, besides greed, is self preservation – so when necessary, friendship is easily discarded.

Bobby Stella, a main player in the skim removal, had everything to lose if Vandermark decided to cooperate with the FBI. Vandermark was a liability, and Stella was confronted with a major problem as extensive Grand Jury investigations were underway in Las Vegas and in his native Chicago. The last thing in the world he needed was to go to prison because of some low life slot cheat. Bobby, acting out of self preservation, may have gone to Lefty and told him where Vandermark was staying. Rosenthal didn't need to have it spelled out for him. He, better than anyone, understood what damage the slot master could wreak if he turned state's witness against the whole crew of skimmers. Given the facts, Outfit boss Joey Aiuppa the ultimate judge in such matters and understanding the potential damage Vandermark could do, gave the go-ahead to whack him.

On a hot, late August or early September night in 1976, only days before Vandermark was to turn himself in to authorities, professional hit men Big John Fecarotta, Harry Aleman (son-in-law to mobster Joseph Ferriola), Butch Petrocelli, and Jimmy La Pietra made their move. Paul Schiro, who was intimately familiar with the Phoenix area and happened to be a close friend of Vaci, helped plan the hot and assisted the group by locating a good desert burial spot where they could plant the body. Schiro was given a key to room #140 by the amicable Vaci, and the hit team entered unannounced and grabbed Vandermark. It was futile for him to struggle. He didn't have a chance. They strangled him in his room. Then they placed him in a wheelchair they had brought with them. They put a blanket over him and wheeled him out into the night, where he was thrown into a car and never seen again. When Vaci was questioned by Vandermark's ex-wife and, later, by me, he lied and denied that Vandermark had ever stayed at the Arizona Manor. He also denied stealing the money out of Vandermark's safe deposit box, as Mrs. Vandermark knew that her husband's money was kept there and it was missing.

Interestingly, in 2002, Rosenthal was asked about Vandermark and he responded sarcastically, "George Vandermark was last seen in Iran." Las Vegas Metro continues to have an "endangered - missing person" notice on Vandermark in their records. The flier reports that he was last seen in "September of 1976 in the area of 24th Street and Camel-back Road in Phoenix." This is near where the Arizona Manor was located before it was torn down. The flier also states, "It is estimated that Vandermark skimmed 7 million dollars from the Stardust and kept 3 million for himself." After being killed by the Chicago assassins, the helpless vagabond was buried somewhere in the Arizona desert. I was able to obtain his dental records and they were sent to the Maricopa County Medical Examiner's Office for comparison with any and all teeth found in male skulls recovered in the county. Although they had several unidentified skulls, no match was ever made. The law was unsuccessful in solving the crime, but, fortunately, the self cleaning oven of the mob took care of most of Vandermark's killers. William "Butch" Petrocelli was strangled and had his throat slit by Frank Calabrese Sr. in Chicago in 1980. Big John Fecarotta was also eliminated by the Outfit. Harry Aleman was sentenced to 300 years in prison for a series of murders, and only Jimmy La Pietra escaped justice, but died of natural causes in 1993.

Frank Rosenthal was forever banned from Nevada casinos, but remained in Vegas and developed a daily pattern of behavior. For a time, he continued to run the Stardust by long distance, but that didn't last when the property changed hands. He went back to placing bets on his favorites, and later in the evening he would meet friends at the bar inside Tony Roma's restaurant on east Sahara Avenue, just off the Strip. The bar is very small and intimate and is surrounded by dining booths but provides some privacy to those standing or sitting at the bar. The place gave Lefty and his friends a spot to get away from the hustle of the 24 hour town.

On the night of October 4, 1982, Lefty had concluded his meeting with his drinking pals and exited Tony Roma's. He was in a good mood and life was simplistically smooth. He was out of the casino business, but he was doing alright and he certainly had plenty of money to tide him over. As was his custom, he entered his 1981 Cadillac Eldorado carrying a takeout order of ribs and started the engine. The moment the car started there was a deafening bang, then flames came roaring out of the dashboard vents. Lefty opened the door to escape the flames and hit the ground rolling on the pavement of the parking lot to put out his burning clothes. Not thinking clearly, he stood up staring in awe as his car was consumed in blue and yellow flames. Two men came out of nowhere and knocked him to the ground. At first he thought they were there to finish him off, but they only wanted to help. As with much of Lefty's life, luck had played an enormous part in his success, and now Lady Luck had kissed him again because the two men happened to be Secret Service Agents who had just finished a late dinner. The heat from his burning car was so intense that the gas tank ignited within seconds, lifting the heavy vehicle off the ground and tearing much of the metal to scrap. Lefty was in shock - he was seen wandering around the parking lot like a man in a catatonic trance. His head was bleeding, he had cuts on his left arm and leg where he had hit the pavement, and he had slight burns and soot all over his face. He had miraculously escaped an assassination attempt, because the C-4 explosion had fortuitously been deflected by the Cadillac's factory installed steel underbelly on the driver's side of the car. The question that has never been answered is, who tried to kill Lefty?

The big money, at the time, was on Tony Spilotro because of Tony's adulterous relationship with Geri, while others thought Chicago had ordered the hit. Cullotta has the strong opinion that it wasn't Tony's doing because he once asked Frank to have Lurch Neumann kill Lefty, then he wanted Matecki to do it, then he called it off. He must have realized that the Outfit heat would land directly on him if Lefty was killed. Frank then expanded his opinion to me. "Tony never used bombs. It wasn't his style. I think Geri put one of her California biker friends up to it. She hated Lefty and she had asked Tony to kill him for her so I know she wanted him dead." I agree, to a degree, with Frank - Tony never used bombs, but I have a different theory as to who ordered the hit. I believe that Nick Civella was behind the bombing and he had ordered it before he passed away in May of 1983. He had personally been disrespected by Lefty when he threw Civella's hand-picked casino manager, Carl Thomas, out of the Stardust. Thomas would have put Civella in the driver's seat at the Stardust, even ahead of Chicago. Civella had plenty of access to mechanics who could have planted the bomb. Recall that Tuffy De Luna once told Joe Agosto, when referring to Lefty Rosenthal, "He's dead!" After the near fatal bombing, Chicago mobsters and friends of Lefty must have stepped in and told Civella not to take any further action, as Lefty had gotten the message and had been scared out of Vegas forever.

Lefty and Geri were divorced in September of 1980, and she left for Los Angeles just before the bombing attempt on his life. She was a drug addicted mess and soon burned through the money Lefty had given her. A short time after the bombing, Geri, screaming hysterically, fell dead in Los Angeles from an overdose of the toxic mix of cocaine, Valium, and alcohol. It was reported that she was hanging out with motorcycle-types in order to obtain drugs and was in a constant addled state. In the end, the once ravishing beauty had too many demons to contend with and they overwhelmed her.

Forever banned from his beloved casinos, and after receiving the very clear message from the bombing, Rosenthal moved to Laguna Niguel, California, in early 1983 in order to help his daughter and son with their love of swimming. Both were world class swimmers and needed personal trainers to push them to the next level. Unfortunately for them, they never quite made the cut for the U.S. Olympic team. Ironically, Lefty's Las Vegas house in the Country Club Estates was sold to Suge Knight, the CEO of Death Row Records, who represented hip hop artists including Tupac Shakur, who was gunned down in Las Vegas in September of 1996. Knight has been in and out of prison since that time and eventually filed for bankruptcy and lost the house.

In 1985, I was conducting surveillance on Bobby Stella Sr., and observed him meeting with a man I didn't recognize at the time. Stella had been subpoenaed before a Federal Grand Jury during the Argent investigation but refused to testify, even under a grant of immunity. The duplicitous judge, Harry Claiborne, refused to find him in contempt, ruling, "He is too old and frail to go to jail." In spite of the judge's ridiculous finding, the frail old man was still meeting with skim conspirators nearly ten years later. Also, as an aside, some time later I brought a case against Bobby Stella, Jr., the old man's son, and two others, and they were convicted of operating a "ponzi scheme" in violation of the Interstate Wire Fraud statute.

I determined the man who had met with Bobby Stella, Sr., was none other than Melvin "Mal" Vaci. Bells went off in my head as I was fascinated by the fact that after so many years the two men continued to maintain close contact. Vaci was described as "a sweetheart" by those who knew him. He was congenial, always smiling, and a real people person, but he had one flaw - he talked too much. Vaci, a Chicago native, had worked at the Stardust as a junket representative until 1984 when he was fired. Frank Cullotta told me that he once met Vaci in the Stardust and, after exchanging pleasantries, Vaci told him that Spilotro had gotten him the job and he and Bobby Stella were stealing out of the joint. Cullotta looked at him as if he had committed the unpardonable sin and remarked, "Why are you telling me about that? It ain't any of my business. I don't want to know about anything that goes on in this place."

When the Stardust was eventually cleaned up and most of the bad actors removed, Vaci moved to Phoenix, Arizona, and became the manager of the Arizona Manor Hotel. The facility had a very popular lounge, and Vaci was the toast of place. His pals, Bobby Stella and Paulie Schiro, often hung out there, receiving drinks on the house. The Arizona Manor had closed, and apparently Vaci had come back to Las Vegas for reasons unknown to me. My plan was to assemble sufficient probable cause to place a tap on both Stella's and Vaci's phones and then prime the pump by interviewing Vaci about Vandermark, thereby causing the two men to discuss Vandermark and, hopefully, cause them to talk about the murder and other matters of investigative interest. I went so far as to prepare a rough draft affidavit to support the wiretap request, when the dark ghosts stepped in and Vaci abruptly moved back to Phoenix, causing my initial investigative plan to fall flat.

Ironically, a few years after my retirement, I received a phone call from two Phoenix detectives who had obtained a copy of my old, rough draft Vaci affidavit from the Las Vegas FBI office and wanted to meet with me to discuss the evidence supplied in the affidavit. We met, appropriately, at Tony Roma's restaurant on Sahara Avenue in Las Vegas where Lefty had nearly been blown to hell. The two men grilled me on the affidavit and wanted to know who my informants were. I told them that I couldn't provide that information. The FBI had committed to keep the identity of the sources secret, as they would never have provided information if they thought they would be exposed. The detectives were understandably upset, but my hands were tied. I can understand how the police could accuse the FBI of non cooperation, a common complaint, but the Bureau makes an ironclad commitment to its informants, a contract that is simply a matter of trust. We don't just make promises and then cast our sources aside as police often do. For the most part, our informants are on a different level than common street criminals. If informants lose confidence in the Bureau's ability to keep their identity secret, we would never have any informants and, therefore, we would essentially be blind.

I had been working on the Vaci case with U.S. Strike Force Attorney, Lawrence Leavitt, a brilliant prosecuting attorney. After investigation by myself, Dennis Arnoldy, and Jerry Doherty in Phoenix, where we located and interviewed old employees of the Arizona Manor, I decided to subpoena Vaci before the Federal Grand Jury in Las Vegas. The subpoena was served and Vaci appeared before the investigative body, but he refused to answer many of the questions and hid behind the 5th Amendment. We then sought and received Department of Justice authority to grant Vaci immunity from prosecution for anything he said in the Grand Jury, thereby forcing him to testify, as we were willing to have him as a witness as opposed to a defendant. The new subpoena was served on him, placing him in an invisible box with no escape, a confinement of his own making. Vaci, always a man who talked too much, did it again. He ran to his pals, Stella and Paul Schiro. He should have known better, but he made exactly the same fatal mistake as Vandermark had made.

Not long after being served with a second subpoena, on June 6, 1986, the 73-year-old Vaci left his employment at Ernesto's Back Street Restaurant in Phoenix, and as he approached his parked car, Nick Calabrese, who had been ordered to kill Vaci by Outfit bosses, grabbed the frail old man. Calabrese, aided by Jimmy La Pietra, opened the sliding door of a cargo van and forced Vaci into the death chamber. Spilotro crew member Joey Hansen was driving the van, and as they sped off, Calabrese pointed one of the Tamiami .22 caliber High Standard semi automatic pistols, fitted with a silencer, at Vaci. The helpless man begged for his life and swore, "I'm not gonna tell the grand jury anything." But Calabrese had a job to do. He felt no pity for his victim and robotically pulled the trigger, but the gun jammed. Calabrese fumbled with the weapon momentarily. We are left to imagine the horror of those last few seconds for Vaci, but the assassin was able to un-jam the gun and shot Vaci in the head six times. The van sped toward the isolation of the desert, but Calabrese began to worry about being stopped by the police, so he wrapped the body in a green plastic tarp that was spread on the floor to collect the victim's blood. Hansen pulled the van over to the side of the road and Vaci's well-dressed body was dumped down an embankment into a semi-dry canal. In his haste, Calabrese had unwittingly wrapped a Smith and Wesson .38 caliber revolver in with Vaci's bloody body, and it was recovered by police during their crime scene investigation. The FBI later learned that Outfit boss James "Jimmy Light" Marcello had financed the operation in Phoenix. When the job was complete, Nick Calabrese called his brother, Frank, and reported the success by saying, "You know, I haven't been feeling too well. But last night, I had some soup."

Homicide detectives determined the .38 caliber gun was not the murder weapon, but found it had been stolen in Chicago, and thus the arrows pointed to a Chicago connection for the murder. What was suspected, and eventually verified, was that Paul Schiro, once a friend of Vaci's, had been involved in setting him up for the hit and had followed the murder van in a car. Further, John Fecarotta, Jimmy DiForti, and Frank Schweihs had also taken some part in the conspiracy to kill the helpless Vaci. When I first learned of Vaci's murder, I realized that because of my persistence in attempting to solve the Vandermark murder by subpoenaing Vaci, I had played an unwitting role in his demise.

Meanwhile, the Rosenthal family left Laguna Niguel and moved to Boca Raton, Florida, where Lefty took over the management of Croc's Restaurant and Bar and where he, in semi retirement, set up a sports service website and returned to his first love, handicapping sporting events. He was also hired as a consultant for author Nicolas Pileggi and movie director Martin Scorsese in the making of the hit movie, *Casino*. When asked about the authenticity of the movie, Lefty responded, "I was a full time consultant for Universal Studios, and a very fine writer/author, Nick Pileggi and worked with the great one, Robert DeNiro." When asked how he liked the finished movie, he responded, "I've only seen the movie twice. The first time at Universal's private studio and in the Big Apple with the author and screen writer,

Nick Pileggi. I was focused on accuracy and portrayal… The way you saw it in the movie is just the way it happened." Not long after the release of the movie, Lefty moved to a condo in Miami Beach.

In the meantime, Glick sold the Stardust to Al Sachs, operating as Trans-Sterling Corporation, The skim continued to some degree particularly through the fill slip scam, but Gaming and the FBI maintained their pressure on the place. Agent Lynn Ferrin told me that the new casino manager, Lou Salerno, was convicted of fraud for forging fill slips that were estimated to have resulted in a skim of up to $30,000 per month for the Outfit. On December 5, 1983, the Gaming Control Board announced the " . . . filing of an 18 count complaint against the Stardust Hotel, doing business as Trans-Sterling Corporation and Allan Sachs … culminating a two year skimming investigation . . ." Gaming pulled all key employee licenses and a forced sale was again ordered in July of 1984. With this termination notice, an historic era had ended in Las Vegas.

Mob control of Las Vegas casinos had been scrubbed clean by the disinfectant of the law. Corporations moved in and took over most casino operations, realizing the huge financial potential of these cash-cows. Today, only one of the Argent properties still exists. The Hacienda Hotel-Casino was torn down in 1993 to make way for the spectacular Luxor Hotel-Casino. The Marina no longer exists, and the Stardust was purchased by Sam Boyd in 1984, doing business as the Boyd Group. The casino and hotel were imploded in 2007 to make room for the new Echelon Place Casino. Only the Freemont remains, and it has changed ownership several times. Even though the mob had lost its power over the casino industry, it is like a rubber ball and always bounces back in one way or another. I believe strongly that the necessary focus on terrorism should not be an excuse for the FBI to let up on organized crime investigations, particularly when the various families have been weakened.

CHAPTER 11

Sin City is Forever Changed

"The mob lost and law enforcement won . . ."

--Oscar Goodman

With the mob out of the casino business, the end of the line had come for Tony Spilotro and the Outfit bosses decided he had to go - one last pile of debris to be cleaned up. With the unsuccessful attempt on Tony's life in Las Vegas, he was ordered back to Chicago on the pretext that he was to be made a boss and his brother, Michael, was to be made a member. Cullotta informed me that he didn't buy the story because Michael was detested by the Outfit guys, including Joey Ferriola, one of the bosses. Cullotta stated emphatically, "They wouldn't have made Michael, and he and Tony knew it. Plus, Tony knew he was in trouble but what could he do? He couldn't run. He couldn't say 'no, I won't come.' He had to go – take his chances. There was no place for him to hide. I think they called Tony back to plead Michael's case cause they were gonna kill him and maybe they said; Maybe you can talk us out of it." Tony, a man with no options, left for Chicago to meet his fate. Both street-wise brothers knew there was potential for a death sentence, so Michael put a small .22 caliber pistol in his pocket as insurance should there be trouble. Cullotta told me that Michael's wife had informed him, after the brothers didn't come home, that Michael said to her before he left for the meeting, "If we don't come back in a while, we're in big trouble."

On a muggy Chicago day in June of 1986, Jimmy Marcello,

the Outfit boss who had taken over after Joey Aiuppa's death, drove Tony and Michael to a house in Bersenville, Illinois, a suburb of Chicago. Perhaps the fact that the boss himself was chauffeuring them quieted their concerns about potential problems. Ironically, Tony had once told Cullotta, "Never go down in the basement with nobody – they'll kill you." Apparently Tony didn't take his own advice, because that is exactly what he and Michael did. When the two men entered the basement with Michael in the lead, they found it full of mob guys who were smiling approvingly. Then things changed in the blink of an eye. Michael noticed that all the men were wearing black golf gloves, an ominous sign, but his observation was too late. Nick Calabrese dived at Michael and grabbed his legs and held on like a linebacker making a tackle, while Frank "Mooch" Eboli produced a length of rope and pulled it around Michael's neck. The death struggle was on. Michael screamed, but the sound was choked off as the rope was pulled tightly around his throat. Michael, in spite of his karate expertise, was now helpless, and his gun remained secured in his pocket. The assembled piranhas moved in and began pounding him in the face with their fists and feet. The soft tissue of his face oozed blood, so each hateful blow drove blood spatter outward. Tony, who was also being held by a number of men, screamed and begged them to stop, but it was hopeless. Then, in complete submission, the once tough Little Guy relented and asked if he could say a prayer before they started on him. The last thing Tony saw was the battered body of his brother as the wolf pack reenacted the blows and kicks on him. The once arrogant hitman who was willing to do anything to be noticed by Chicago mobsters had overplayed his hand and paid the ultimate price. He was the guy who had popped another man's eye out by crushing his head in a vise. He was the guy who willingly set up the Tamara Rand murder and committed many other brutal murders to do the bidding of Outfit bosses. Now it was the Outfit that repaid him for his deeds. Many believed that Tony had been sent to Las Vegas to oversee the skim. This is not true by any means. He came voluntarily – he oversaw nothing but his own greedy acquisitions. He was a thug, a low-life killer who took it upon himself to spy on Argent operations and murdered people who posed a threat to the Outfit at the request of his superiors. After all his bloody deeds, he was the guy who ended his life with a desperate prayer on his lips. His massive wounds were earned because of disobedience – he had been told not to do anything that would bring heat on the Argent gold mine, but he had disobeyed and paid the ultimate price.

Both Spilotros were beaten beyond recognition, their faces swollen and obliterated. The bodies were carried up the stairs and dumped in the trunk of a car like two sacks of rancid meat and driven 60 miles south to Indiana, where they were thrown into a grave previously dug in a farm field by Big John Fecarotta and others. The murders of the brothers were clearly personal. It wasn't enough to just shoot the two men; they had to be severely punished - paid back for the problems Tony had caused in Las Vegas. Tony was responsible for much of the heat placed on the Outfit and had acted as a lone wolf, doing his own thing and disregarding orders. Because of him, the Outfit's giant piggy bank had been snatched away. I asked Cullotta why Michael was killed along with Tony, and he explained that they killed both brothers because if they had let Michael live, he would certainly have retaliated, and the killers realized that.

Not long after the brutal murders, farmer Mike Kinz was driving his tractor on his land just outside Enos, Indiana, when, from his high perch, he noticed a small patch of ground along a tree line that didn't have any corn sprouts growing on it. The rest of the field was covered in fresh, green, four-inch sprouts. Something was definitely wrong, and he assumed some poacher had killed a deer and, after taking what meat was wanted, had probably buried the remainder of the carcass in his field to hide the evidence. It had happened before and he was getting tired of it, so he called his friend, a game warden. The warden arrived and began to investigate. As he walked around the area, he found drag marks leading from tire tracks on a dirt road to the grave. There were also many shoe prints around the site. The warden began digging with his shovel in the soft, fertile soil, when he struck something solid. He was sure he had found a deer carcass until he scraped away the soil and, to his surprise, saw what appeared to be white skin. He continued to dig and found the bodies of two men dressed only in their under shorts and stacked one on top of the other. Their clothes had been removed possibly as an additional degradation, but probably to dispose of possible blood residue or other forensic evidence. The bodies were reasonably fresh, but their faces were so damaged and swollen that the warden assumed they may have been shot in the face. The police were called, and in turn, they contacted the FBI. The FBI was able to match the dead men's fingerprints with those on file for Michael, age 41, and Anthony Spilotro, age 48. An autopsy performed on the battered bodies indicated that both Michael and Tony had multiple contusions over their entire bodies. Michael's right lung was almost completely filled with blood, his right kidney was torn, his nose was broken, and the vulnerable bones of his face were shattered. Tony had suffered much the same injuries.

Mobsters are killed for a variety of reasons, and their bodies are either left out in the open or dumped in the trunk of a car to eventually be discovered. The victims are usually shot or have their throats slits or, on a rare occasion, are blown up, but the murder of the brothers had been beyond brutal, and great lengths had been taken to hide the bodies by burying them in a five-foot deep grave, necessitating substantial digging. Mobsters are inherently lazy; they don't like manual labor – but this was a special case. I asked Cullotta why the killings were carried out the way they were and why the bodies were so carefully hidden. He explained, "The way they beat them, that was hatred, that was years of bottled up hatred. The bosses who ordered the hits also were involved in the killings. That's very unusual – they hated Tony. I think it was Joey Ferriola who pushed hard for it, and when Lombardo agreed, they killed them. They hid the bodies 'cause if they were found, the spotlight would automatically come back on the Outfit guys and there would be a big investigation. Everybody knew Tony and Michael were dead before the cops found the bodies, so the message for everybody was to shape up and keep their mouths shut." Frank was right. Everybody, except attorney Oscar Goodman, knew the mob had killed Tony and his brother, but we had to wait for over 20 years before the murder was conclusively solved.

Only four months after the Spilotro murders, Nick Calabrese had had enough of John "Big Stoop" Fecarotta's bungling and obtained the okay to kill him for his stupidity in the jackpot problem in Bullhead City, Nevada. Furthermore, Big John had begun to show signs of reticence about doing any more murders and was suspected of cooperating with the FBI. Mob hit man Nick Calabrese made arrangements to meet Big Stoop on the pretext of doing a hit on someone. Fecarotta got in the driver's side of the work-car and Calabrese moved to the passenger's side. As he did, Nick pulled a .38 caliber revolver out of a paper bag and turned to his left, pointing the gun at Fecarotta, who struggled valiantly as the gun was fired. Fecarotta was struck in the side but he was able to knock the gun out of Nick's hand. Fecarotta jumped from the car but Nick pulled another revolver from his waistband and chased Big John down an alley. He finally caught up with the wounded man at the door of a bingo hall, where he finished him off with several shots to the head.

Once the death struggle was over, Nick realized that he had shot himself through his lower left arm with the first shot into Big John. He noticed his blood running down over his left glove, so he hurriedly pulled his gloves off and stuffed them into his back pocket as he fled the scene. In his haste, he didn't notice that the gloves fell out of his pocket as he ran. The gloves were later recovered near the crime scene by police. They assumed, wrongly, that the gloves were covered in Fecarotta's blood, and the crime remained unsolved.

In Las Vegas, the Strawman case was effectively over and Tony Spilotro was nothing more than a bad memory, but our investigations continued. George Togliatti was appointed as the new Las Vegas OC supervisor. He believed that letting up on mob investigations was foolish and wanted to strike a knockout blow to any LCN control in Las Vegas. He understood his men and used them for the benefit of the Bureau. He never assigned a case to me, but allowed me, as the Organized Crime Program Coordinator, to run my own cases. He was wise enough to rely on his people without burdening them with nonsense and was always supportive.

With the Outfit's control of Las Vegas in the bag, I began to focus on various New York LCN members residing in Las Vegas in 1986. It has always been my philosophy that any confirmed LCN member, no matter what his age or status, is a viable target for FBI investigation because LCN guys never really retire. A perfect example of aged mobsters never stopping their criminal activities is Sonny Franzese who was indicted in 2010, at the age of 93, for shaking down strip joints. He was asked if he realized he would die in prison. His terse response says it all. "Who cares?! I gotta die someplace." There should never be a safe harbor for these killers. First, each LCN member has taken the secret oath swearing loyalty to a criminal enterprise. Second, the LCN requires participation in a murder prior to being made. Even the old timers, as proven by the old men convicted in the Kansas City Argent trial, are career criminals and murderers. They never retire. Some are, as they say, "put on a shelf," having proven to be useless to the organization. However, they had once made their bones and continue to be crooks. The LCN has no retirement program for its elderly members. The aged men, therefore, have either saved great sums of money derived from criminal activity, or they continue to receive money from long term criminal enterprises where they have their hooks securely implanted.

During our all-out assault on organized crime, other crimes were also being committed in Las Vegas. One of the most cruel and heartless crimes is kidnapping. The victims are robbed of their innocence and sometimes killed in horrific ways, but the entire family is severely victimized by the abominable act. The uncertainty is crushing, the family pain is unfathomable, and the malignant effects of personal violation last forever. A seventeen year old girl was kidnapped after completing a modeling gig at the Meadows Mall in Las Vegas. She had been too nervous to allow her parents to attend her first modeling job, so she asked them to stay home. A vile serial kidnapper and murderer was passing through Las Vegas and stumbled upon the modeling session and, like all cruel predators, he was always on the hunt for new prey. He was somehow able to convince the naive girl that he was a professional photographer, and she willingly went with him for a photo shoot. She was never heard from again. We were quickly able to identify the kidnapper, Christopher Wilder, a man from Florida who had been traveling across the country kidnapping, torturing, and murdering his female victims. From that point on, we knew it was only a matter of time before her body would be found.

I was assigned the unenviable task of interviewing the distraught parents to glean any and all information about their missing daughter. This may have been the most difficult assignment of my career. I continued to stay with the family during the day, and Jerry Doherty who had single handedly arrested an FBI Top Ten Fugitive while assigned to a previous office, took over during the night shift while our investigation was ongoing. This excruciating vigil went on for days. The agony, the pain, the insufferable melancholy that permeated the house was almost more than I could endure. The mother nearly went mad and coped by riding around with various psychics who, like vultures, came to prey on the helpless woman. Day after day, they searched for the girl's body in wet places the psychics had seen in visions. The father, a large, formidable man, suffered in silence, but from time to time he retreated to his bedroom where I could hear him sobbing quietly. The effects of a kidnapping have long term consequences on the family and more often than not lead to divorce. Wilder kidnapped, sexually assaulted, tortured, and murdered 11 women and was placed on the FBI's Top Ten List, which was telecast to all police agencies, and the cowardly perpetrator was finally cornered by police in New Hampshire in April of 1985, where he struggled with an officer and was able to pull his gun and shoot himself in the chest. The bullet passed through him and into the heroic officer, who miraculously survived. Our fears for the kidnap victim were realized months later when the weathered remains of the poor girl were found in the California desert.

Dark fate sometimes sets the stage for future tragedies, and between April and October of 1980, thousands of Cubans came to the United States in what was known as the Mariel Boat Lift. Many of these huddled masses were trying to escape the bonds of Communism. The poor, criminals, psychotics, and others from the island nation of Cuba made their way to south Florida any way they could. Castro cleared his jails and mental institutions by allowing the inmates to escape to the United States. Many of the escapees came in rickety boats and rafts, and some didn't survive the arduous journey across 90 miles of treacherous ocean. Castro didn't care if they lived or died, he was rid of them. A south Florida newspaper reporter had photographed a lone Marielito, Cuban male riding a large inner tube and holding an American flag as he approached the Florida coast. The front page photograph and accompanying story were inspirational. They provided a riveting account of the man's escape, courage, and hope for the future. No one questioned how one man, without drinking water or a paddle, could have traveled the dangerous waters from Cuba to Florida in the deadly heat of the Caribbean in nothing more than an inner tube. No one bothered to inquire how the man was able to carry a good sized American flag on his perilous voyage, or how he obtained the flag to begin with, as it's illegal to have an American flag in Cuba. But the facts didn't get in the way of a good story, as the eye-catching newspaper photograph was inspiring to all who saw it. The stirring photo portrayed a man who loved the U.S. and held its banner high.

In the midst of our attack on organized crime, a tragedy of unspeakable proportions occurred that shook the Las Vegas Division to its core. Ten years after arriving on our shores, the inner tube refugee moved to Las Vegas to find his American dream. This pretender entered a Las Vegas bank armed with a pistol and ordered everyone to the floor. As dark fate would have it, on June 25, 1990, Special Agent John Bailey, age 48, a Vietnam veteran and a 21 year veteran of the FBI, was in the bank manager's office obtaining some records in another investigation. Normally, a bank robber is allowed to exit the bank before any action is taken by law enforcement to minimize danger to innocent people inside. However, the robber was acting erratically and was exhibiting very dangerous behavior, so John took action in an effort to stop the robber before innocent lives were lost.

Tragically, there was a shootout inside the bank and John was hit three times, knocking him to the floor, where, despite heroic efforts by bank personnel, he drowned in his own blood. Dennis Arnoldy was assigned the case, and his matchless efforts resulted in the killer being brought to justice. The murderer escaped to Mexico shortly after the killing, but the Mexican cops found him as a result of Arnoldy's information and returned him to the U.S., where he was tried for murder in a Las Vegas courtroom. It was learned that the contemptible man was very familiar with killing. He had served in the Cuban Army during its occupation of Angola, where he had learned the art of killing. An ironic twist on the tragic story of John's death was that some time before, one of John's neighbors had passed away and the man's wife had given John some of her deceased husband's like-new shoes. We teased John about wearing "dead man's shoes," but after his murder, we no longer found the joke to be funny.

I was on vacation with my family in Yellowstone National Park when I received word that John, my friend and fellow Las Vegas FBI agent, had been killed. The news was devastating, as it brought back memories of the shooting of Dick Carr in Milwaukee. Agents were instructed to stay away from the trial so as not to affect the outcome of the legal proceeding, but after the Cuban was found guilty, thanks to the persistence of case agent Dennis Arnoldy, a contingent of FBI agents and John's friends filled the courtroom for the sentencing. The killer had originally been accepted into this country as a flag waving patriot, but things are not always what they seem on the surface. The judge solemnly sentenced Jose Echeverria to death, but as the convict was being taken from the court by deputies, he turned and railed against the United States and the FBI. As a result, all of us stood as one and glared at the human scum as he was led away. The killer has remained on Nevada's death row for over 20 years at the expense of the state, but the agent's two daughters have grown up without their father, and our country has lost a true patriot.

It's natural for law enforcement to question how and why a fellow agent lost a gun- fight and was killed. As a result, every FBI-involved shooting requires an official inquiry. This is done for several reasons, but mainly to learn from possible mistakes so that those mistakes are not made again. I will not second guess John or his actions, but suffice it to say that the FBI constantly trains with firearms so that if the need arises, the crook will die and not the agent. Unfortunately, this doesn't always happen. This training takes place regularly and requires passing scores in several tactical courses. Qualifying scores are required with hand guns, shotguns, and rifles. Remarkably, studies of police involved shootings show that most gunfights take place within seven feet, but with the super adrenalin charge that flows through the body always has an effect on concentration. When I first came into the Bureau, we were issued a Smith and Wesson (S&W) Model 10, .38 caliber, six-shot revolvers. This was an efficient gun but was outdated having been in use since the 1950s. I eventually bought myself a S&W Model 66, .357 Magnum revolver that packed a much greater punch than a .38. The crooks were going to much more sophisticated weapons, semi-automatics with a magazine capacity of 10 bullets or more, while we were using six-shooters. The Bureau realized this problem and began issuing S&W 9mm semi-automatic pistols, and I was issued one. It was a fine gun, but I had seen so many instances where police around the country had shot bad guys with a 9mm and the guys had survived to fight some more, so I requested a 10mm semiautomatic. It was a heavy pistol but was extremely accurate, and I knew that if I needed it, it would do the job. Luckily, although there were several instances where circumstances could easily have escalated to a level requiring deadly force, it was never necessary.

Sometime after John's death, the FBI moved into a new building on Charleston Boulevard in Las Vegas. Planning and arranging for the dedication of the new building was carried out by Jerry Doherty, a close friend of John Bailey, and since the new building was to be named after John, Jerry strived to faithfully honor him and his memory. On such occasions, politicians clamber to be part of the event to show their support for law enforcement. Many officials were invited, but when Senator Harry Reid's office called to inquire as to why the Senator hadn't been invited, Jerry informed the caller that John didn't care for the Senator, and as such, Reid wouldn't be invited to the event. I was sitting next to Jerry when this conversation took place, and I was struck by the courage of such a decision. The caller was mortified and asked to speak with the SAC about the clear personal snub. To the eternal credit of the SAC, he stood behind Jerry, and Reid didn't attend.

I asked Jerry why John had such hard feelings for the Senator. He explained that John had investigated a bribery case in which a man named Jack Gordon, former husband of La Toya Jackson, tried to bribe Reid, the then Gaming Control Board Chairman, to approve Gordon's gaming devices sometime around 1978. I once interviewed La Toya Jackson when she accused Gordon of physically abusing her and wanted revenge for the beatings. She accused him of several crimes but they were unsubstantiated, and as they were local crimes, I referred her to the police. It was my impression that she seemed to be a very sad person. Thanks to John Bailey, Gordon was convicted of attempted bribery and served three years in prison, and John was thanked profusely by Reid for his efforts. According to Jerry, sometime later, John attended a speech given by Reid in which he attacked the federal government and the FBI for intruding into the affairs of Nevada. This infuriated John, but to make matters worse, after the speech Reid approached John and glad-handed him as if they were long lost friends. John considered this to be the ultimate in phoniness and hypocrisy. He felt Reid would say whatever he needed to be popular to a particular group and was completely disingenuous.

I often remembered the wise words of a veteran agent who warned me about the guys in the white hats and his words have proven to be absolutely dead on. One of the most frustrating elements of being an FBI agent was getting a prosecutor to take a serious interest in a case and committing to its prosecution. There are far too many federal cases that fall through the cracks because a prosecutor declines charging the case. Federal prosecutors are graded on their success of convictions, fines, and restitutions, and as such they all have very good paper statistics, usually on the level of 80 to 90 % conviction rates. This success rate for many of the attorneys is based on the fact that many cases end in plea bargains, and only airtight cases are prosecuted. Admittedly, some FBI agents present cases that have no chance of success in court, or cases that may have been shoddily investigated, but there are certainly times when a good case has been declined or neglected by prosecutors. Some grand jury work and aggressive prosecution could result in more convictions of criminals, and probably more acquittals as well, but that is how the system is meant to be.

An example of this neglect to prosecute an important case

even though the Bureau had expended money, manpower, and time occurred in an undercover case targeted at a crooked attorney. An informant had told me of a Marina Del Rey, California, lawyer who frequented Las Vegas and represented himself as a man who could launder large sums of money for various criminal enterprises. He took a piece of the laundered funds and became very wealthy in the process. At my direction, the informant introduced two undercover agents to the attorney. George Togliatti, using the alias Mike Meli, and Jerry Doherty, using the name Jerry Butcher, posed as Detroit mobsters who wanted to launder heroin money in such a way as to show it to be legitimate. The attorney represented that he could take their money to the island of Montserrat in the Caribbean and deposit the funds into a secret bank account in that small nation, where they could then access the funds for their use. The undercover plan was approved by the Bureau, and a quarter of a million dollars in cash was provided. It was determined that George and Jerry would travel with the attorney to Antigua and tape record their conversations for evidence against him. The attorney would then fly to Montserrat on his own and make the banking arrangements. I would travel separately as an agent, but without any authority in either nation, and, of course, I had no authority to carry a weapon in either of those countries.

I traveled ahead of the trio and stayed at the same resort as they did, but kept my distance. I then flew to Montserrat ahead of the attorney on a very turbulent flight in a small puddle-jumper airplane. The wind and rain bounced us around like a cork in the sky, but we finally arrived, and as we landed, a man sitting in the rear of the plane cried out, "Thank you, Jesus!"

The passengers laughed but were happy to have arrived safely. The next morning I met with the Chief Inspector of Police and the British Governor of Montserrat and we laid a plan to have the attorney stopped at customs, searched, and questioned. The plan was executed flawlessly, and the attorney was held for several hours. When questioned about the money, he lied about the source of the $250,000 dollars in his possession. The money was seized and was later turned over to me. The attorney was shaken to his core and terrified of what his mob clients might do to him for losing their money. The tape recording of him rationalizing the loss is hilarious. He explained, "They took the money. There was nothing I could do. They wouldn't listen to anything I said. I promise I'll make it up to you. Just give me some time." The agents continued the charade and appropriately yelled and threatened but gave him a month to come up with the money, which, by the way, he never did.

I flew back to Antigua and had the responsibility to ensure that the Bureau's money was securely returned to the FBI, while the attorney left for home unable to bear the threatening presence of the pretend mobsters. Jerry and George took advantage of the sun and beach while we waited for our return flight, and I sat in the room looking at the briefcase stuffed with $100 bills. I couldn't take sitting in my room while my companions enjoyed the resort, so I walked to the beach in my swim trunks carrying the stuffed briefcase. We sat in the sun with the money between us and had a good laugh.

The next day, our flight was scheduled to leave in the afternoon, and as we stood in line waiting to have our carry-on luggage scanned, the x-ray machine broke down. This left one lone uniformed security guard scanning the packages with his eyes as they passed on the conveyor belt. I thought it was hilarious as he watched the packages and suitcases go by, and I jokingly thought to myself, *This guy must have x-ray vision.* Suddenly things were not so funny as he grabbed my briefcase from the conveyor belt and ordered me to unlock it. I looked at him for a second. I had no other option or he would have seized the case, so I complied. When the case was opened, his x-ray eyes got wide as he stared at the contents. I did what I had to do, knowing the money could easily have been confiscated or stolen. The director would be very unhappy if that happened, so I flashed my credential and said, "Official business." I closed the case, grabbed it out of his hands, and walked to the plane parked on the tarmac some 50 yards away. I didn't dare look back and expected armed police to take me into custody at any moment, but, miraculously, nothing happened. When the plane took off, I may have been the happiest man on board and I mentally joined the man in the puddle jumper plane as I thought to myself, *Thank you, Jesus.* Even to this day, I chuckle at the experience.

A week or so later, Agent Bill Mathews and I interviewed the subject attorney in Marina Del Rey and showed him posed mug shots of George and Jerry, but he stonewalled and denied ever having met them. The case was presented to the AUSA for prosecution, but nothing ever happened. He was so overworked, or so he said, that the case was never taken any further. We appealed many times for action, but it never came. The case eventually slipped through the cracks into a black hole, and the crooked attorney walks free to this day. It isn't possible to describe my anger and frustration with this sorry result.

I was down in the dumps about the frustration of non-prosecution of my crooked attorney case when I discovered a fledgling career prosecutor. Jerry Doherty and I attended the initial court appearance for defendant, former Los Angeles Police Officer Steve Homick and co-defendant Michael Dominguez, who had been charged with racketeering for two contract killings in Los Angeles and three Las Vegas murders. The Las Vegas killings were brutal. Doherty had determined that Homick had invaded a house and forced a woman to tell him where her jewelry was located, and after robbing her, he shot her dead. Moments later, a deliveryman knocked on the door and Homick invited him in and cold-bloodedly shot the man to death for no reason. The third murder occurred when Homick and Dominguez tried to force an 80-year-old man to give them the location of his money stash, which, by the way, didn't exist. They beat the poor old man with an iron rod, then put him in his bathtub filled with ice cold water, and repeatedly pushed his head under the water in an effort to get him to comply. As a result, the poor old man died of a heart attack in his own bath. Dominguez confessed to Doherty, "That old guy was tough. He wouldn't tell us anything. He just stared at us when we pushed him under the water." These two hired guns had also killed a husband and wife in California at the request of their sons. The sons were sent to prison, and one of them, climbing the heights of hypocrisy, filed a lawsuit in federal court demanding he be served kosher food, as it was important for the observance of his religion.

The killers were very bad guys and they were surrounded in court by U.S. Marshals as brand new Strike Force Attorney Jane Shoemaker walked into the small courtroom of the U.S. Magistrate

Judge for the hearing. She had a stack of files tucked under her left arm and was substituting for the assigned prosecutor in the case. Initial appearances are simple affairs where the indictment is read to the defendant and the attorneys are allowed to argue bail. When it came time for Shoemaker to speak, despite the silence in the courtroom, we could barely hear her as she timidly presented the government's position of no bail. Jerry turned to me and asked, "What have we got here? She's scared to death." I agreed with him, but our initial assessment turned out to be completely wrong. Homick was sentenced to death in California and Nevada, but remains on death row. Dominguez was sentenced to life in prison and spends 23 hours a day in his cell in the Pelican Bay prison of northern California.

After Jane's first public performance, she quickly evolved to become one of the very best prosecutors I had the pleasure to work with. She was smart and extremely prepared in the law, but more than anything, she had the heart of a prosecutor. As a result, we became a team – I brought the cases and she vigorously prosecuted them. I would often call Jane to discuss cases, and frequently the office receptionist was a substitute and didn't know me. She would go through the requisite questions: "Who are you? May I ask what you want to talk to her about? Let me see if she's available." After waiting for some time, I decided on another method of attack to circumvent the receptionist's questions. From that time forward when a substitute receptionist was on duty, I would say, "This is doctor Magnesen. I need to speak with Jane Shoemaker please. Tell her the test results are in." This immediately got me through every time. When I retired, the Strike Force presented me with a plaque that stated in part, " . . .

Gary 'the doctor' Magnesen." On another occasion, a new SAC had been assigned to Las Vegas. He didn't know me, and one day I ran into him in the FBI office and he questioned, "Doctor, what are you doing here?" At first, I thought he was making a joke, but then I found out that when the SAC had visited Jerry Doherty at his home while he was recuperating from a serious illness, I happened to be there and the SAC had somehow assumed I was Jerry's physician.

Las Vegas has long been a destination for mobsters to come and recreate, but in the 1990s we had an influx of "old mustaches" from the Big Apple that made Vegas their permanent residence. They came to Sin City for the sun and to get away from the hassles and problems of the big city. They wanted to settle down and live out their lives in peace, but we knew who they were and we wouldn't allow them to forget their crimes committed over a lifetime, so we targeted them. We hung photographs of our known LCN members on the walls of our squad room to remind us of their presence. From approximately 1990 to 1996, we investigated and convicted no less than seven New York LCN members who made the mistake of settling in Las Vegas. This is a remarkable statistic, as Las Vegas has no LCN family and we were essentially left with picking up the scraps that had moved to Las Vegas.

There is one case that stands out in my mind as it is near the top of my despicable scale. It involved a mobster wannabe punk who preyed on elderly, lonely widows. After endearing himself to them, he was able to convince the poor souls that he could make them wealthy if they would invest in his race horses. The victims trusted him completely and gave him their life savings, which he took home to his flight attendant wife, who thought he was a professional gambler. The problem was that he had no race horses, and once the money was obtained, he dropped the widows like so much excess baggage. I obtained an indictment against him and developed a source in the neighborhood who told me that the con-man took his flight attendant wife to work every day, then returned home. I called the neighbor and he informed me that he had seen the man come home and park in his garage, so I took two first-office agents with me and we went out to arrest the guy. After ringing the door bell for some time, it was obvious he wasn't coming to the door, so we went about trying to gain access to the house. I found a sliding patio door in the rear and was able to jimmy it open, and as we had probable cause that he was home, we made entry. We searched the house and found the degenerate sound asleep in an upstairs bedroom. I grabbed him by the arm and yanked him out of his slumber and onto the floor. His wide-eyed disbelief as he stood exposed in his striped boxer shorts made the whole case worthwhile.

Another one of my cases involved drug dealer Joseph Balzano, the night manager of the now closed Crazy Horse topless bar on Paradise Road in Las Vegas who sold some cocaine to undercover agent Rick Bacon. Straw man and attorney Joseph Monteiro had been set up as the front man for the place but it was actually owned by Vito Di Filippo, a Bonanno family capo. The original owner, Tony Albanese, had disappeared, and his skull with a bullet hole had been found by hikers in the California desert sometime before. Balzano was arrested on the drug charge, and he knew he was in deep trouble because he had been warned by Di Filippo that if he ever dealt in drugs again, he was a dead man. After being released on bond, Balzano locked himself in his house, surrounded by various friends, because he knew he was in big trouble. One of his friends, not realizing the depth of the situation, had a craving for ice cream and went to the store dressed in Balzano's jacket and driving his car, but he never came back. A day later his body was found face down in the scrub of the Las Vegas desert. His hands were handcuffed behind his back and he had been shot several times in the head with a .22 caliber rifle. Metro's homicide detectives surmised that someone posing as police officers had grabbed him in the parking lot of the grocery store where Balzano's car was recovered and took him out and finished him, thinking they had Balzano. The killing was clearly a professional hit, but was never solved.

Balzano was devastated by the loss of his friend, but he had nowhere to turn, so he weighed his options and decided to cooperate with the FBI. After debriefing Balzano on his criminal career, Dennis Arnoldy and I were preparing to transport him from the old Federal Building to jail. As we walked him to the Bureau parking lot behind the court building, an elderly Nevada Supreme Court Justice, who was allowed to park his vehicle in the lot as a courtesy, approached us. He had had a few too many in the bar across the street when he stumbled upon us. Balzano, in a good mood, smiled at the judge and asked, "How you doin, Pops?" The judge, apparently in a foul mood responded, "What the hell do you mean, Pops?" and tightened his fist and approached Balzano. Joe started laughing, but Dennis and I had to get between the two and informed the old judge, "This is a federal prisoner; you don't want to get involved with this." The judge came to his senses and got in his 1964 red Ford convertible and angrily drove off. The judge had no idea who he was dealing with. Balzano's testimony resulted in charging Di Filippo and front man Joseph Monteiro with extortion. They went to trial and Joseph Monteiro was convicted, but the jury hung up on Di Filippo. One of the jurors refused to vote for guilty because he said Di Filippo was "too old to go to jail."

Our offensive against the LCN was contagious. Everyone on the squad wanted a piece of the action, and as success breeds success, everyone wanted to play a vital role in the many cases we made. Our Las Vegas squad became a team, a relentless band in much the same way as had in done in Milwaukee. I have always considered the Las Vegas Division to be the biggest little FBI division in the United States. The work is voluminous and worthwhile, but the constant pressures of crime fighting can be physically and mentally draining. Humor is an effective defense mechanism against some of the horrible cases we had to deal with. Our practical jokes helped vent the pressure and, I believe, built camaraderie. One morning about two weeks before Christmas, I arrived at my cubicle and found a Christmas ornament hanging from the ceiling. I recognized it immediately as a Norwegian, straw ornament shaped like an angel. I asked who had hung it, but of course, no one would say a word. For the next five mornings, I found a new straw ornament in the shape of a reindeer or other Christmas symbol. I can imagine how everyone waited for me to arrive each morning to see my response. All I could do was shrug and ask, "Come on, who's doing this?" It wasn't as if it was a big deal - I was accumulating nice ornaments. Finally, Joe Degnan confessed. He explained that his wife had bought the ornaments at a garage sale.

Degnan, an agent and an attorney, developed a case on a big dope dealer who we learned had 9 children by 9 different women. He was heartless and was sent on a long stretch in prison. Later Joe investigated a case on Fredrick "Rick" Rizzolo, owner of the Crazy Horse Too topless lounge who had been closely associated with Bonanno Capo Di Filippo and LCN member Vincent Faraci. Rizzolo had worked with Balzano and Vito Di Filippo at the old Crazy Horse club and subsequently had become a millionaire. Degnan was transferred before the case was indicted but Bob Bennett picked up the ball and successfully brought it to prosecution, which ended in the conviction of Rizzolo, a high rolling whale who gambled many of his millions on Las Vegas casino tables.

A whole series of cases against LCN members were made possible because Special Agent Bill Matthews, a CPA, had organized a brilliant undercover operation where mob guys could obtain fraudulent credit lines from the old Maxim Casino. The participants provided false personal information and received thousands of dollars in credit to gamble with. They played the tables a little, then took the remainder of the chips to the cage and cashed them in. The operation was very successful and resulted in numerous convictions thanks to Bill and Jane Shoemaker's prosecutorial efforts. The crown jewel of Matthews' efforts was the conviction of Charlie "Moose" Panarella, a Colombo family capo.

Special Agent Michael Howie and I, as co-case agents, developed a case in which various Nevada guys obtained slot machines and shipped them to New York City, where they were used in gambling operations run by the LCN. In another major case, we used my well placed informant who set up a social club where the informant's pals hung out. Howie, a work horse and former clerk in the Los Angeles Office, handled the excellent but very difficult informant masterfully. Many of the source's pals were various mobsters, including Peter Milano, the Los Angeles LCN underboss. The informant wined and dined his guests daily, at the Bureau's expense, and they discussed past crimes and future illegal projects. All the conversations were taped and eventually used against them in court. The case was extremely productive and resulted in the convictions of several men, including Milano. Additionally, the murder of Herbie Blitzstein, former henchman for Tony Spilotro, was also solved as a result of loose talk in the FBI-sponsored social club.

Natale "Big Chris" Richichi, a Gambino family capo, and very close confidant of once Gambino boss, John Gotti, moved to Las Vegas for the warm weather. He was getting old, and the cold of New York City had taken its toll on him and his wife. His son, Sal, lived in Los Angeles, where he made and distributed porno films. Richichi bought a home inside the walls of the Las Vegas Country Club Estates and settled in. The New York Division had given us a heads up that Big Chris was coming, and when he arrived our surveillance squad busied themselves with determining his movement and contacts. We learned that he daily drove his dark chocolate-brown Mercedes 550 SL to an old friend's house and they would drive around town with no apparent destination. My first target was Richichi's home phone, and after extensive work, with the able assistance of first office agent John Chaddick, an affidavit was prepared and approved and we began listening to his conversations. We learned early on that he would contact an old New York mob buddy before picking him up. We had monitored enough telephone conversations that indicated they discussed criminal activities inside the car so I made that a target. In addition, Big Chris was in regular contact with Kenny Guarino, a major distributor of pornography in Rhode Island and New England who provided Richichi with his beautiful car. Guarino owned a sprawling estate on Narragansett Bay and sailed a 50-foot yacht worth $650,000. He grossed $8 million a month from his porno business and had contact with former Gambino boss John Gotti and other mobsters, and, of course, Guarino and Richichi were financially connected at the hip.

After receiving court authorization, we embarked on one of the most difficult microphone installations of my career. The target Mercedes was always parked in the driveway in sight of Richichi's front window. We learned that he stayed up late at night, sometimes into the early morning hours, so we had a very narrow window of opportunity to install the microphone. I am not authorized to disclose the methods and techniques of the installation, but it was accomplished. Dark fate came into the picture when, within days, Big Chris' friend went to the doctor and was diagnosed with a fast moving bone cancer that had spread throughout his body. He was hospitalized and never came out alive. As a result, the daily drives ended abruptly. The dark ghosts had struck again, protecting their shady mob associates. Then, before we had an opportunity to remove the microphone from the Mercedes, we intercepted a phone call from Guarino saying he had ordered a new car for Big Chris and a truck would pick up the old one that afternoon. I drove down to the area and found an auto-hauler truck parked near the house and the Mercedes was already loaded. I engaged the driver in small talk about the fancy cars he had aboard, including a red Corvette and a beautiful green Jaguar convertible. I asked where he was headed, and he replied, "Back east. The Corvette goes to Pennsylvania, the Jag goes to Maine, and the Mercedes goes to Rhode Island." We notified our Rhode Island office, and they, at a later date, obtained judicial authority to remove the microphone.

Richichi had run the Gambino family's pornography empire out of south Florida for years, and he continued to have his hooks into porno through Kenny Guarino, who, by all rights, should have been paying off the Boston mob, but the Gambinos owned him and refused to give him up to Boston. It was a simple matter of which LCN family was stronger. We knew from various phone conversations that Guarino was sending Richichi what he referred to as "food" through Federal Express. Our investigation determined that all Fed Ex deliveries to Big Chris were flat envelopes, nothing that could contain food. So we were sure the food was actually a reference to cash, Richichi's piece from the porno business.

In the middle of everything, Big Chris began dealing with a mobster named Frank Nesci from Long Island, New York, who was working on a construction scam. Chris recommended a construction job in Las Vegas, so Nesci came to Vegas and stayed at the Flamingo-Hilton, where a meeting with Chris was scheduled in his room. With the excellent assistance of Agent John Chaddick, a veteran Marine Corps officer, we hustled and received emergency authorization for a microphone and a video camera to be placed in Nesci's suite. We were under tight time constraints and completed the installation only a short time before his check-in. We had set up for monitoring in an adjacent room, but because of a glitch by a hotel desk clerk, the room assigned to Nesci was the very room we were in. We were waiting with anticipation for the target to arrive when our room door was unlocked by the bell hop. Luckily, we had secured the chain lock on the door, so it could only be opened a few inches. There we were, sitting with tape recorders and a video screen for the whole world to see. If the door had been opened a few inches more we would have been compromised, but this time, the good angels smiled upon us and we weren't detected. Before long, Richichi arrived and the two men began discussing their plans, when a phone call came in for Nesci. To our chagrin, the dark ghosts had come back. We could only hear Nesci's side of the conversation as he said, "Oh, where are they now? I'll come right home." He hung up and mumbled something to Richichi and they both left the room. We had no idea what had happened, but we worried that they had somehow been tipped off.

We subsequently learned that the New York City FBI was conducting massive raids on the Gambino Crime Family, including the arrest of Gambino boss, John Gotti, and Nesci had returned to participate in the cover up. Some days later, we monitored Richichi speaking with Guarino on the phone. Guarino said, " Sammy Bull. He turned."

Richichi, in shock, responded, " . . . I can't believe it! … This is bad news. This is very, very bad news. I mean all around. I mean for me and you, you know what I'm talking about?"

Guarino: "Yeah, I guess he's in that same circle."

Richcichi: "He's three, top three."

Guarino: "You're kidding?"

Richichi: "Yeah. He's second."

Guarino: "Unbelievable."

Richichi: "I can't believe this.... everything is over, there."

Richichi, in this terse conversation, explained that "Sammy the Bull"[Gravano], Gotti's underboss, had rolled over and was cooperating with the FBI, and this was devastating news. As a side note, Gotti was eventually convicted in federal court in New York City and was sentenced to life in prison where he hired members of white supremacist gang the Aryan Brotherhood to protect him from other prisoners. The mob boss mistakenly discontinued his insurance payments, and he was attacked by another inmate and beaten badly. He died in prison of throat cancer not long after.

Later, we also placed a microphone in a Dunes Hotel suite where Guarino and Richichi were to meet, but the meeting never happened. We also obtained authorization for a microphone to be placed at an outdoor table where Richichi sat with other mobsters at the annual Las Vegas San Gennaro Feast but they kept switching tables, so we weren't able to make the installation. Chaddick was transferred to Chinese language school, so I told supervisor George Togliatti I needed an able assistant to help with the Richichi case.

Not long after, George asked me to come into his office. He introduced me to Caroline "C.J." Kelliher, a first office agent who had just graduated from FBI training school. George said, "Caroline is a former Marine Corps officer who served in the Gulf War." I shook her hand and said, "Nice to meet you. Welcome to Las Vegas." Then I sat down and George dropped a bomb. "I want you to be her training agent." I slouched down in my chair and made a face. "George, I'm too busy for this. I don't have time to train another new agent." I could see Kelliher stiffen. George continued, "She can help you. She'll be a good agent." Kelliher and I left George's office, and she was steaming. She blurted out, "What's wrong, don't you want to work with a woman?" I looked at her intently. "What does you being a woman have to do with anything? If you pull your load, I don't have a problem." I know she didn't believe me, but it was true. We soon came to an understanding, and she worked out very well. I always stressed two major points with trainees. These were: always watch your back – there are some very bad guys out there, and be relentless in your pursuit of bad guys – never give up.

When it came time to search Richichi's home, I decide we would use a ruse to get the door open so we wouldn't have to knock it down. Richichi had bragged over the phone that he never came to the door for anyone, so it was decided that C.J. Kelliher would go to the door and ring the bell. Big Chris peeked through the blinds and saw a young lady, and as he had developed a taste for ladies over the years, he broke his rule and opened the door and we were inside in an instant. Unfortunately, the search produced very little evidence, but Oscar Goodman showed up and monitored the whole process. Later, Kelliher was transferred to another squad where she developed an informant who solved a major casino robbery.

Before long, we intercepted a conversation between Big Chris and Guarino where they discussed Guarino sending "food" to Chris to help with his legal expenses. Guarino told Richichi that to be safe, the food would be sent to Richichi's son, Sal, in LA and he would have one of Sal's teenage sons drive the package to Las Vegas and deliver it. On the appointed day, we observed Big Sal's son arriving at Oscar Goodman's office, and later he went to his grandfather's house. We were convinced that the attorney's fees sent from Guarino, had been delivered, and prosecutor Jane Shoemaker determined to go as far as it took in an effort to force Goodman to produce his financial records for the Richichi case, thereby proving his attorney fees came from Guarino's porno business. A grand jury subpoena was served on Goodman, and he, understandably, went ballistic at what he considered to be an attack on attorney client privilege. Unfortunately for him, the 9th Circuit Court of Appeals had ruled that attorney financial records are not covered by the constitutional privilege, so the fight was on. In spite of the ruling, Goodman went before the grand jury and respectfully declined to produce the records.

In April of 1994, Goodman found himself before Federal Judge Philip Pro to answer for his contempt of court by refusing to divulge the source of Richichi's attorney's fees, as the mobster hadn't had a legitimate source of income for decades. Goodman put on a good front. He said any sanction wouldn't bother him, as he was defending his client's rights, so he fought on. Goodman informed the court that, "I cannot tell the court that I personally received any monies; my office did. The receipt was for the monies actually received; those monies were deposited in the bank."

About one month later, Goodman was again before Judge Pro. The courtroom was packed with media and attorneys on both sides of the issue, waiting to see what was going to happen. It was high drama. Judge Pro found Goodman to be in contempt and ordered that he be taken into custody until he complied with the grand jury's demand. The government didn't want to make Goodman a martyr, so Pro stayed his order until all appeals were exhausted. Then Jane Shoemaker decided to ask the court to impose a fine instead jail time, and one month later Judge Pro had had enough, so he ordered Goodman to pay a $25,000 fine plus $2,500 for each day he went without compliance. The order could go on forever unless Goodman relented. Goodman responded to reporters after the hearing, saying "If they think money means more to me than jail time, they're nuts. What they couldn't do to me with the threat of jail, they can't do to me with the threat of money." Goodman bravely held out for 10 days, but then his fortitude crumbled. After paying $50,000 in fines, he had had enough and gave in, to a degree. He provided a form containing very limited information, which never divulged the actual source of the funds, but technically he had complied. The government could have fought on but, in the end, we didn't need it. Richichi, age 75, was convicted and sent to prison, where he passed away in the solitude of his cell knowing that the FBI had arrested him only months before he was to move to Costa Rica to live out his life on the shores of the Pacific Ocean and where he would have been out of the reach of the FBI. Oscar Goodman is now the popular mayor of Las Vegas, a city he loves.

Chicago's political "pay to play" corruption is legendary. For example, in 1986 a massive FBI undercover investigation, code named "Gray Lord," resulted in the conviction of 17 Chicago judges, 48 lawyers, 10 deputy sheriffs, and 8 police officers. The undercover operation included several FBI agents, who were also attorneys, posing as crooked lawyers who worked the Chicago system, developing evidence against dirty officials. In 1987, another FBI case, code named "Gambit," resulted in the indictment of Chicago 1ˢᵗ Ward, "machine," Alderman, Fred Roti and his assistant, Outfit associate Pat Marcy. They had conspired to sell judgeships and for years had taken kickbacks for favors provided. Things haven't changed much in the Windy City, as the bumbling, impeached governor, Rod Blagojevich, has been indicted for the same pay to play schemes. Interestingly, in 1978, mob boss Joey Aiuppa made a comment about the Outfit's influence in Chicago, "We've got everyone in Chicago wrapped up except the FBI. Wouldn't this be a great place if it wasn't for the 'G?'"

The Chicago FBI kept plugging along, persistently probing the weaknesses of the Outfit, when, in 1999, Chicago mobster Frank Calabrese Jr., who was serving time in prison, had had enough of "the life." So, with some trepidation, he communicated by letter with the Chicago FBI organized crime squad and offered his cooperation. A seven year investigation resulted from the communiqué, as Frank Jr. surreptitiously recorded countless conversations between himself and other mobsters, including his father, Frank Sr., who was also serving time in prison. One conversation that piqued the interest of Chicago agents was when the father and son were discussing Tony Spilotro. Frank Sr. told his son that Joey Aiuppa had ordered the killing of Tony Spilotro because he was committing unauthorized crimes in Vegas and, worst of all, Aiuppa learned that Tony was sleeping with " . . . that guy's wife. That's a no-no. That's a no-no. That was the nail in his coffin." The FBI investigation pressed on and looked into the murder of Big John Fecarotta. The investigators caused the examination of the bloody glove dropped near the murder scene and recovered by police. The glove was removed from the Chicago Police Department's evidence vault and submitted for DNA analysis, and it was determined that Nicholas "Nick

Calabrese's DNA was identical to the blood on the glove. "Nick", an Outfit member, and Frank Sr.'s younger brother was visited in jail by the FBI and ordered to submit to an X-ray of his left arm, where they saw healed scar tissue proving a through-and-through bullet wound, the result of his accidental self inflicted injury while struggling with Fecarotta. Calabrese knew the murder of Fecarotta, cinched by the forensic evidence, would put him on death row, so after some consideration, he determined that his self preservation trumped his oath of omerta and he rolled over.

Crooked cops are despicable. In my opinion they are worse than mobsters, as they can cause great damage and often give up undercover agents and details of investigations to the bad guys. Chicago Police Officer Anthony Doyle, whose real name is Anthony Passafume, and Cook County Sheriff's Deputy Mike Ricci had inside information about the FBI's investigation so they tipped off Calabrese Sr. that the FBI had obtained the bloody glove and his own brother might be indicted for Fecarotta's murder. Frank Sr., after learning of this fact, told his son, Frank Jr. "I don't wanna see nothing happen to him, but let me tell you something. If somebody feels it's, it's either them or him, he's gone. That's the bed he made." Unlike his brother, the misguided code was alive and well with Frank Calabrese Sr. Nick's cooperation had far reaching results. When Paul Schiro, the multiple murderer and Spilotro's former crew member, learned that Calabrese had turned, he told an associate, "Calabrese could put me away forever."

On June 19, 2007, the final chapter in Tony Spilotro's sordid life came to an end in a federal courtroom in Chicago. Assistant United States Attorney Mitch Mars, with the able assistance of FBI Special Agent Michael Maseth, brought an indictment of

14 Outfit mobsters. Two defendants died before trial, including Deputy Sheriff, Mike Ricci. Also, hitman Frank Schweihs was too ill for trial and died at the age of 75 in July 2008. Joey Lombardo went into hiding for nine months but, in agony, secretly met with dentist Vincent Spilotro to have an abscessed tooth treated. Vincent was Tony and Michael Spilotro's brother and held deep hatred for those who had killed his brothers. As a result, Vincent dropped a dime on Lombardo and he was arrested by the FBI and later was convicted.

Frank Calabrese Jr. testified in the trial known as "The Family Secrets Case," and his damning tape recordings were presented. Prolific hitman Nick Calabrese, even though he admitted to taking part in no less than 14 murders, was the star witness in the trial. He provided graphic testimony as to the murders of the Spilotro brothers, John Fecarotta, and many others. He amplified the details of the Spilotro hits when he explained that mob boss James "Little Jimmy" Marcello had delivered the men to their meeting with death. Nick Calabrese went on to testify that he, Joseph Ferriola, Joey Lombardo, Jimmy La Pietra, John Fecarotta, John Di Fronzo, Louis Marino, Louis Eboli, Ernest Infelise, and Sam Garlisi all took an active role in the deadly pummeling of the Spilotros. He added that Fecarotta, Albert Tocco, Albert Roviero, Dominic Palermo, and Nick Gussino had participated in burying the two battered bodies. A virtual "whose who" of the Chicago Outfit had taken part in the ten against two ambush, a predatory pack that pounded the men to death, literally giving their stamp of approval for the hit. The mass participation in the murders by so many high ranking members is, as far as I am aware, unprecedented.

At Nick Calabrese's sentencing the Chicago prosecuting attorney addressed the court on behalf of his star witness. "On the one hand, he's a cold blooded killer who operates in an almost robotic fashion. While without question, he committed terrible deeds, Calabrese never was a guy celebrating later at a bar." Then he added, [Calabrese] "showed us the underbelly of Chicago." Some may question such support by the government for a cold blooded killer. Unfortunately, sometimes the government is left without an alternative and makes deals with criminals who have committed heinous acts. The overriding consideration is: could the prosecution of other cold blooded mobsters who are part of an ongoing criminal organization be successful without the help of an equally guilty witness? If the answer is no, then the government is obligated to proceed with the cooperation for the overall good of society. This is often a very difficult choice, but it has to be made.

Calabrese pleaded guilty to a lesser charge with no excuses. He made no rationalizations, but explained curtly to the court, "I chose my path in life." He was sentenced to 12 years in prison after testifying about 22 mob murders, four attempted murders, five bombings, and providing 60 names of Chicago made members. A hard blow had been struck against the Chicago mob, but the festering canker that is the Outfit hasn't been finished off, and until it is, it will continue to devour members of civil society. An interesting aside is that after Frank Calabrese Sr. was convicted and sentenced to life in prison, the FBI searched his house in Oak Brook, Illinois (as a result of the government seizing his home) in March of 2010. There they discovered a compartment hidden behind a large family photograph. A treasure trove was found inside the wall space, and $728,000 in cash, 1000 pieces of jewelry, and seven guns were retrieved. Additionally, $26,000 in cash was seized from a locked desk drawer. In the case of Calabrese, crime certainly paid him well for many years.

The high profile Family Secrets racketeering case ended with the conviction of Outfit boss James Marcello, who had taken over for Joey Aiuppa. He received a life sentence, Joseph "The Clown" Lombardo received life, and Frank Calabrese Sr. also received a life sentence. Several others pled guilty in the massive case and, crooked Chicago Police Officer Anthony "Twan" Doyle was sentenced to 12 years in prison for providing the mob with inside police information. Spilotro crew member, Paul Schiro, was convicted of conspiring to murder Mel Vaci for participating in the planning of the hit and acting as a lookout. The 71-year-old Schiro was sentenced to 20 years, a virtual death sentence. He was already serving time in prison, along with former Chicago Chief of Detectives William Hanhardt, for a 2001 jewelry theft. Tony Spilotro and his crew of killers are gone. They began their criminal careers as teenage punks in the tough city of Chicago, but it took nearly 55 years to finally convict one of them for murder. It happened to be for the homicide of Emil Vaci, a little man who knew too much and who had refused to testify in my investigation of the Jay Vandermark murder.

In the words of Frank Cullotta, "When the FBI gets onto you, you're in trouble. Everybody knows it. Tony knew it. They put a tight case together and there isn't anything you can do." Cullotta also told me, "The Outfit talks about honor – there is no honor. It's all about money and power." He added, "Chicago left Rosenthal alone after the bomb. He had learned his lesson and had left town. That's what they wanted. He was out of their hair. They must have thought he would never turn against them. Maybe if he had been charged with something, they would have changed their minds." Frank Cullotta has been reborn; he is a new man. He is engaging and pleasant to deal with. He even acted as a consultant in the movie, *Casino,* in 1995 and he played a role near the end of the movie. He explained that the character of Nick Santoro in the movie was supposed to be Tony Spilotro, and Sam "Ace" Rothstein was a portrayal of Frank Rosenthal. Frank is a success story for the FBI. He is filled with memories of the past, but has no desire to return to the dark side of the street.

Screen writer Nicholas Pileggi wrote the forward to the book, *Cullotta,* by Dennis Griffin. A partial quote by Pileggi states. "Frank Cullotta is the real thing. I found that out when working on *Casino,* a book about the skim at the Stardust Hotel in Las Vegas… Cullotta turned out to be an invaluable resource. His memory was phenomenal. He's the kind of person who remembers his license plate numbers from decades ago, and this is a man who usually owned three or four cars at once… Martin Scorsese, the director with whom I wrote the script for *Casino* realized Cullotta's value immediately and hired him as a technical advisor during the production of the film, which was shot on location in Las Vegas… He had Cullotta recreate the Lisner murder scene on film. The man you see in the film, chasing the victim around the house, emptying bullets into his head, and finally tossing him in the pool, is the real Frank Cullotta, the same man who did the actual murder for which he was given immunity. I cannot think of another film in which the killing being depicted on screen is reenacted by the man who committed the original murder."

Lefty Rosenthal was running out of gas. He began to slow down and moved into a Miami Beach condominium, where he ran an Internet, sports tout service. His social life was relegated to hanging out at the 112 Restaurant almost nightly. As he once said, "When I find a place I like - I stick with it." In his latter years he became somewhat philosophical about his gambling life. When describing his management style he said, "The Chairman and I held to the theory that there are three ways to operate a public corporation, 'The right way, the wrong way, or our way." In discussing Las Vegas he stated the obvious, " . . . the number one industry, obviously, in the state of Nevada is casino gambling. There would be no Nevada without gambling." He also came to recognize the ills of gambling when he admitted "Las Vegas has the highest suicide rate in the nation. It can be a real heart break ridge." Then he told a story that had haunted him for many years. "I remember one situation where a family, a husband, wife and two children had saved up for a vacation to Vegas. They saw a sign '49 cent breakfast.' They waited in line for breakfast and the father went to the blackjack table while they waited. Within minutes, the guy lost $18,000. He was so broke that he had to ask for money to buy gas so they could get back home. We got his $18,000 and gave him a small pittance so they could get home. That's a heartbreaking story but it happens on an everyday basis. The glitz of the town is seducing. It sucks you in and has destroyed many a man."

Rosenthal never seemed able to admit that his actions and his past were to blame for his negative treatment by Nevada gaming officials. He once said, "In retrospect, his [Spilotro's] reputation and the fact that we were boyhood friends – there was no way for me to overcome." He also once mused about relying on others, "If you want a good friend, buy a dog." When asked about his fondest memories he replied, "Becoming a father ranks first. Divorce, runs second. Third, the miracle at Tony Roma's." He was once asked about the importance of money in his life. He replied, "Money can buy just about anything other than loyalty, health, and happiness." On October 13, 2008, the legend died of a heart attack while at home at the age of 79. I wonder if he won his last bet?

On October 30, 2008, Jane Ann Morrison wrote her column in the *Las Vegas Review Journal*. She stated, "…Now that Rosenthal is dead, three former law enforcement sources with first-hand knowledge confirmed what was long suspected. Lefty Rosenthal was an FBI informant, whether his attorney knew it or not. While Rosenthal was alive, no one would confirm it. Nobody wanted to be the one who got Lefty whacked… it is confirmed Rosenthal was a 'top echelon' informant, someone with first hand knowledge of the top ranking bosses. Rosenthal's code name was 'Achilles,' one source said… it is a sly reference to the handsome Greek warrior who was invincible except for his heel… I couldn't confirm exactly when he started informing to the FBI, but the relationship was lengthy and useful. His information helped the FBI develop a lot of organized crime and casino skimming cases. Rosenthal was an informant even before the 1982 bombing of his Cadillac outside Tony Roma's restaurant on Sahara Avenue . . . Later he told the Chicago Tribune he rebuffed the offer to become a federal witness. 'It's just not my style. It doesn't fit into my principles.' …He talked about everything and everyone, whether he had first hand knowledge, like he did at the Stardust, or second – and

third-hand knowledge like at the Tropicana, one source said…
The indictments were many, so were the convictions. Despite the
extensive wiretapping, Rosenthal was never charged, even though
authorities described him as the man who 'orchestrated the skim
at the Stardust.' … He may not have testified, but he definitely
talked." Unfortunately, I am not authorized to comment on
Morrison's revelation.

There exists a class of individuals who, by their very nature,
are understandably viewed with scorn by criminal peers. These
men are derisively referred to as stool pigeons, stoolies, snitches,
turncoats, informers, and rats. They are hated and feared at the
same time because they hold inside information about crimes and
perpetrators that can lead to years in prison. Hatred by criminals
is one thing, but this visceral hatred is often embraced by defense
attorneys, as well. To these defenders of criminals, the once
crooks who roll over and cooperate with law enforcement are the
lowest form of life, dirty scum often referred to as "filthy rats."
I've often wondered how this mental twist in otherwise normal
attorneys can be so hateful. It's as if the attorneys have sided with
the crooks and have reached far beyond defending his clients. It's
as if the cooperating witness has personally turned against the
attorney. Am I saying that mob witnesses are always honest and
wholesome? Of course not. They are what they are. They were
once career criminals, men who lived the life, and very few of
them come willingly to law enforcement because they have seen
the error of their ways. They come for various reasons; they may
come over as an act of revenge against more powerful criminals
who have wronged them, they come because they want special
treatment in a particular matter or to mitigate criminal charges

against them, they may come for the money the FBI may offer, or they come because they like to play the game.

Most of the time, cooperating criminals are required to testify against associates in open court as part of their plea agreement. They receive some sort of immunity for many of their crimes and usually plead to one felony charge. This is usually a source of consternation for the defense, but think about it, if the government required a witness to plead guilty to every crime, then said, "You testify and we will send you to prison for the rest of your life," how many witnesses would agree to such a ridiculous deal? Sometimes a mobster is convicted for many crimes, including murder, and then requests a deal so as to save himself from the death chamber and agrees to testify against former associates. In these cases, the witness is required to testify, but remains in a witness protection prison for the rest of his life.

There are many levels of informants. There is the street snitch, who drops a dime on a fellow dope dealer. There is the criminal who hears about a planned bank robbery and informs police. There is the confidential source who introduces an undercover officer to a drug dealer so a buy can be made. Then there are certain men who function on the highest levels of criminal cabals. For example, the brother of a drug lord, the bodyguard of a worldwide terrorist, or a high level mobster who is embedded in the LCN and can provide a constant stream of high level intelligence. These priceless human assets are referred to as Top Echelon Informants in the FBI and their identity is aggressively protected. Except in very rare situations, these informants would never testify in open court. These men are not Boy Scouts, but they provide invaluable eyes and ears inside the belly of the beast.

There have been many organized crime figures connected to the development of Las Vegas, but another key player on the neon stage that is Las Vegas is Steve Wynn. Wynn, the son of Mike Weinburg, past owner of several East Coast bingo parlors. Weinburg was a degenerate gambler who owed $350,000 to various bookmakers when he passed away in 1963. Steve Weinburg, who changed his name to Wynn, was able to pay off the debts and began a remarkable climb to remake Sin City. His first significant acquisition was a run- down, sawdust gambling joint located on Freemont Street called the Golden Nugget. The place was literally remade and brought fresh air to the floundering Glitter Gulch. He then went on a building spree and invented the Las Vegas classy, themed mega resort. He began with the Mirage, then the Treasure Island, the Bellagio, the Wynn Las Vegas, and finally the Encore. A major paradigm shift had occurred in Vegas, and many other resorts followed his lead. As a result, corporations have taken over the Strip, and the neon city has changed forever. Many retired agents are now employed by casino corporate security departments, where they oversee employee wrongdoing and vet all vendors for any organized crime connections.

Fame and money sometimes draw the bottom feeders in our society, and in 1993, Kevyn Wynn, daughter of Steve, was kidnapped by a group of crooks, and a ransom was paid by Wynn for the return of his daughter. The Las Vegas Division of the FBI poured in its investigative assets and arrested the perpetrators, and Kevin was returned unharmed. This was the only major Las Vegas case I played no part in. Some have said Wynn is mob connected, but extensive investigation by the Bureau has failed to develop any real evidence confirming that rumor.

One of the most devious and ridiculous slogans ever devised is "What happens in Vegas, stays in Vegas." This marketing cliché not only gives a totally false impression of a wide open, "everything goes" city, it causes additional problems for the police as people come to Vegas and act like idiots. Furthermore, what happened in Las Vegas when the mob controlled many of the casinos certainly didn't stay in Las Vegas. The demise of the straw men and the skim was purchased with the blood of witnesses and many guilty men as they maneuvered for power and self-preservation. A mob-free Las Vegas was purchased by countless law enforcement heroes, many of them sacrificing their entire careers for the victory. Even long time FBI nemesis, Las Vegas Mayor Oscar Goodman, admitted to *Las Vegas Review Journal* columnist John L. Smith, on August 14, 2009, when discussing the mob in Las Vegas, "The good news is, at least as far as some people are concerned, we know the end of the story. The mob lost and law enforcement won..."

There are those, even today, who fondly long for the old Vegas – the way it used to be, but the old Vegas is nothing more than a glitzy facade. The old Vegas, with the power of the Outfit controlling much of the economic heart of the city, brought corruption in its many forms: corruption of the courts, of the police, of unions, politicians, and even the FBI. Is it logical to assume that the owners and dealers of early Las Vegas casinos were pure as the driven snow? They were transplants who learned the art of gambling in illegal operations throughout the nation. Early gaming enforcement was all but non-existent, and these operators and slippery dealers used every trick available to separate money from gamblers. Furthermore, the gaming control structure of Nevada was lulled into the fiction that the status quo was acceptable for the economic welfare of all. In the old Vegas there were many cold blooded murders committed against witnesses who were positioned to harm the shadowy men who secretly controlled many of the casinos while Las Vegas straw men smiled for the public and were the happy face of the mobbed up casinos. There was a bombing where the lives of innocents could easily have been lost. There were untold murders committed in the self cleaning oven of the Outfit as mobsters were rubbed out to eliminate problems and maintain control within the Outfit. There were millions of dollars siphoned out of the casinos and packed back to the Midwest, where it was used to perpetuate the Outfit and all its contaminations of society. Entire careers were spent by FBI agents and others grappling with the virus that is the mob. And when the FBI made its move against the corrupt power structure of the old Vegas, it was greeted as the enemy, a pox on the city by disparaging city fathers, and yet, I am not aware of another instance where the FBI has had such a profound impact on a major city. The stealthy lawlessness of the Outfit, the open assassinations of potential witnesses, the untangling of sweetheart political deals tied to hidden ownership are gone. In the end, the sharp talons of the parasitic vampire known as the mob have been cut, drying up the flow of skim that nurtured the monster. Sin City is forever changed, thanks to men and women who fought a war against the forces of darkness and, at least in this one instance, won.

On May 15, 1996, I turned in my credentials, badge, and my Bureau issued Smith and Wesson 10 millimeter semi automatic and walked out of the Las Vegas FBI building carrying a scuffed cardboard box containing sparse personal belongings. After nearly

26 years as an FBI agent, the strength and reputation of the Bureau were no longer mine. My beloved FBI career was over, and as soon as I left the building, as is Bureau policy, the entrance code to the external doors was changed. I had a sense of melancholy as I drove home, even though I knew it was time to hang it up. I had fought the good fight, and as Theodore Roosevelt once said, I had "known the great enthusiasm, the great devotions and had spent myself in a worthy cause." I knew I had made a difference. I had been responsible for using Title IIIs in ten separate cases, tapping 13 telephones and installing 11 microphones while attempting four more that were dry holes. Each of the ten cases had led to convictions. These statistics could possibly be a Bureau record. I had brought justice to many and had put a lot of bad guys in jail. But I was tired, and it was time to move on. I would surely miss the camaraderie, the laughs, the adrenaline rushes, the sense of high achievement, and most of all, I would miss the FBI's band of heroes.

CONVICTIONS

In the end, a career in law enforcement can be gauged by results. The following organized crime-associated individuals were convicted in federal court in cases where I was the case agent or, in a few instances, where I was assigned as co-case agent:

Max Addonis
Maurice Altamuro
Anthony Amico
Frank Balistrieri – Milwaukee, LCN boss
John Balistrieri
Joseph Balistrieri
Joseph Balzano
Joseph Basile
Steve Cino – Los Angeles, LCN soldier
John Conte – New York, Lucchese LCN soldier
Alphonse Cuozzo
Michael Di Bari
Steve Di Salvo – Milwaukee LCN soldier
Charles Disney
Russell Enea
Seymour Freedman
Gus Gallo
Kenny Guarino
Herb Holland
James Jennaro
Bobby Jernigan
Dennis Librizzi
Sam Librizzi

Joseph Logue

John Mascia – New York, Gambino LCN soldier

Jerry Marcigliano

Joseph Monteiro

Karen Monari

Carl Miselli

Dominic Nesci – New York, Gambino LVN soldier

Tom Oden

Elwood O'Grady

Richard Panella

Sally Papia

John Pisciune

Anthony Pullara

John Ricci

Natale Richichi – New York, Gambino LCN capo

Jack Schlecter

John Sciandra

Michael Sergio – New York, Genovese LCN soldier

Gaspare Speciale

Robert Stella Jr.

Max Walker

BIBLIOGRAPHY

Griffin, Dennis, *The Battle For Las Vegas, The Law Vs. the Mob*, Huntington Press, Las Vegas, Nv., 2006.

Griffin, Dennis, *Cullotta, The Life of a Chicago Criminal, Las Vegas Mobster, and Government Witness,* Huntington Press, Las Vegas, Nv., 2007.

Hemingway, Ernest, *On Blue Waters, Esquire Magazine,* April 1936.

Magnesen, Gary, *The Investigation, A Former FBI Agent Uncovers the Truth Behind Howard Hughes, Melvin Dummar and the Most-Contested Will in American History,* Barricade Books, Fort Lee, NJ, 2005.

Pileggi, Nicholas, *Casino, Love and Honor in Las Vegas,* Simon and Schuster, NY, NY, 1995.

Smith, John L., *Of Rats and Men*, Huntington Press, Las Vegas, Nv. 2003.

NEWSPAPERS

The Chicago Tribune
The Las Vegas Review Journal
The Milwaukee Magazine
The Milwaukee Sentinel
Sports Illustrated

ABOUT THE AUTHOR

Gary Magnesen was born in Bergen, Norway, during the German occupation of that country. His family left Norway in 1948 and settled in Salt Lake City, Utah. After graduating from college, he joined the Federal Bureau of Investigation in 1970. He worked in Minneapolis and Milwaukee before being transferred to Las Vegas in 1980. He was appointed as the Organized Crime Program Coordinator and retired in 1996. He was the recipient of numerous commendations and awards for his investigative work.

Magnesen is the author of *The Investigation*, a book about Howard Hughes and the validity of the Hughes will discovered by Melvin Dummar. Magnesen resides with his wife in the southwest United States.

LaVergne, TN USA
26 October 2010

202339LV00005B/136/P